Science for the People

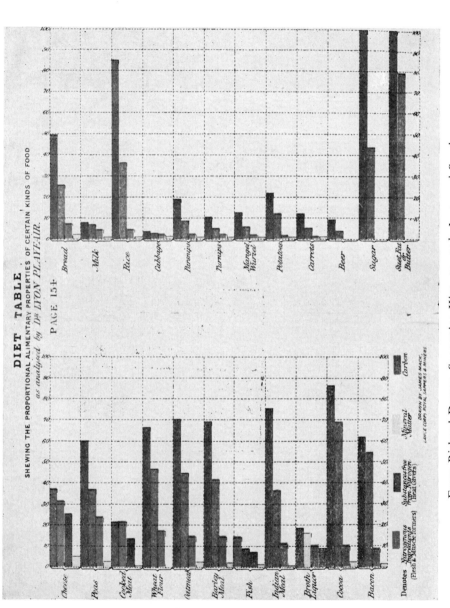

From Richard Dawes, *Suggestive Hints towards Improved Secular Instruction* (1853)

Science for the People

The origins of the school science curriculum in England

DAVID LAYTON

London . George Allen & Unwin Ltd
Ruskin House   Museum Street

ISBN 0 04 507001 6

Printed in Great Britain
in 11 point Times Roman
by Clarke, Doble & Brendon Ltd
Plymouth

*Science has never been fully accepted by humanity.
It has been tolerated because of the material
benefits it can provide. But now it is being
increasingly questioned whether these practical
benefits of science are indeed benefits. . . .
We are coming to the realization that at this time
the furtherance of science itself is no more
important than its communication to humanity as a
whole. Yet as we go out to proselytize we recognize
the time is late, for the world is on the verge of
turning against us.*

Richard L. Wolfgang,
Professor of Chemistry, Yale University,
until his death in 1971 : Chairman, Panel on
Chemistry for Citizens, International
Conference on Education in Chemistry,
July 1970, Snowmass-at-Aspen, Colorado

*Today we study the day before yesterday, in order
that yesterday may not paralyse today and today
may not paralyse tomorrow.*

F. W. Maitland

To E.M.L.
      D.M.L.
      A.M.L.
      M.R.L.

Preface

Because of its use of historical data it would be gratifying if this book should prove of interest to historians of science and of education. Certainly it has benefited from many discussions with scholars in these two disciplines. Its prime concern, however, is neither with the history of science nor with the history of education, as such. Rather it is a contribution to a relatively new and growing field of educational studies whose focus – to borrow Sir David Eccles' phrase – is the secret garden of the school curriculum. Its existence stems from an interest in a limited but important sector of educational experience, that associated with the learning of science and with the contribution which scientific knowledge can make to the general education of children.

Rather more than a decade of curriculum development, supported by human and material resources on an unprecedented scale, has not removed the impression that science is still failing to achieve its full potential as a branch of education in schools. As an indication of the sense of shortcoming, reference might be made to the title of the volume recording the proceedings of the 1970 International Congress on the Education of Teachers of Physics in Secondary Schools – *Teaching Physics – An Insoluble Task?* Clearly all is not well, but, equally, all is not lost. The mark of interrogation supports a measure of hope for the future.

In the belief that it is useful to step back occasionally from the ferment of activity associated with present-day problems, an attempt has been made in this work to explore the complex factors that shaped the school science curriculum at one particularly crucial stage of its development. For a variety of reasons, not least the richness of available source material, the period chosen for study was the mid-nineteenth century, when the foundations of a state system of mass education were being laid and when the first organized movement for the establishment of science as a school subject took place. It could equally well have been the turn of the century, when administrative decisions of considerable significance for the place of science in the secondary school curriculum were taken, the inter-war years associated with the rise of the general science movement or the 1950s when the first stirrings of present-day curriculum reform activities were observed. If this preliminary exploration should serve to stimulate further inquiries into the decision-making processes which operate in one corner of the secret garden, it will have more than satisfied the author's best hope.

It is a pleasure to acknowledge the help of several friends and colleagues in the preparation of this book. Dr Peter H. J. H. Gosden, Reader in Educational Administration and History, Dr Jerome R. Ravetz, Head of the Division of the History and Philosophy of Science, Dr Maurice P. Crosland, Reader in the History and Philosophy of Science, and Mr George Taylor, Teaching Fellow, all of the University of Leeds, have commented on earlier drafts of the manuscript and saved me from several types of error. Dr W. H. Brock (University of Leicester), Dr Roy MacLeod (University of Sussex) and Professor Arnold W. Thackray (University of Pennsylvania) have all read portions of the work and provided helpful comment. To Professor William Walsh, Head of the Department of Education, University of Leeds until 1972, I owe a special debt for counsel and support over a period of several years. Finally, I thank the University of Leeds for granting me study leave during the 1970–71 session, the period when much of the research for this book was brought to fruition.

Manuscript sources

I record my thanks to the librarians and archivists of the following institutions for their unfailing help and for permission to consult the sources listed:

College Archives, Imperial College of Science and Technology
The correspondence and papers of Lyon Playfair
The correspondence and papers of T. H. Huxley

Archives of the Royal Society
Correspondence and papers of Henry Moseley
Referees' reports by Moseley
Referees' reports on Moseley's papers

Library of the Botany School, Cambridge
Bound volume of letters to J. S. Henslow

Library of the Royal Institution, London
The Correspondence of John Tyndall
The Journals of John Tyndall 1843–72 (3 vols.)
The Journal of Edward Frankland, 1848–49 (1 vol.)

Library of the Royal Society of Arts, London
Collection of letters to Lyon Playfair
Council Minutes

Library of the University of Manchester
Papers and correspondence of Sir James Kay-Shuttleworth

Library of University College, London
The papers of Francis Galton

Library of University of St Andrews
Correspondence and papers of J. D. Forbes

Library of the Victoria and Albert Museum
Cole Correspondence
Cole Pocket Diaries

10 *Manuscript Sources*

Public Record Office
  Science and Art Department Minute Books

Record Office of the National Society for Promoting Religious Education in accordance with the principles of the Church of England
  King's Somborne School file
  Hitcham School file
  Church School Inquiry 1846–47

Contents

Chapter 1

Education and Science
before State Intervention

Teachers, according to Robert Lowe, were 'most dangerous
and unsatisfactory judges' of educational objectives, quite
unfitted for the task of prescribing a course of study. This
was no caustic appraisal of an adolescent and callow pro-
fession whose shortcomings encouraged vituperation and
disdain. Teachers were disqualified from assuming the role
of arbiter in curriculum matters because, as Lowe pointed
out, 'It is in the nature of teachers to recommend that
which they know best themselves . . . there is nothing in
the occupation of a teacher which tends to give that larger
acquaintance with men and things which enables a man to
discover what are the wants of society in respect of instruction and how these wants might be supplied'.[1]

Equally, however, for Lowe the state was incompetent to
take decisions on the objectives of schooling and the content
of instruction. There was no justification for its intervention
between parents and the schools which served their children.
To act in this way would be to usurp the right of parents to
decide the most suitable instruction for their own children.
State control of the curriculum would give to the central
power the prerogative to train the mind of the people, as
unpalatable a state of affairs as vesting this authority in the
hands of teachers.

Lowe's own view, derived from his political belief in
laissez-faire, was that educational objectives should be determined by a process of free trade, in which diverse local
provision and natural selection would operate to secure the

survival of schools offering what the consumers valued. The action and reaction of supply and demand would produce schools with objectives and curricula in tune with the wants of society.

The context of Lowe's remarks on the control of the curriculum was the debate about the future of endowed schools in the nineteenth century. The principle of free trade which he advocated presupposed the existence of an already educated population of parents, or, at least, a population of parents capable of judging what was an appropriate education for their children. In the case of the labouring poor, according to Lowe, no such presupposition was warranted, and hence there was no illogicality in advocating state influence on the elementary school curriculum.

The extent to which the state should interfere in educational matters was a crucial issue which divided opinion in the nineteenth century. At one extreme it was contended that there were only two classes of children – prisoners and paupers – with regard to whom the state could be considered in *loco parentis*. At the other extreme, the voluntary agencies were judged inadequate for the task in hand and it was argued that the state had both a right and a duty to apply a part of its resources to the education of the people. It was fallacious to assume that a desire for education would spontaneously assert itself like that for food, clothing and shelter. If this were the case, an ignorant man's appetite for knowledge ought to be in proportion to his destitution. But all experience showed that this was not so. Where there was mental, moral and religious deprivation, there was no demand for education. A state of brutish ignorance and unrelieved barbarism could only be redeemed by a concerted national effort involving the creation of a system of well-staffed schools.

Although the voluntary system achieved significant educational advances in the early decades of the nineteenth century, there is little question that the quantity if not the quality of educational provision improved noticeably following the establishment of the Committee of Council on Education in 1839 and the evolution of a policy which associated

grants with specific objectives and the fulfilment of prescribed requirements. In his 1851 Census Report on Education, Horace Mann drew attention to the extraordinary
educational advances achieved in the previous half century.
'The records and the recollections which describe society so
recently as fifty years ago bear testimony to a state of ignorance and immorality so dense and general that, if any
member of the present generation could be suddenly trans-
ported to that earlier period, he would probably be scarcely
able . . . to believe himself in England, and would certainly
regard the change which half a century has witnessed in the
manner of the people as but little short of miraculous?'[2]

Much of this progress was attributable to the work of
Sunday and Day Schools, many of the latter under the
guidance of religious agencies such as the National Society
and the British and Foreign School Society. Nevertheless,
their contribution left ample room for improved standards
of educational provision as the following vignette indicates.
The author, Harry Chester, was assistant secretary to the
Committee of Council on Education, with particular responsibility for the administration of the building grants.

'When the Committee of Council on Education was first
created, in 1839, so little attention had been given to the
planning of schools, that they were commonly erected by
the village bricklayer and carpenter, by rule of thumb, without any plans at all. The organization of schools had been
little studied. A minimum education was given at a minimum cost. Babes of eight and ten years old were set to
teach other babes of the same age; the national infantry
was still drawn up in Dr Bell's hollow squares; writing desks
were few, scanty and fixed to the walls; and Dr Bell's original
plan of teaching poor children to write, by marking out
letters with their fingers in shallow troughs of sand, had not
long been abandoned. Of apparatus there was little but a
few slates; of maps there was perhaps one, a meagre map
of Palestine; of books, there were scarcely any but the Holy
Bible. In the Holy Bible, used as a primer, little children
were drilled in spelling and reading; and their arithmetic

was too often drawn from the same source. . . . "There were twelve patriarchs, twelve apostles and four evangelists; add the patriarchs and evangelists together; subtract the apostles, what is the remainder?" "Solomon had so many wives and so many concubines; add the concubines to the wives, and state the result." '

'The buildings were low, thin, dingy, ill-drained, often without means of warming, often without proper conveniences; with no furniture but a teacher's desk, a few rickety forms, a rod, a cane, and a fool's cap; the floor was almost invariably of brick – the worst kind of floor, as it is tenacious of moisture, cold to the feet, easily abraded into red dust, and soon worn into holes. There were rarely any porches or lobbies for the caps and cloaks of the children. If there were a house for the teacher, it was seldom such a house as a teacher at the present day would like to inhabit.'[3]

Chester was writing in 1860 by which time government specifications for school buildings were well established and school books, apparatus and equipment had been improved immeasurably both in range and quality. Indeed, in an attempt to achieve for education what the Great Exhibition of 1851 had done for manufacturers, an international Educational Exhibition of school appliances had been held in London in 1854.[4] Accompanying this improvement in the material resources available to education, a new corps of teachers had been raised under the encouragement of the regulations of 1846. These were Kay-Shuttleworth's 'pioneers of civilization', the products of the pupil-teacher system and the recently established teacher training colleges. It was no longer necessary for the schools of the people to be staffed by untrained men and women, the former in many cases driven from the rougher struggles of life because of ill health or some physical defect.

New resources created opportunities for the achievement of new objectives and the mid-century was a period of considerable curriculum activity in elementary schools, one important aspect of which – the attempt to establish science as a basic ingredient of a general education – is the subject of this book. The conflict of studies, more usually associated with endowed and public schools in the 1860s[5] and with events such as the publication in 1867 of Farrar's *Essays on a Liberal Education*, was rehearsed in detail in the early 1850s with its focus on the curriculum of schools for the labouring poor. Likewise, the controversy over the relative merits of scientific and literary studies, although its roots may be traced much deeper than the nineteenth century, resonated at the node of the elementary school curriculum some years before it engaged Huxley and Arnold later in the century.

In subsequent chapters it will be argued that decisions taken during the 1850s, and certainly before the introduction of the Revised Code in 1862, determined the bias of the elementary school curriculum for the remainder of the century and indeed so thoroughly infected educational dispositions towards science as a school subject that traces are readily discernible today. At this point it is sufficient to note that the opportunity for concerted curriculum change in elementary schools arose as a consequence of state intervention. Decisions about the availability of material resources, the qualifications required of teachers, and the conditions to be fulfilled in order to secure grant were taken centrally by the Committee of Council on Education. In terms of these parameters, the practicable objectives of schooling were determined and the shape of the curriculum was fashioned.

Before proceeding to examine in more detail the vicissitudes of the movement for the establishment of science as an essential component in the education of the people, it is necessary to look briefly at two further proemial questions. The selection of scientific knowledge and skills for inclusion in the school curriculum inevitably involved drawing upon the repository of knowledge and skills accumulated by the scientific community. One question, therefore, relates to the state of development of scientific knowledge at the time in question and the prevailing views on the sort of intellectual activity involved in the pursuit of science. In terms of these, limits would be set on the objectives which could be

B

achieved by the study of science in schools. Secondly, it needs to be asked to what extent science was already taught in schools before state intervention occurred; what, if any, traditions of science teaching existed and what teaching skills and material resources, such as books and apparatus, were available? Factors such as these might be expected to give direction, at least, to subsequent developments.

II

The relationship between science and the society in which it is practised is undoubtedly complex. Appeals have been made to a variety of cultural factors in order to explain observations on the differential growth of various sciences and the course of their historical development. In a letter to Faraday in 1844, shortly after a triumphant tour of Great Britain, the German chemist Liebig commented on a national characteristic of English science: 'What struck me most in England was the perception that only those works that have a practical tendency awake attention and command respect; while the purely scientific, which possess far greater merit, are almost unknown.'[6] Liebig's observation did less than justice to some commanding figures such as Dalton and Faraday, but it reflected a widely held opinion that, in the early nineteenth century, England was a land of applied science. Liebig's point had in fact been made eleven years earlier by Edward Bulwer, Lord Lytton, writing on *England and the English*.[7] The doctrine of free trade, advocated by Lowe in connection with the education of the middle and upper classes, but regarded as inapplicable to the education of the labouring classes, appeared to be operative in the field of science. In his discussion on the state of science, Lytton, who acknowledged a debt to Charles Babbage, distinguished three levels of scientific activity. The first, characterized by the highest intellectual endeavour, was concerned with the discovery of abstract principles of a wide generality. The elevated minds who laboured at this level would not be remunerated naturally by the public: furthermore, it had to be accepted that national encouragement would be unlikely to increase their number. A second class of intellect was applied to the discovery of less general principles which could be more readily applied to industrial and technological situations. These principles, 'the parents of the useful', nourished the third class of mind. Rarely found in combination with either of the other two, its concern was the application of scientific knowledge to purposes of practical utility and for this exercise a modest knowledge of science, coupled with workshop skills and manual dexterity, would normally suffice. Yet despite a dependence upon the other two, this was the only class of scientific intellect which received public remuneration and whose welfare could therefore safely be left to public encouragement. 'Pure' science, like education for the labouring classes, could not be sustained adequately under a voluntary system and required state support. Lytton's subsequent argument that there should be something in the constitution of the state that would encourage science in 'the higher grades' need not detain us here. Particularly through the influence of Sir Robert Peel a beginning was made to state patronage of science in the way of pensions, awards and, from 1849, an annual parliamentary grant-in-aid of £1,000 for the promotion of scientific research.[8] What is of greater consequence for the present study is that the mid-century institutions of science which were supported by government funds reflected the concern with practical applications which had been the subject of Liebig's comment. England, still heavily agricultural, a trading estate of coal, minerals and canals, had institutionalized its concern for civil science in bodies such as the Geological Survey, the Mining Records Office, the Museum of Practical Geology, the Government School of Mines and the Royal College of Chemistry.[9]

The administrative homes of the Geological Survey are of interest because they reveal the increasing tendency towards a federation of science and education. Initially under the Board of Ordnance, the Survey was transferred in 1845 to the Office of Woods and Forests. Following the Great Exhibition of 1851 and the verdict of the Exhibition Commissioners that there was need for a system of scientific and artistic instruction to the industrial population, a Department of Science and Art was established under the Board of Trade. Along with other scientific institutions maintained by the government, the Geological Survey was brought into administrative unity with the new department in 1853. Three years later with the transfer of the Department of Science and Art from the Board of Trade to the Education Department of the Privy Council, the Survey acquired yet another new master.

Much was hoped of the closer association of these government supported institutions with educational developments during the 1850s. Unfortunately there were intrinsic strains which prevented an immediate and fruitful union. For instance, the antecedents of elementary education and of the sciences in question were not so easily overlooked. More than 70 per cent of the public elementary schools recorded in the 1851 Census returns were supported by religious bodies, notably the Church of England. Yet the 'Royale Hammereres' of the Survey and their mineralogical, palaeontological and zoological colleagues of 'the Jermyn Street gang' represented those very branches of science which currently seemed most threatening to religious beliefs. Geology was particularly suspect. As Basil Willey has recalled, 'Sir Charles Lyell suffered social ostracism for the "uniformitarian" heresy in his *Principles of Geology* and "reconcilers" like Buckland and Hugh Miller had been hard at work trying to "harmonize" Genesis with the "testimony of the rocks".'[10] When the members of the British Association for the Advancement of Science met for their annual meeting in 1855, they were told by the Duke of Argyll in his presidential address that 'in respect of elementary education we (i.e. the advocates of science) are generally opposed, as aiming at the displacement of religious teaching'.[11] The holy alliance of science and religion, a characteristic of the diffusion of scientific knowledge in eighteenth-century England, had become somewhat attenuated by the time of state-aided education for the labouring classes in the nineteenth century.

From our position today it is perhaps difficult to appreciate the structure of scientific activity in the mid-nineteenth century, and particularly the dominating position occupied by geology. When the statutes of the Royal Society were revised in 1847 with a view to stimulating the intellectual activity of the Fellows and establishing more stringent criteria for membership, a zealous inner ring of reformers founded the Philosophical Club of the Royal Society. This might be seen as comprising the hard core of Fellows most actively concerned in scientific research. Of the forty-seven original members, no less than fourteen were geologists or workers in the associated fields of mineralogy and palaeontology. Medicine and physics each provided seven representatives, followed by botany with four, and mathematics, chemistry and zoology with three each.[12] As the Secretary of the Linnean Society had pointed out to the members of the Society's Zoological Club some years previously, in a country where institutions and activities were free to develop with minimum interference from the central authority, not all sciences would be encouraged to the same extent. Botany and zoology would find support only in so far as they contributed to useful ends such as the extermination of insects destructive to timber in the dockyards. In contrast, sciences rich in applications, for example mechanics, would stand pre-eminent. 'Steam engines and Chronometers' were the symbols of free states.[13] By the mid-century, chemistry also had established its claims. The Royal College of Chemistry, instituted as a private venture in 1845 but nationalized in 1853, was intended to serve the needs of agriculture, in particular.

In science, as in education, the issue of government intervention proved divisive. Whilst some leaders of the scientific community urged the need for a Board of Science and an increased amount of state encouragement for abstract science and its cultivators, others were reluctant to depart from the principles of voluntaryism and *laissez-faire*;[14] and, as in education, the voluntaryists lost ground. In consequence, at the time when concerted attempts were being made to introduce science into the school curriculum, scientific knowledge in England was in process of transition; an emphasis on science in its applications to practical affairs was slowly yielding to one in which science was pursued for its own sake.

It should be added that the movement from 'applied' to 'pure' science was assailed on grounds other than the change entailed in the means of support. The introduction of 'modern' continental mathematics into Cambridge, its naturalization there in the hands of Herschel, Babbage, Peacock, Whewell and Airy, and its close association with experimental physics was viewed with alarm by figures as distinguished as the logician Sir William Hamilton and the scientist Sir David Brewster. On the question of pure mathematics being an effective agent for training the mind in logical habits of thought, Hamilton's view was incisive. 'A mathematician in contingent matter', he wrote, 'is like an owl in daylight.'[15] Brewster's objection was of a different order. The closer association of physical science with the disembodied symbols of algebra would result in science becoming detached from practical affairs and technology, the relationship with which had been its particular strength, especially in the Scottish universities. A danger existed that scientific inquiry might become subordinated to pure mathematics, making facts of nature 'mere pegs on which to suspend festoons of algebraic drapery'. If science was to succeed as an instrument of general education it was important that it retained its relevance to common life.[16]

There was, of course, no resisting the power of mathematical physics in the hands of men such as Stokes, Cayley, J. C. Adams, Kelvin, P. G. Tait and, pre-eminently, J. Clerk Maxwell. Nevertheless, whether for purposes of research, teaching, administration or examinations, the relationship of science to mathematics and of the various sciences to each other were matters of active concern to scientists of the mid-nineteenth century. The literature of the period includes frequent references to the classification of the sciences and to what constituted an acceptable account of scientific activity. Mill and Whewell debated the issue of 'methods of discovery' in successive editions of their respective works on *Logic* and *Philosophy of the Inductive*

Sciences and when, in the summer of 1854, both the Royal Institution and the Society of Arts arranged courses of lectures on science and education, the relationship of the sciences to each other and to other branches of knowledge was a central theme. As will be seen later, the views held on these various topics were of considerable significance to the task of selecting scientific knowledge for inclusion in the school curriculum.

III

Turning from a consideration of the state of science in England to that of the teaching of science in elementary schools before state intervention, the available evidence suggests a picture of almost total neglect. It is true that both public and private schools were established at an impressive rate during the 1830s and 1840s; of the 15,000 or so elementary schools in existence in England and Wales at the mid-century over a third had come into existence during the previous decade.[17] Nevertheless, throughout this period of rapid expansion the curriculum of elementary schools remained largely untouched by science and by those contemporary achievements in engineering and the industrial arts which, a short time later, were to provide Samuel Smiles with much of his subject matter. The early age at which many working-class children started school and the limited duration of their education were widely regarded as formidable constraints on any attempts to progress beyond the rudiments of reading, writing and ciphering. Happily, in a handful of experimental schools, notably those established by men and women who had come under the influence of continental educational reformers such as Pestalozzi and Fellenberg, the possibility of improvement was demonstrated.

One notable development took place at the school in Cheam established by the Protestant clergyman, the Rev. Charles Mayo and his sister Elizabeth.[18] Convinced that childhood was a period of ceaseless activity of the perceptive faculties, they argued that intellectual education should commence with the exercise of these and that lessons should be based on the study of common objects. With the aims of quickening the powers of observation of their pupils and of encouraging skill in the arrangement and classification of objects, the Mayos pioneered a form of teaching which they regarded as preparatory to instruction in science. The innovation was significant in that Mayo's work led to the foundation in 1836 of the Home and Colonial School Society, through which his influence extended into the field of teacher training; furthermore, a series of texts and lesson guides were prepared, in support of which publishers and apparatus manufacturers produced cabinets of objects such as minerals, natural and manufactured products, shells and familiar chemical substances. The Mayos' small book entitled *Lessons on Objects as given to children between the ages of 6 to 8*, first published in 1831, had achieved a tenth edition by 1845 by which time at least eight firms were advertising collections of objects.[19] In the hands of a skilled teacher, experience showed that 'no lessons produce more continued interest or more enlarge the minds of children than those of Objects'. Children whose early education had included such lessons reacted unfavourably to the more traditional studies which followed later and the Home and Colonial School Society was obliged to extend its work upwards to the age of ten and beyond.[20]

The 'object lesson' was a recurring pedagogical device in educational practice during the nineteenth century. Unfortunately it was susceptible to distortion and travesty. Not all who claimed to employ it enjoyed the Mayos' clear conception of its aims and of its relationship to subsequent instruction in science. Indeed, it was frequently emphasized that any resultant understanding of science was fortuitous and that the association might even be harmful. As a writer in the Society's Quarterly Educational Magazine put it, 'The object is not to make the children zoologists, or mineralogists, or botanists. Scientific knowledge is of course communicated, but it is only incidentally, and is an adjunct to the main object of the lesson. Those infant teachers who make a parade of their scientific knowledge, and delight to show visitors how much the children know of pachydermatous animals, and monocotyledonous plants, absurdities which are often witnessed, caricature the purpose of these lessons. . . . The chief object . . . is to cultivate the faculty of observation, this being the first faculty developed in the infant mind.'[21]

However, this was far from the whole story. Even the cultivation of 'the faculty of observation' was secondary to the ultimate goals of religious understanding and moral improvement. The following extract from a lesson on 'scriptural natural history' given in the Home and Colonial Schools in the 1840s illustrates the complex web of objectives within which scientific knowledge made one of its entries into the school curriculum. The children, having been shown a piece of silver and some silver ore, are led through an account (bearing only superficial resemblances to that of the commercial process) of the refining of the ore to yield pure metal.

Teacher 'Yes, the heat melts it; and then what becomes of all the earthy substances which are mixed with the silver? (A pause.) They rise to the top and the silver remains at the bottom. And what do you think the man who is refining the silver does then to get rid of the impurities? I think some of you have seen your mothers do something of the same kind.'

Children 'Skim it.'

Teacher 'Yes, the man skims off what is at the top. Now, what is it that separates the impure substances from the silver?'

Class 'The heat of the fire.'

Teacher 'Tell me the two things about which the refiner is careful.'

Class 'He is careful not to take the silver out of the fire till it is pure; and he is careful not to keep it there when it is pure.'

Teacher 'And how does he know?'

Class 'When it is pure it reflects his image.'

Teacher 'Now, dear children, I have given you this lesson

on refining silver, to lead you to understand what Jesus Christ does for us. Listen to this passage of Scripture. Speaking of the Lord Jesus Christ, it says, "He shall sit as a refiner and purifier of silver, and he shall purify his people, and purge them as gold and silver, that they may offer to the Lord an offering in righteousness." (These words were read by the teacher twice.) Who is spoken of here?'

Class 'Christ.'
Teacher 'Who shall "sit"?'
Class 'Christ.'
Teacher 'As what shall he sit?'
Several voices   'As a refiner.'

And so on to an understanding of the purification of unclean hearts from sin by Christ's Holy Spirit.[22]

Before leaving the topic of 'object lessons', certain related developments in Scottish education require brief comment because of the influence which they later exerted on the teaching of science in England. Reference has already been made to the bias towards applications which characterized Scottish science in the early nineteenth century and which Sir David Brewster had championed in opposition to the Cambridge school of mathematical physics.[23] A similar emphasis on useful knowledge characterized the introduction of science into Scottish elementary education. In the model school attached to his Glasgow Normal Seminary, David Stow had introduced lessons on natural science applied to everyday life from the time of the establishment of that institution in the late 1820s.[24] Oral lessons, illustrated by apparatus, models and experiments, were timetabled as the first exercise each afternoon for both boys and girls. Superficially the form of the lessons was similar to that developed by the Mayos and in early editions of Stow's book, *The Training System*, much was made of the religious and moral conclusions which could be drawn from science lessons. Progressively, however, emphasis was laid on the acquisition of useful knowledge which would enable pupils to understand better the nature of the world around them and of the tasks which would occupy them in employment. Even in the drudgery of manual labour a workman would have the consolation of being able to follow his routine with understanding. Through appreciation of the mechanical principles underlying his equipment and machinery, it was thought that he would become more adaptable and better able to meet difficulties. There was even the prospect that more Watts and Arkwrights might emerge if the minds of those from humble origins could only be suitably nourished and exercised by science. The problem of understanding technical terms and abstract concepts was not deemed a barrier provided an abundance of familiar illustrations, analogues and concrete instances could be supplied. In the case of girls, with the prospect of household tasks as their future preoccupation, scientific knowledge could be usefully applied to the improvement of standards of domestic hygiene and economy. Why a room was better ventilated by opening the top rather than the bottom of a window, how to make or mend a fire so as to save fuel, and whether the top or bottom of the coal ought to be poked in order to induce steady burning were but a few of the homely questions to which an elementary knowledge of science could provide answers.

The prime goals of this teaching, according to Stow in later editions of his book, were the acquisition of useful knowledge and the development of an ability to apply this knowledge to everyday occurrences. It was not only legitimate but highly desirable that learners should use their powers of reasoning on the world around them. A similar emphasis characterized the so-called 'Intellectual System' of Wood's Edinburgh Sessional School and when, in 1837, Kay-Shuttleworth sought to revitalize the workhouse schools under his care in the Eastern Counties of England, it was to Scotland that he looked for staff. Of one of his first appointments, Horne, who later played an important part in the training of elementary school teachers, he wrote, 'This enthusiastic Scotch youth, brimful of elementary technical knowledge, and an expert in Mr Wood's methods, was a phenomenon in these small workhouse schools.'[25]

The educational value of science as 'useful knowledge' was recognized in a further development in England during the 1830s. In the first publication of the short-lived Central Society of Education, Baldwin Francis Duppa, the Society's secretary, gave an account of what he termed 'Industrial Schools for the Peasantry'.[26] The established religious providers of education were criticized as having limited the curriculum to 'literary instruction' and Duppa described with approval the work of several agricultural schools in which manual activities, elementary science and nature study were introduced because of their relevance to agricultural labour. The full impact of science on agriculture did not take place until later, following the foundation of the Royal Agricultural Society in 1838, Liebig's report to the British Association in 1840, and the publication in the same year of an English edition of his book on *Chemistry in its Applications to Agriculture and Physiology*. The agricultural schools of the 1830s were too early to enjoy the full benefit which accrued from the revival of agricultural science, but they represented an important variation on the prevailing theme of civilizing the agricultural labourer by scriptural literacy. An attempt was made to educate by building on the interest of the children in the world around them and by encouraging a study of 'things' rather than of 'words'.

The scale of these and other early innovations in English education was severely limited; although they contained the germ of future developments there is no escaping the conclusion that, by the mid-century, science had made little progress in establishing itself as a basic element in general education. Where scientific knowledge did appear in the curriculum it frequently served religious and moral ends, as in the object lessons of the Home and Colonial School Society, or was introduced because of its utility, as in the Scottish systems and the early agricultural schools in England. Elsewhere it was justified, as by the Mayos, in terms of the exercise of postulated faculties of mind, such as those of 'observation' and 'classification'. There was little recognition of science as a distinct mode of understanding, in Faraday's words 'flowing in channels utterly different in their course and end to those of literature'.[27]

Yet this limited assimilation of science into the schools leaves us with a problem. Just as there existed a measure of literacy among working men in the nineteenth century which cannot be accounted for in terms of the existing educational institutions, so there was diffused a not insignificant quantum of scientific knowledge which it is equally impossible to account for in terms of formal education. When Francis Galton conducted his inquiry into the nature and nurture of some 180 scientists whose education had taken place in the early nineteenth century he found only thirteen instances in which the influence of masters, tutors and professors had encouraged a taste for science, and of these, eight referred to teachers in Scotland.[28] One third of Galton's sample of distinguished scientists had not attended a university and it was impossible to distinguish these from the remainder on grounds of scientific distinction. However, in contrast to the case of literacy, where the autodidactic tradition was markedly working class, the self-motivated and non-institutionalized pursuit of scientific knowledge was an activity which transcended all class barriers. Men like William Whewell, Richard Owen and Edward Frankland, at various stages all pupils at Lancaster Grammar School, owed little to the formal curriculum of their schools. Apart from science books borrowed from the library of the Mechanics' Institute, Frankland records how his reading of *Sandford and Merton* gave him his first impetus 'to observation as distinguished from hearsay' and how the home workshop of his great uncles, one of whom 'grew cucumbers by steam', held an early fascination for him.[29] Whewell,[30] like Richard Dawes whose work is the subject of the following chapter, received extra-curricular tuition at the feet of the blind Quaker mathematician, John Gough of Kendal, to whom Dalton attributed an extraordinary mastery in 'astronomy, optics, pneumatics, chemistry, natural history in general, and botany in particular'.[31] G. B. Airy,[32] the Astronomer Royal, son of an excise man, was introduced to certain aspects of science through the contents of his uncle's library where he found Nicholson's *Dictionary of Chemistry*, a source also of Humphry Davy's chemical knowledge. Alfred Russel Wallace's self-education in science began, like Frankland's, with *Sandford and Merton*, embraced influences from an Owenite 'Hall of Science', and was deflected towards botany by a publication of the Society for the Diffusion of Useful Knowledge.[33] In the opinion of Charles Darwin, the most valuable part of his education at Shrewsbury was spent in the tool-shed of the garden, assisting his brother as they worked through the experiments in the back of Parkes' *Chemical Catechism*.[34]

Behind this front rank of researchers and professional scientists there existed the 'mute, inglorious Miltons', self-taught weaver-botanists, lighthouse keeper-astronomers, and cobbler-instrument makers. No doubt this element in the autodidactic tradition was well burnished by the evangelists of work and stories of Lancashire weavers throwing the shuttle with Newton's *Principia* before them were calculated to strain the credulity of even the most fervent apostles of self-help. The fact remains, however, that the biographies of nineteenth-century scientists and of working men provide much evidence of self-teaching of science and dissemination of scientific knowledge through informal channels. In his introduction to *Practical Botany* (1826), William Johns, a surgeon, described a long-established Rochdale Botanical Society 'composed chiefly of labouring mechanics' – among whom was enrolled 'John Mellor, of Royton, than whom no man perhaps is better acquainted with the habits of the rarest British plants'.[35] A few years later, in neighbouring Oldham, another mechanic, J. Riley, describing himself as 'an uneducated working man' and 'self-taught', was writing a text on the slide rule for his fellow mechanics, cotton spinners and engineers, all of whom in his opinion would find useful a knowledge of 'instrumental arithmetic'.[36] Looking back over the early decades of the century, a writer in the *Educational Expositor* for 1855 could point to many instances of eminent natural philosophers arising from the lower ranks of life. The barriers of class were no obstacle to advancement on the pathway of science as Dalton, Faraday and Hugh Miller had demonstrated. Moreover, the motive behind these scientific labours was rarely the hope of financial betterment for there were few, if any, jobs in which the prospect of 'getting on' was improved by the possession of scientific knowledge; certain aspects of applied science might prove useful, but it was frequently the un-educated, loud-voiced rough who was promoted foreman by his employers. Where science was pursued it would seem that the love of learning was a prime incentive; a belief was cherished that, whatever the station in life, the quest for knowledge dignified existence and afforded an entry into a fellowship which transcended the more wordly barriers of rank and employment. Science was an open society. As the *Educational Expositor* declared, 'He who cultivates any department of science can claim kindred with the master spirits of the world, and can aid in the development of truth.'[37]

Two points of relevance to the present study arise from this brief examination of the autodidactic tradition in science education. The first is that, by the time of state intervention in the field of education, there existed an appreciable scien-tific literature which could be described as 'popular' being concerned to bring scientific knowledge within the grasp of the common reader. It included periodicals such as the scientific *Mechanics' Magazine* which, in the 1820s, had achieved a considerable success and provoked numerous competitors.[38] In a similar tradition, the *Magazine of Science and Schools of Arts* appeared each Saturday throughout the 1840s. Although it is difficult to estimate the circulation of such journals, the more general *Penny Magazine* of Brougham's 'Steam Intellect Society' found 200,000 purchasers whilst the substantial *Penny Cyclopaedia*, with its commissioned articles by leading scientists, had a circulation of 75,000 at the beginning of the issue.[39] Of books available, a typical example was Mrs Jane Marcet's *Conversations on Chemistry*, first published in 1806 and the precursor of works on natural philosophy and botany by the same author. It achieved sixteen editions in less than forty years, sold more than 150,000 copies in America alone, and numbered the young Faraday amongst its admiring and grateful readers.[40]

From works such as these anyone with a basic measure of literacy, and a somewhat greater degree of application, could, in theory, acquire a knowledge of science. In character the material available was descriptive and non-quantitative. Mathematics might have been indispensable to Newton, but it was thought a mistake to consider it essential for a beginner in science. Particularly, in works by Scottish authors, such as James Rennie's *Alphabet of Physics* (1833)[41] and the Rev. R. Fraser's *Scientific Wanderings or The Elements of Physics* (1843) a virtue was made of the fact that science could be enjoyed and a valuable general education obtained without the intrusion of mathematical reasoning. Mechanics, astronomy, hydrostatics and pneumatics were dealt with, as in the extraordinarily popular *Scientific Dialogues* of the Rev. Jeremiah Joyce,[42] by conversational expositions of quantitative results such as the laws of motion; diagrams and references to applications were plentiful, but mathematical symbols and formulae rarely sullied the printed page.

The second point arises from the first. The dependence upon the printed word for the transmission of science led to an ironic situation in which the use of observation and experimentation to acquire knowledge was more read about than practised. The spirit of the Royal Society's motto, '*Nullius in verba*', had found an echo in the educational theories of the early century, with the advocacy of 'things not words' and 'doing, rather than reading'. Yet, as Richard Altick has pointed out, paradoxically the antiverbalism of the period was manifested in books and children read about the way in which other children learned by direct observation and experience.[43] It was all very well to follow the account in Joyce's *Dialogues* which described how Charles' father turned on the air pump with the result that Charles could not withdraw his hand from the top of the cylinder which was being exhausted. No doubt Charles was learning something about air pressure and the way in which experimental evidence could be employed to support his conclusions. The unfortunate reader without access to the appropriate apparatus had really no alternative but to accept things on the authority of the text, apart from the limited extent to which scientific knowledge could be verified in terms of everyday experiences.

In fact there were in existence numerous philosophical instrument-makers plying their trade, especially in and around London. E. G. R. Taylor lists over forty names for the quinquennium 1835 to 1840.[44] There was, however, little in the way of apparatus especially designed for purposes of scientific instruction. It was a frequent complaint from those involved in the teaching of science in mechanics' institutes that there was a lack of suitable equipment for the task, particularly in relation to physics. Chemistry was perhaps better served. Darwin's account of his schoolboy experimenting was by no means an isolated example of practical chemistry by juveniles. The adolescent Kay-Shuttleworth established a home laboratory for the study of chemistry[45] and from similar records it is clear that suitable chemical apparatus was available. There were even attempts to simplify equipment for individual experimentation by members of a class. When Dr D. B. Reid came south from Edinburgh in 1836 to advise on the improvement of ventilation and sound transmission in the House of Commons, he gave a series of lessons on elementary chemistry to boys of the Borough Road School. They were instructed in Reid's 'flat glass' micro-chemical techniques and the lessons culminated with a practical class in which the pupils successfully analysed an unknown chemical substance.[46] Such an emphasis was rare, however, and the lack of appropriately designed and suitably priced apparatus was a factor of considerable influence on the selection of scientific knowledge for inclusion in the school curriculum and on the choice of teaching method.

IV

It has been the aim of this chapter to describe the condition of education and of science prior to and around the time of

c

state intervention in education, with particular reference to the teaching of science. Once a system had been established in which government grants were associated with specific objectives and the fulfilment of prescribed requirements, the possibility arose for curriculum change on a national scale. As will be seen a movement emerged which had as its objective the establishment of science as a central element in the education of the labouring poor. Considerable resources were marshalled; new books were published, kits of scientific apparatus were produced and teachers were appropriately trained. The three chapters which follow are each concerned with the work of a pioneer of science education whose activities had a significant influence on the course of this movement.

Chapter 2

Richard Dawes and Applied Science

Throughout the nineteenth century the advocates of science teaching in elementary education acclaimed two exemplars. In their opinion, at the fountain head of science education stood the work of Richard Dawes, Dean of Hereford, and John Stevens Henslow, Professor of Botany in the University of Cambridge. When the claims of natural science as an essential component of elementary education were being urged by the Royal Commissioners on Scientific Instruction in 1872, the pedagogical achievements of Dawes and Henslow were singled out for approbation[1] and individuals such as Sir John Lubbock, who repeatedly brought the question of science teaching in elementary schools before the House of Commons, paid frequent tribute to their authority in this field.[2]

Superficially their lives ran on closely parallel lines. Born before the turn of the century within a few years of each other, they entered the University of Cambridge, Dawes at Trinity, graduating as fourth wrangler in 1817, with Henslow his neighbour at St John's and sixteenth wrangler in 1818. Each remained at the University after graduation. Dawes became Fellow, mathematical tutor and bursar of the recently established Downing College; Henslow was appointed to the chair of mineralogy which he vacated in 1825 to become Professor of Botany.

The intellectual network of early nineteenth-century Cambridge has been described by Walter F. Cannon who attributes to it a leading role in 'up-grading natural science as a total professional discipline' and in linking science 'to the full set of intellectual activities in England'.[3] Within this close-knit community Dawes and Henslow shared the same circle of acquaintances over a period of some sixteen years. In the late 1830s, and within a year of each other, each received the gift of a valuable living, Dawes at King's Somborne, Hampshire, and Henslow at Hitcham, Suffolk.

With the move to their rectories, both men, now in middle age, made a break with the old pattern of life. Dawes' links with Cambridge were permanently severed. Henslow's withdrawal, less complete, nevertheless deprived the university of an important stimulus to the cultivation of science and papers on botany or other branches of natural history disappeared from the pages of the *Transactions* of the Cambridge Philosophical Society which he had earlier helped to found. Apart from a period during the Easter terms when he lectured during the week, he resided at Hitcham until his death.

King's Somborne and Hitcham were parishes with unusually heavy poor-rates, a symptom of extensive social and moral problems. Towards the solution of these, the new rectors established village schools whose work they supervised with outstandingly successful results. In each case a distinguishing feature of the curriculum was the introduction of science. But at this point the parallelism stops. From the first Dawes embraced the opportunities provided by the regulations which governed state aid to education, in contrast to Henslow whose school remained unassisted by grant until a few years before his death in 1861. Dawes' work quickly attracted attention and was widely publicized; in so far as the inspectorate in the Education Office upheld any model for imitation it was taken from King's Somborne. Henslow's educational labours were pursued in rustic isolation, remaining relatively unknown until the mid-fifties. When eventually they received official recognition this came not from the Education Office of the Committee of Council with its concern for elementary education, but from the Department of Science and Art, established in 1853 with the object of encouraging industrial instruction. Dawes' influence was exercised predominantly within the field of education for the labouring poor, whereas Henslow's experiment in his village school bore fruit, not in similar institutions, but in a number of the great public and endowed secondary schools later in the century. Finally, and, as it transpired, crucially for the future development of science teaching, there were fundamental differences in the objectives and content of the science which each man introduced in his schools. A more detailed examination of the educational practices and theories of Dawes is undertaken in what follows; a consideration of Henslow's work is the subject of the succeeding chapter.

Richard Dawes was a Yorkshireman, born at Hawes in Upper Wensleydale.[4] The origins of his scientific interests can be traced in part to the early tuition he received, along with William Whewell, from Dalton's erstwhile mentor, John Gough of Kendal. Whewell took up residence at Trinity College, Cambridge, in the autumn of 1812, a year before Dawes, graduating as second wrangler in 1816. For a time Dawes would appear to have been his pupil. Although it is clear that a close association was maintained with the major scientific and mathematical figures in Cambridge throughout his eighteen years at Downing, and that colleagues such as Peacock, Whewell, Sedgwick and Henslow were frequent visitors to the Downing Combination Room, Dawes made no original contributions to scientific knowledge himself. No doubt his duties as bursar took up much of his time, for these involved not only the supervision of the college accounts but also the active stewardship of the heavily mortgaged Downing estates in surrounding Cambridgeshire. Nevertheless, he participated in many of the reforming movements of the times, and notably that for the admission of dissenters into the university. His involvement in this cost him the mastership of his college and led to his departure from Cambridge. The Master of Downing was elected by the Archbishops of Canterbury and York, and the Masters of St John's and Clare Hall, from among those who had been professors or fellows. Dawes' long and efficient service was regarded as giving him a strong claim when the vacancy occurred in 1836, but his liberal vote on the issue of nonconformists proved the bar to his election.[5] He married almost immediately, retiring to the college living of Tadlow. Shortly afterwards he was presented with the valuable rectory of King's Somborne, Hampshire, by Sir John Mill, a former student at Downing.

Cambridge had provided Dawes with few opportunities for teaching. The historian of Downing records that, for much of its early life, the college 'acted as a kind of un-endowed hostel'.[6] The few students in residence almost invariably prepared for the ordinary degree of B.A. with a view to entering the church, in which most of them prob-ably had good prospects of advancement. When Dawes left, he was noted as a man of liberal views and independent thought: his education and experience over the past quarter of a century had brought him into close contact with many of the most eminent scientists and mathematicians of his day. Yet he had published nothing himself and there is no hint to suggest he had given serious thought to educational problems. Certainly there is little evidence from the Down-ing period to indicate either the passionate concern for the education of the labouring classes which was to dominate the remainder of his life, or the powerful advocacy of science as an instrument of secular instruction which was the hallmark of his later practice and writings.

It is not possible to do more than speculate on the changes which occurred during Dawes' early years at King's Som-borne. He found there an agricultural parish of some 1,100 people, undistinguished from similar parishes, except by an unusually heavy poor-rate. There was no squire or other representative of the gentry resident in the parish; in con-sequence, not only did the burden of social and moral leader-ship fall on the rector, but there was little prospect of eleemosynary aid for any enterprise he might plan. At a personal level, although Dawes and his wife were people of warm and generous disposition who enjoyed the company of children, their own marriage was childless. Dawes, in effect, adopted the young Edward Frankland as his son from the time of their meeting in 1847, but Frankland's future career as one of the leading English chemists permitted him to stay with the Dawes at irregular intervals only.[7] Educational work occupied Dawes increasingly throughout his years at King's Somborne, and later when he moved to the Deanery at Hereford. 'The Dean is working for the rising generation as hard as ever', wrote Mrs Dawes to their friend, the physicist John Tyndall, shortly before her husband's death. 'In that consists his happiness.'[8]

The establishment and growth of the National Society Schools at King's Somborne is a well-documented story. Opened in October 1842, with the aid of a government grant, the schools went from strength to strength. In 1848 the Minutes of the Committee of Council on Education contained a long account of their organization and curriculum by Henry Moseley, one of Her Majesty's Inspectors.[9] Permission was granted for this to be reprinted the following year by Groombridge & Sons, Dawes' publishers. Moseley reiterated a point previously made in the report of John Allen, after an earlier inspection. The unprecedented popularity and success of the schools was not a consequence of unique technical skills exercised by the teachers and the rector. The significance which the inspectorate attached to King's Somborne was that its success was independent of virtuoso performances by those in control; rather, it resulted from the adoption of principles which could be applied equally well in other situations by ordinary teachers who had been appropriately trained.

Paramount among the educational objectives which Dawes set for his schools was, of course, the improved moral and religious condition of the pupils. But his judgement on the most effective instruction needed for the attainment of these ends was untrammelled by doctrinaire considerations about the role of the Bible and scriptural books. Experience early demonstrated that the greater the amount of secular knowledge bearing upon the everyday life of the learners, the greater was the success achieved.[10] The sense of accomplishment which resulted from the effective application of reasoning powers to familiar things bred self-respect and integrity, the necessary correlates of behavioural propriety.

Dawes' view of the labouring classes was at once realistic

and humane. He had no delusions about the habits of life which prevailed among many of his parishioners. Yet his educational prescription was devoid of condescension and this, in Moseley's view, was the secret of his remarkable success. His schools were not instruments for moulding children into conformity with a culture that was imposed from above. Dawes had 'shown his knowledge of the springs of opinion amongst the poor by consulting their independence', and by adapting the education he offered to their wants.[11] Furthermore, this education was to be evaluated by precisely those criteria which would be applied to the education of any other class. The touchstone was not the amount of knowledge imparted but, in Dawes' own words, the tendency which this knowledge had to make his pupils 'alive to the humanities of life, to fit them for their industrial occupations, to raise them in the scale of thinking beings, and make them feel what they owe to themselves and to those around them?'[12]

Cardinal to the success of the schools was the emphasis which Dawes placed on a grasp of language. This was the basic skill through which education could be continued in the home outside school hours and long after children had left school. The concept of 'every fireside a school' was also important because it made possible the involvement of parents in the work of their children. However, a knowledge of language was to be acquired through the use of secular reading books, as opposed to the Bible and scriptural works; the latter remained the most important part of education, but they were displaced as essential vehicles for the understanding of grammar and the teaching of reading. The importance of suitable reading books, and of children possessing these, was continually stressed by Dawes and the per capita figures for expenditure on books and stationery by the King's Somborne schools are impressively high compared with those of other schools.[13] At the time of the opening of the schools, he examined all the available published texts and was led to purchase a number of works from the British and Foreign Society, although his own schools were in union with the National Society. Because of the high price of the British and Foreign Society texts, these were sold at less than cost price to the children of labourers in his parish. The major source of his books, however, was the Commission of National Education in Ireland. The Irish reading books were astonishingly cheap and, by contemporary standards, excellent in the range of secular information which they contained.[14] The material proved interesting to the children, who soon became ready purchasers. The contribution of the Irish books to the success of his school was frequently acknowledged by Dawes and his regard for Irish education was further enhanced when he undertook an extended tour of Irish National and other schools in 1846.[15]

A particular feature of the Irish reading books was the amount of geographic and scientific knowledge they contained. The *Sequel* to the *Second Book of Lessons*, which the King's Somborne children bought enthusiastically, included passages on the discovery of America, world geography, natural products and the zoology of birds and quadrupeds. The more advanced *Fifth Book of Lessons*, used with the first class of boys in the school, was highly scientific in content, containing chapters on physical geography, geology, vegetable and animal physiology, and natural philosophy (including astronomy, hydrostatics, pneumatics, optics, electricity and chemistry).

Such material was necessary if Dawes was to realize a principle of curriculum planning which he regarded as fundamental to the success of his schools. The information imparted was to be 'connected with the every-day concerns of common life'; the subject-matter of secular instruction needed to be drawn from 'things which interest them at present, as well as those likely to interest them in future – such as a description of their clothing, how it is manufactured, etc., the articles which they consume, from whence they come, the nature of the products of the parish which they themselves and those about them are helping to cultivate'.[16]

From this interest in 'common things' it was a small step to explanations 'of a philosophic kind' with reference to the action of pumps, the expansion and contraction of solids and liquids, the pressure of steam, and why, for example, it was possible to tell when a kettle was boiling by placing one end of a poker on the lid and the other against the ear.[17] The response to this informal teaching of science was so remarkable that within two years of opening his schools, Dawes was led to plan an additional classroom which was, in effect, a rudimentary laboratory. When this was built it housed various sectional and glass models of equipment and machinery, an air pump, apparatus for illustrating centrifugal force, chemical apparatus, an electric machine, Leyden jars, a voltaic battery, prisms, lenses, a magic lantern and numerous other pieces of equipment. 'In subjects of this kind, and to children,' Dawes wrote, 'mere verbal explanations . . . are of no use whatever; but when practically illustrated . . . by experiment, they become not only one of the most pleasing sources of instruction, but absolutely one of the most useful.'[17] All subsequent experiences confirmed him more securely in this judgement on the value of scientific knowledge applied to an understanding of familiar things. Once the mechanical difficulties of reading had been overcome and the principles of simple arithmetic understood, there was no kind of knowledge more likely to raise the character of a village school than this. Instead of directly attacking the ultimate moral and religious goals of education, the great aim of the teacher ought to be 'to make the children observant and reflective; to make them think and reason about the objects around them . . . to instruct them in the school of surrounding nature, and to bring their minds to bear upon the every-day work of life'.[18]

Such objectives required teachers in possession of knowledge and skills which, in the 1840s, few had had the opportunity to acquire. In *Hints on an Improved . . . System of National Education* (London, 1847), written as the schools entered their fifth year, Dawes described how he was obliged to instruct his own staff and their apprentices in a knowledge of elementary science and its applications so that they might implement his curriculum reform. In the same year he wrote what was in effect a schoolmaster's guide to the teaching of science in elementary schools, *Suggestive Hints towards Improved Secular Instruction making it bear upon Practical Life*, which achieved a wide circulation, quickly ran through six editions and became a prescribed text for students in training colleges. The Irish National Board went further and presented a copy to all their teachers in training. It represented, in Dawes' words, 'an attempt to introduce into our elementary schools more of science and a knowledge of scientific facts bearing upon the arts of life and of everyday things than has been hitherto done'.[19] In this pioneering manual of science teaching, Dawes characteristically presented his case not by theoretical argument but by a wealth of practical examples of scientific knowledge bearing upon observations and events within the experience of elementary school children.

Understandably not all branches of science lent themselves equally well to his task. 'Natural history' and 'geology' were thinly represented compared with 'mechanics' and 'agricultural chemistry'. But it was under the heading of 'natural philosophy', which for Dawes included properties of matter, heat, light, sound and parts of chemistry, that the richest seam of applications lay. Experiments using simple apparatus, tables of data, and questions to stimulate discussion and further investigation were included in a long chapter occupying a quarter of the book. Not all the scientific information given will withstand a scrutiny in the light of modern knowledge, but an infusion of vitality and enthusiasm carries the reader over page after page of fertile and ingenious teaching material. The work is clearly the tested product of an experienced and gifted educator. Here was knowledge at work in a manner which engaged the intelligence of children of the labouring poor, of whom it had previously been taken for granted that they should have 'no business with anything where the mind is concerned'.[20]

This Baconian emphasis on the utilitarian value of scientific knowledge was a distinguishing feature of Dawes' educational practice. The extent to which it led him to transcend the more familiar literary mode of instruction is indicated by the considerable collection of scientific apparatus used in the King's Somborne schools and by the extensive tables of numerical constants and scientific data which decorated the plastered walls of the classrooms.[21] The activities of his pupils included participation in 'conversational lectures' based on scientific experiments, as well as practical exercises. Typical of the latter is his account of the invasion of the rectory lawn by a group of young scholars in order to measure the dimensions of the garden roller and hence, from a knowledge of the specific gravity of iron, compute its weight.

Table 1

Numerical constants: written on the plastered walls of the classroom of King's Somborne School

(Taken from R. Dawes, *Suggestive Hints toward Improved Secular Instruction*, London 1847)

Circumference of a circle, dia. 1	3·14159
Area of do.	·7854
Circumference of a circle, dia. D	(3·14159) D
Area of do.	(·7854) D^2
Length of Arc 1° dia. 1	·008726645
Sol. cylinder Ht D and dia. of Base D	= (·7854) D^3
Sol. of sphere = $\frac{2}{3}$ of cylinder	= (·5236) D^3
Surface of do. dia. D	(3·14159) D^2
A body falls by gravity	16 1/12 feet in 1 sec.
A body falls by gravity	(16 1/12) t^2 in t sec.
Length of a pendulum vibrating seconds in lat. 51° 31′	= 39·1386 inches
Velocity of sound	1,142 feet in 1 sec.
Velocity of a cannon-ball	2,000 feet in 1 sec.
Velocity of light	200,000 miles in 1 sec.
Velocity of rotation of point at equator	1,520 feet per second
Velocity of a point in lat. 51°	830 feet per second
Velocity of a musket-ball	1,280 feet per second
Velocity of a rifle	1,600 feet per second
Velocity of a 24 lb shot	2,400 feet per second
Velocity of quick train railroad	88 feet per second
Velocity (mean) of rivers	3 or 4 feet per second
Velocity rapid river	13 feet per second
Velocity of a brisk wind	10 miles per hour
Velocity of a high wind, about	40 miles per hour
Velocity of a hurricane	80 miles per hour
Most rapid flight of a swallow, about	80 to 90 miles per hour

Table 2

A list of some of the philosophical and other apparatus used
in the King's Somborne School

(Taken from R. Dawes, *Suggestive Hints towards Improved Secular
Instruction*, London 1847)

A geological map of England.
A pair of globes.
A compass, a spirit level, a measuring chain, and models of the
simple geometrical solids.
A set of mechanical powers, lever, wheel and angle, etc.,
apparatus for illustrating centrifugal force, etc.
A pair of common bellows.
Glass model of a common pump.
Glass model of a diving-bell.
Air-pump and receivers, etc. with other apparatus for various
experiments.
Brass bottle-balance for weighing air, gases, etc.
Apparatus for finding specific gravity of bodies.
Apparatus for showing elasticity of steam.
A sectional model of a steam-engine.
Apparatus on heat, etc. – barometer, thermometer, pyrometer.
Apparatus for showing the different conducting powers of
metals.
Leslie's parabolic reflectors.
Three plane circular discs of white metal, on stands, one
smooth, one scratched, one blackened for experiments on the
absorption and radiation of heat.
A vessel in the shape of a cube, with faces of different kinds for
ditto.
Leslie's differential thermometer.
A magic lantern, with astronomical and other slides.
Glass prisms, lenses, etc. of different kinds.
A small chemical apparatus.
Pneumatic trough, bell-jar, etc., with stop-cock, etc., for collect-
ing and decanting gases, retorts, etc.
Spirit-lamp, argand-lamp, oxy-hydrogen blowpipe, Davy lamp.
A voltaic battery – apparatus for showing Oersted's experiment
– the principle of the electric telegraph – magnets, etc.
A small electric cylindrical machine, glass and sealing-wax, rods,
and pith-balls, stools, with glass legs, Leyden jars, discharging
rods, electrometers, etc.

For his illustrations of the applications of scientific knowledge Dawes drew upon a wide range of sources including many of the works which had sustained the autodidactic tradition referred to in the previous chapter. The most recent revision of Joyce's *Scientific Dialogues* was commended as suitable for pupil teachers, whilst schoolmasters themselves were advised to study the volume on *Heat* in Lardner's *Cyclopaedia*.[22] Not surprisingly, in view of the marked Baconian influence it exhibited, one of his major sources of industrial applications of scientific principles was the *Preliminary Discourse on the Study of Natural Philosphy* by Sir John Herschel, the distinguished scientific son of an equally famous father. Herschel shared with Dawes a rare insight into the needs of the labouring classes, together with a profound belief that the capacity for improvement had not been denied to those of humble origin. The Baconian maxim, 'Knowledge is Power', which had appeared on the title page of the first number of the *Mechanics' Magazine* in 1823 was liberally exemplified in the *Preliminary Discourse*. 'Between the physical sciences and the arts of life', Herschel asserted, 'there subsists a constant mutual interchange of good offices, and no considerable progress can be made in the one without of necessity giving rise to corresponding steps in the other'.[23] Significantly, it was this one point which led Whewell to criticize Herschel in an otherwise eulogistic review of the *Preliminary Discourse*. Scientific knowledge was an end in itself, and not a means; and Whewell questioned whether an emphasis on applications of scientific knowledge might not interfere with the success of scientists 'in ascending to laws of a more exalted generality and higher speculative beauty'.[24]

The *Preliminary Discourse* was the introductory volume to the Natural Philosophy division of Dionysius Lardner's *Cabinet Cyclopaedia*, the whole work comprising 133 volumes published between 1829 and 1849. Lardner himself contributed the texts on *Heat* and *Hydrostatics and Dynamics*, whilst that on *Optics* came from the pen of Sir David Brewster. A graduate of Trinity College, Dublin, the irrepressible Lardner held the chair of natural philosophy

in University College, London, for a short period during
which he assembled a remarkable collection of scientific
apparatus to illustrate his lectures. His love affair with the
wife of a cavalry officer contributed to his eventual translation to Paris where he resided from 1845 until his death
in 1859.[25] The *Cabinet Cyclopaedia* was but one of several
ambitious publishing ventures from which he derived a
substantial income. The science volumes in the series were
designed to provide 'a series of works on popular and practical science, freed from mathematical symbols and technical terms, written in simple and perspicuous language, and
illustrated by facts and experiments which are level to the
capacity of ordinary minds'.[26] Their appearance provoked
considerable comment. As a thinly disguised caricature of
Lardner explained in the Yellow Plush Correspondence,
'It's the littherary wontherr of the wurrld . . . It's the
Phaynix of Cyclopajies – a litherary Bacon . . . shining in
the darkness of our age; fild with the pure end lambent flame
of science . . . a monumintum . . . bound in pink calico, six
shillings a volume.'[27]

Through these and similar works elementary schoolmasters were to be prepared for science teaching. The proposed curriculum reflected that concern with the practical
applications of science which has been noted as characteristic of the Scottish tradition in science teaching, exemplified
at the more advanced level by Brewster and at the elementary level by Stow. At the same time there was much in
common with the adult movement for teaching science to
artisans in Mechanics' Institutes and with the activities of
the Society for the Diffusion of Useful Knowledge. In contrast, although Dawes was undoubtedly familiar with the
work of the Home and Colonial School Society and had
visited schools on the continent, there is little to suggest
that there had been influence from these sources. His educational writings were singularly free from the theoretical
speculation about the nature of childhood and the development of mental faculties which was to be found in the work
of the Mayos and others who derived their inspiration from
continental reformers. Indeed, Dawes betrayed more than

a hint of scepticism towards academic discussion of issues related to the education of the 'lower orders'. 'The real difficulty of the question is not with the people, or the classes to be educated', he maintained, 'but in getting it out of the hands of talking men, and into those of the practical and working ones.'[28] On the question of the education of the teacher and where the balance should lie between acquaintance with the nature of children and knowledge of the skills of teaching on the one hand, and personal education and academic attainments on the other, he was firmly of the view that the better educated a man, the more likely he was to succeed as a teacher.[29]

One further aspect of Dawes' curriculum innovation requires examination. Reference has already been made to the use of Irish reading books in his schools and to his visit to Ireland in the summer of 1846. From the time of its establishment in 1834, the Board of Commissioners of National Education in Ireland had attempted to encourage the introduction of the teaching of agricultural science in elementary schools, although little progress had in fact been made by the early 1840s. With the tragic famines of 1845–7 a powerful stimulus was given to further developments in elementary agricultural instruction on a scientific basis. As the Board's Report for 1847 recorded, 'What before the blight of the potato crop was a matter of undeniable usefulness, is now, by this casualty made a matter of indispensable necessity.'[30] In the succeeding years considerable resources were directed towards the establishment of a system of agricultural instruction.

Simultaneously, a collateral movement emerged in Scotland. Following a public meeting in October 1844 in Glasgow, an Agricultural Education Committee had been established. As an aid to schoolmasters who might wish to introduce the elements of agricultural science into their schools, a small book *The Catechism of Agricultural Chemistry and Geology* was written by Professor J. F. W. Johnston, who also lectured to teachers on the necessary scientific background knowledge and on the method of teaching the subject.[31] The title of the book misleads in suggesting an exclusive reliance upon a verbal mode of teaching. In fact the text was supported by a specially designed and inexpensive set of chemical apparatus which enabled the necessary experimental work to be carried out. Although information about the sale of apparatus is difficult to obtain, the text was undoubtedly widely used. First published in 1844, it had achieved a 23rd edition by 1849, and was translated into nearly every European language.[32]

In England, also, there were considerable stirrings in the field of agricultural education particularly as Liebig's work became more widely known through Lyon Playfair's translation of *Chemistry in its Applications to Agriculture and Physiology* and through Liebig's own visits to this country in the early forties. An English Agricultural Society had been founded in 1838 and granted a royal charter in March 1840. One of those most active in the promotion of this development was William Baring, later Lord Ashburton, whose country seat at Alresford was little more than twelve miles from King's Somborne. Ashburton was also a prime mover in the founding in 1845 of the Royal College of Chemistry, an institution which was conceived as having a special responsibility for the advancement of chemistry particularly in its relations to agriculture and industry. In the opinion of Hofmann, the first professor of chemistry in the new college, Ashburton was the most able of its Council members[33] and, according to Carlyle's biographer, 'it seems as likely as anything can be that when Peel returned to power as Prime Minister, which seemed impending when an accident killed him, Ashburton would have been one of his ministers, and probably the head of a new Education Department'.[34] His part in the movement for the teaching of science in elementary schools will be considered in a later chapter; it is sufficient at this point to note that the study of agricultural chemistry – or, as Liebig preferred to call it, 'the chemistry of agriculture' – was a subject likely to have the strong support of at least some of the landowners in the neighbourhood of King's Somborne and Dawes was not disappointed with the reactions when he arranged a introductory course of six talks on the subject, illustrated by

D

experiments, for teachers and farmers in the region. The course was held in the autumn of 1847, a year after his Irish visit, and the lecturer, who later succeeded Hofmann in the chair of chemistry at the Royal College, was a young man of twenty-two, Edward Frankland, recently appointed to the staff of Queenwood College.[35]

Queenwood was on the doorstep of King's Somborne, a mere four miles to the west. Originally founded in 1839 by Robert Owen, and known as Harmony Hall, the institution was closed in 1845 because of financial difficulties. In the following year it was purchased by the Quaker, George Edmondson, and re-opened in August 1847 as 'an odd mixture of an ordinary junior boys' school and a technical college for older boys and young men'.[36] The school possessed a printing office, a carpenter's shop and black-smith's shop: apart from conventional studies, there was a wide range of pure and applied sciences in the curriculum including inorganic and organic chemistry, agricultural chemistry, botany, vegetable physiology, 'the steam engine' and 'railways'.

Frankland's future lay in chemical research; he resigned from Queenwood in the autumn of 1848 to work in Bunsen's laboratory at Marburg and, later, with Liebig at Giessen.[37] On returning to England, he became professor of chemistry at Owens College, Manchester, eventually succeeding Faraday as Fullerian professor of chemistry at the Royal Institution. His short period at Queenwood was sufficient, however, to inaugurate a friendship with Dawes which lasted unbroken until the latter's death twenty years later. There was a fruitful exchange of ideas, books and apparatus between the two men, Frankland assisting in the scientific education of the older boys and pupil teachers at King's Somborne, Dawes providing tuition in scientific German for Frankland (and, later, his friend John Tyndall) in preparation for his future chemical education. Frankland was one of the important links through which Dawes was kept informed of events within the world of science. His letters written when staying with the Dawes at Hereford give evidence of a genuine filial affection; Dawes was described as 'perhaps, the dearest friend I have ever had' who 'always called me his son' and on his death, Frankland was at his bedside.[38]

In passing, it should be remarked that the staff of Queenwood, around the mid-nineteenth century, must have been one of the most distinguished in the history of school science teaching. In addition to Frankland, John Tyndall, later to become Professor of Natural Philosophy at the Royal Institution, taught at Queenwood during Dawes' period at King's Somborne. Again a friendship developed out of their common interest in science and education. When Dawes died in 1867, it was to his memory that Tyndall dedicated his new volume on *Sound*.[39] Frankland and Tyndall were followed by T. A. Hirst (who eventually succeeded de Morgan as Professor of Pure Mathematics at University College, London), Robert Galloway (later to hold the chair of chemistry at the Royal College of Science, Dublin), H. Debus (previously Bunsen's assistant at Marburg and later Professor of Chemistry at the Royal Naval College, Greenwich) and William F. Barrett (who held the chair of physics at the Royal College of Science, Dublin, from 1874 to 1909).

Elementary instruction in agricultural chemistry was introduced by Dawes at King's Somborne following Frankland's pioneering course. Johnston's *Catechism* was adopted as the text and experimental work was carried out to illustrate points such as the differences between organic and inorganic materials, the varying composition of soils, the essential food requirements of plants and animals, and the recently discovered circulation of carbon in nature. The pneumatic techniques for the manipulation of gases, developed by eighteenth-century chemists such as Cavendish and Priestley, were introduced into the mid-nineteenth-century classroom. In consequence it was possible for Dawes and his schoolmasters to teach the chemistry of substances such as hydrogen, oxygen, water, carbon, carbon dioxide, chalk, coal gas, nitrogen and ammonia by the use of experimental methods which were to remain substantially unchanged for over a century. Furthermore, although the agricultural applications of chemical knowledge were of obvious relevance to the interests of pupils in rural schools, the potential of chemistry as a branch of instruction was by no means limited to this. In the rapidly growing industrial towns there existed what Herschel had described as 'a condensed population' whose housing and sanitation were undescribably squalid, whose diet was impoverished to a degree which seriously endangered health, and whose ignorance of the basic facts of hygiene prevented its members from achieving even those limited measures of melioration which existed within the constraints of their abject poverty. To the solution of these urban problems chemistry also had a contribution to make.

Food, air and water, the staples of life, had all been subjected to chemical investigation. Typical of work in the first category was Lyon Playfair's analysis of different kinds of food, showing their alimentary values; his results were summarized in a coloured diagram which Dawes incorporated as the frontispiece of *Suggestive Hints*. In the realm of pneumatics, the discoveries of Priestley, Scheele, Lavoisier and Black had paved the way for a scientific understanding of respiration, transpiration and the movement of atmospheric gases which Dalton and, later, Thomas Graham, had brought to fruition. It was the opinion of Dr David Boswell Reid, expressed in his text on *The Theory and Practice of Ventilation* (London, 1844), that after mental anxiety and defective diet, imperfect ventilation was the most significant cause of ill health and discomfort among the crowded urban dwellers;[40] that chemistry could now be applied to the improvement of ventilation was a matter of satisfaction. In similar manner, there had been numerous chemical investigations arising from the growing demand for potable water. Playfair, as one of the government scientists attached to the Museum of Economic Geology, was frequently requested by the Board of Health to report on proposed water supplies to towns. When the supply to Liverpool came under discussion in 1846, his chief, the Director of the Geological Survey, Sir Henry de la Beche, urged him to assist in every way possible, thus to demonstrate the utility of the scientific institutions which the government was supporting. 'The whole matter of the supply of water', wrote de la Beche, 'is the application of geology and chemistry to the useful purposes of life, and we could prevent much public loss by attention to it.'[41]

Because chemistry could be applied to the benefit of both urban and rural dwellers there followed a significant revaluation of its importance as a branch of education. To the teachers in elementary schools for whom he had written *Suggestive Hints*, Dawes commended chemistry as a subject which, no matter what the environment and circumstances of education, could be made both interesting and useful, 'perhaps more so than almost any other (knowledge) of a secular kind'.[42] Mechanics and other aspects of physics might be able to provide an impressive store of previous applications, but the instructional potential of chemistry – in Reid's phrase 'the most awakening and fundamental of the physical sciences' – was such as to establish its primacy when considered from an educational point of view.

Before his elevation to the Deanery of Hereford in 1850 Dawes had created at King's Somborne an elementary school curriculum which, by any standards, was achieving remarkable results. Here was no crumb of upper-class education charitably dispensed to the children of the labouring poor. Instruction was related to a culture which was familiar to them and provided opportunities for the use of reason and speculation by drawing upon observations which pertained to everyday life. Understanding and the exercise of thought were not prerogatives of the middle and upper classes. Nor indeed was social mobility, for Dawes anticipated certain aspects of the reform of the civil service by entering into an agreement with the Inland Revenue Board whereby a position was available to a King's Somborne scholar whose educational attainments, irrespective of background, merited the reward.[43]

The principal feature of the King's Somborne curriculum were the stress placed on a mastery of language skills – grammar being taught almost entirely through reading lessons based on secular material – and on the understanding of scientific knowledge which had a direct and practical bearing upon the lives of the learners. 'The Science of Common Things',[44] Dawes' own description of the kind of knowledge that he wished to see schoolmasters possess and that he regarded as an essential component of the elementary school curriculum, was to become an educational catch phrase recurring in a variety of contexts throughout the century.

Chapter 3

John Stevens Henslow
and Systematic Botany

Shortly before his nineteenth birthday in February 1828, Charles Darwin entered the University of Cambridge to prepare for a career in the church. As far as academic studies were concerned his autobiography makes clear that his three years in residence were wasted almost as completely as had been the previous two at Edinburgh, where he had commenced the study of medicine.[1] Nevertheless, Cambridge life had certain redeeming features, not least the acquaintance of a number of distinguished university men who, despite Darwin's undergraduate status, frequently included him in their social activities. Richard Dawes, for example, was one of those whose company Darwin found 'most agreeable' and the omniscient Whewell notably impressed his student companion as they conversed on their way home from dinner with a mutual friend. Dawes, with other senior members of the university, included Darwin on the periodic excursions which were made into the Cambridgeshire countryside. During one expedition in the spring of 1831, stirred by his recent study of Herschel's *Preliminary Discourse* and Humboldt's *Personal Narrative*, Darwin read aloud from Humboldt long passages describing Teneriffe and aired his plans for a voyage of scientific exploration, a project which was to materialize sooner than anticipated with the sailing of the *Beagle* later that year.[2]

Entry to this informal, but, for Darwin, crucially influential intellectual community was achieved through the sponsorship of John Stevens Henslow, Regius Professor of Botany in the university. In the term in which Darwin entered Cambridge Henslow had instituted Friday evening meetings in his home open to all staff and students who were interested in science.[3] These weekly gatherings continued over a period of nine years during which time they were of considerable importance in fostering a taste for science among students in the university. Darwin's attendance at them led to a friendship with the Professor of Botany which was acknowledged in his autobiography as the most important single circumstance in his career. In his final year at Cambridge it also earned for him the sobriquet of 'the man who walks with Henslow'.[4]

Through Henslow's influence he obtained the position of naturalist on the *Beagle*. During the five-year voyage and until Henslow's death in 1861 a correspondence was maintained which proved a source of mutual influence. In response to requests from his former pupil, Henslow ungrudgingly supplied botanical materials, technical information, practical help and scientific counsel. After the publication in 1859 of *The Origin of Species*, although his personal view was that Darwin had pressed his hypothesis too far, Henslow unhesitatingly defended Darwin's scientific integrity and presided with scrupulous impartiality at the celebrated Oxford meeting when Huxley and Hooker demolished the arguments of Samuel Wilberforce. Darwin, for his part, although he palpably outgrew his mentor, displayed an invariable regard for Henslow's beliefs and capabilities which sustained their relationship to the end. In the realms of theory and in the business of 'grinding general laws out of large collections of facts' Henslow was no match for his pupil. As Nora Barlow has pointed out, Darwin could never discuss 'philosophical botany' with his former tutor as he could with his friend Joseph Dalton Hooker, Henslow's son-in-law.[5] Nevertheless, the common ground was cultivated to good effect; Darwin, who wrote on the return of the *Beagle* that he knew no more about the plants he had collected than the Man in the Moon,[6] had at his disposal an inexhaustible source of information on the fine detail of structural botany; whilst Henslow, whose parochial and educational activities diffused his energies over an expanding front, retained to the end of his life a close link with the frontiers of research.

Henslow's relationship with Darwin exemplifies an important point of difference between the contribution to science teaching made in his village school at Hitcham and that made in Dawes' school at King's Somborne. The intellectual network within which Henslow lived and worked was predominantly one of research scientists and university dons. Kinship and amity linked him to the younger Hooker and Darwin respectively; although his own academic influence was diminished on the assumption of his parochial duties at Hitcham in 1837, his formal association with the university was an unbroken one of almost half a century, terminated only by death. Henslow was himself a scientific investigator of distinction whose early papers in the *Transactions* of the Cambridge Philosophical Society had excited the admiration of Lyell.[7] With Sedgwick he had founded the Society in order to encourage scientific research in the university, and served as its secretary from 1821 until 1839 when he ceased to reside in Cambridge.[8] His students included M. J. Berkeley, a notable authority on cryptogamic botany, W. H. Miller, who held the chair of mineralogy in the university from 1832 until 1870, and C. C. 'Beetles' Babington, who succeeded him as Professor of Botany in 1861.

This academic and research orientation in Henslow's interests, in contrast to Dawes' more practical turn of mind, had been noted by Darwin who classified Dawes as one of those friends of Henslow 'who did not care much about science',[9] meaning by this that he was not actively involved in the pursuit of scientific knowledge by original investigations. Despite his later friendships with physical scientists such as Frankland and Tyndall, Dawes stood outside the community of scientific researchers. Scientific knowledge was a product of their activities which he valued highly for its utility and for the aid it lent to the achievement of his educational objectives. But the principles in terms of which he selected and organized scientific knowledge for purposes of teaching were derived less from the internal discipline of the subject than from the needs and interests of the learners.

The detail of his prescription was specific to the children of the labouring poor and would presumably have been modified for the cases of middle- and upper-class education.

Henslow's perspective was different. He was a celebrated member of the small body of scientific investigators then working in England; as such he understood from first-hand experience what intellectual and other attributes were necessary for the successful prosecution of research. His rationalization of the procedure of scientific investigation, in general agreement with the views of Herschel and Whewell, stressed the importance of undertaking a classification of facts and objects from which more generalized summaries and laws could be induced. From these higher level generalizations, more specific consequences could frequently be deduced by pure reasoning. In Whewell's recapitulation, 'This mutual dependence and contrast of induction and deduction, this successive reasoning up to principles and down to consequences, is one of the most important and characteristic properties of true science.'[10] As such, acquaintance with it was an educational objective of prime importance for all classes of learner. In all his educational writings Henslow was at pains to stress that the scientific curriculum developed in his village school with the children of farm labourers was equally applicable to the children of other classes of society. When he was invited by the Prince Consort to introduce the subject of botany to the Royal children, their lessons were identical in all respects with those given to the Hitcham pupils.[11]

A distinction between 'education' and 'instruction' was basic to Henslow's pedagogical thought.[12] Information about the names of plants, their economic and medicinal uses, and their physiology, however interesting it might appear to the learner, was not strictly educational because it was held to have no lasting influence on the mind. Some years later, in his evidence to the Public School Commissioners, the same distinction was upheld by Dr George Moberley, Head Master of Winchester, when contrasting the learning of facts and principles of science with the learning of a classical language. 'The difference which I see,' he argued, 'is, that whilst the one fades away absolutely, and leaves nothing behind, the other gives power. All classical learning tells on a man's speech; it tells on a man's writing; it tells on a man's thoughts; and though the particular facts go, they leave behind a certain residuum of power; and precisely the one great problem educationists have to consider is how to constitute a system of education which will impart to the mind that power to the highest degree.'[13] In Henslow's view, the study of science as a strictly educational weapon which satisfied Moberley's criterion was both possible and desirable. It entailed a personal observation of facts and a mental effort to derive just inferences from circumstantial evidence. In this way enduring qualities would be imparted; 'observant faculties' would be strengthened and reasoning powers expanded.[14]

It did not follow from this emphasis on the potential of science for training the mind, that Henslow had no interest in the applications of scientific knowledge. At one stage of his career he had done considerable work on the damage to crops caused by insects and fungi. Furthermore, his discovery of valuable beds of phosphatic nodules in the coastal area near Felixstowe was a factor leading to the establishment of fertilizer factories in Suffolk, from which the present firm of Fisons Ltd arose.[15] Even as Whewell had criticized Herschel for dwelling too much on what Bacon called '*deductio ad praxim*' – the application of science to the welfare of man[16] – so Darwin found it necessary to chide Henslow for maintaining that 'however delightful any scientific pursuit may be, yet if it shall be wholly unapplied it is of no more use than building castles in the air'. Possibly these words struck a sensitive spot, for they reached Darwin some time after he had embarked upon an extended study of barnacles which occupied eight years of his life. 'I fear the study of the cirripedia will ever remain "wholly unapplied",' he wrote, 'and yet I feel that such study is better than castle-building.' 'I believe there exists, and I feel within me, an instinct for truth; and that our having such an instinct is reason enough for scientific researches without any practical results ever ensuing from them.'[17]

It is clear that Henslow's own teaching at Hitcham incorporated a great deal of 'useful information' and that he missed few opportunities for capitalizing on the botanical knowledge of his pupils. His manuscript notes included a lesson on pneumatics arising from the making of pop-guns from the stem of the elder; an account of soap-making in connection with the ash; of glassmaking, under the saltworts, once burnt for the sake of their alkaline salts; of brewing, under hops; and numerous other applications which justified his son's description of the Hitcham course as one of Systematic Economic Botany.[18] Equally it is clear that this information was regarded as incidental to his main educational purpose of training the powers of observation and rational thought, and of improving the intellectual and moral status of his pupils.

A prime consequence of Henslow's conception of the educational role of science was a stress on individual practical work by the learners. Accurate knowledge of the structure of plants, for example, required a devotion not to books, but to the specimens themselves. Characteristically, Oliver's *Lessons in Elementary Botany*, based on Henslow's unfinished manuscript and published after his death, opened with the Beetonesque instruction, 'Gather, first of all, a specimen of the Common Buttercup'. In this emphasis on practical knowledge acquired by observation and experiment, Henslow had the strong support of workers in the field of natural history and particularly of J. D. Hooker whose views on the teaching of science were trenchantly expressed in a letter to Asa Gray, criticizing the learning of botany from books. 'Reading without observation on the Sciences of Observation is most destructive. The difference between the modes of teaching required for the Natural Sciences and Moral Sciences, etc., has never yet been properly put, and until it is, all hopes of getting the Natural Sciences introduced into Elementary Education are illusory.'[19]

In theory, at least, almost any of the branches of sciences cultivated in the mid-nineteenth century might have lent themselves to Henslow's ends. Accurate observation, patient experimentation, cautious inference and close reasoning were needed for the successful progress of all the natural sciences. In practice, however, there were problems. Chemistry, he argued, could be ruled out because of the insuperable difficulty of obtaining sufficient apparatus and supplies of reagents to enable pupils to perform experiments for themselves. Mineralogy, likewise, would not serve; many mineral specimens were rare and costly; furthermore, the mathematical prerequisites for dealing with the associated problems of spherical geometry and optics were formidable. Both zoology and entomology were open to the objection that animal life was being disregarded. Apart from the issue of dissection, there was the difficulty of ensuring a steady and adequate supply of specimens for class teaching.[20] On the various branches of physics which Dawes had found so educationally serviceable, Henslow was strangely silent; possibly the cost of apparatus for individual experimental work led him to exclude from consideration subjects such as mechanics and electricity. The increasing application of mathematics to the treatment of physical problems, with the associated 'passionless discussions and repulsive formularies', might have been another factor to which he gave weight. Certainly, from his university experience, he would have been thoroughly familiar with the primacy accorded to mathematical physics. When the palaeontologist, Edward Forbes, visited Cambridge in 1843 he found natural history discouraged as much as possible, being regarded 'as idle trifling by the thousand and one mathematicians of that venerated University',[21] and on William Whewell's scale for measuring the degree to which a science had advanced along the road to induction, subjects like botany occupied a lowly place.[22] It was with some satisfaction, then, that Henslow could argue forcibly for the pre-eminence of his professed study when the sciences were considered from an educational standpoint.

By the mid-nineteenth century botany was a large subject which had become differentiated into a number of separate disciplines. Systematic botany, a term used to cover the classification of plants into their natural order on the basis of plant structure, had for some years been the main pre-occupation of botanists. As a greater understanding of plant development and embryology was acquired, morphology emerged as a distinct area of study, but one which nevertheless could serve the ends of the systematists. In England the Garden at Kew with its living collection, herbarium, library and museum, became, under the effective administration of the Hookers, the great co-ordinating centre for systematic comparison of botanical specimens from all parts of the world. Contemporaneously, however, great advances were being made on other fronts. Microscopic investigations were being undertaken into the structure of plant cells and the application of chemistry and physics to the study of the operation of living plants was establishing the subject of plant physiology. As Henslow acknowledged, physiological botany had many attractions; its results were striking and readily appreciated.[23] Eventually, under Huxley's inspiration, it was to play a significant part in a major reform of biology teaching, but at this earlier stage it appeared a relatively minor branch of botany. Furthermore it represented a concentration on the inward parts of plants which seemed likely to detract from a knowledge of their wholes. In the later years of the century, when the battle between systematists and physiologists had resulted in victory for the latter, it was a frequent complaint of those who had trained under the old regime that the young men 'did not know their plants'.[24]

For Henslow, systematic botany not only had a prior claim on the energies of botanical researchers, in competition with other branches of his subject, but it was, *par excellence*, the aspect of botany which could serve educational ends. It provided for its practitioners a thorough training in close observation; but more than this, it required them to understand those general principles which governed the classification of plants and which represented the general inductive laws of his science. Confronted with an unknown botanical specimen, a pupil had to engage in a systematic examination. noting differences, detecting resemblances, exercising memory, judgement and reasoning faculties in order to draw a valid inference. The process was far from the mechanical application of a received scheme; differences imposing to the eye might, in fact, be superficial or trivial, whilst less obvious resemblances might provide the clues by which the plant could be assigned to its 'genus', 'order' and 'class'. The mental operations involved had much in common with those employed by a doctor in diagnosing a disease and by a lawyer in sifting evidence, a similarity which both Henslow and Hooker emphasized in urging the educational claims of systematic botany.[25]

The case was further strengthened when the requirements for individual practical work were considered. Here systematic botany posed few of the problems associated with other sciences. Not only was the cost of apparatus for collecting, preparing and preserving specimens trifling, there was also 'a free Museum on the grandest scale' readily available to anyone in a rural situation, and only slightly less accessible to town dwellers. Furthermore, after the lessons had served their purpose as an instrument of education and the desired skills had been cultivated, there was still profit to the learner from the factual information which had been imparted. This need not be cast aside 'as we find mathematics to be by the bulk of them who have been educated at Cambridge' Henslow asserted,[26] registering a hit at the critics of botany in his university. Botanical information had practical value in a wide variety of circumstances; the emigrant in a colony, the rich man in his garden, the young women in service charged with the care of her employer's children, and the young man on a farm would all find a knowledge of botany useful. Moral gains might also be expected because familiarity with plants was a source of rational amusement for the leisure hours. As a devout and orthodox churchman, Henslow also saw the study of systematic botany as contributing to the strengthening of religious beliefs by demonstrating 'a unity of design amidst vast diversity of detail'.[27]

At the time when Henslow took up residence in Hitcham, it was a large, neglected rural parish which presented many of the social and moral problems that Dawes had encountered at King's Somborne. Shortly before his arrival, unemployed and vagabond labourers were so numerous that the poor rate amounted to an average of 27 shillings for every man, woman and child in the village. So far as schooling was concerned, there was a marked unwillingness on the part of some of the farmers to assist in finding means of educating the children of labourers and an equal aversion on the part of parents to allow their children to attend school as soon as they could earn the smallest trifle in the fields.[28] The humble village school which Henslow caused to be erected and the teacher he employed, both in large measure at his own expense, were part of a larger programme of reform.[29] Perceptively, his first step was not to moralize or preach, but to cater for the recreational needs of his flock by a firework display on the rectory lawn. His scientific knowledge equipped him well for the role of pyrotechnist; the exhibitions became an annual event at Hitcham and a model for developments elsewhere. 'Tell me,' Darwin earnestly inquired in 1853, '(and it is the most important of my queries on Fire Works) what sum of money will procure a fair village display?'[30]

Over the years ploughing competitions, parish allotments and horticultural shows were introduced, often in the face of considerable opposition, but with uniformly beneficial results. A 'recreation fund' was established in order to support village excursions, one of the most ambitious of which was a three-day visit to London at the time of the Great Exhibition of 1851. Another notable trip occurred in the summer of 1854 when Babington, 'that mighty man of minute differences in British Plants', recorded with commendable restraint that, 'Professor Henslow brought 280 of his parishioners to visit Cambridge. They arrived early in the day, walked over the place, dined, and had tea in Downing College Hall and Combination Room, and returned in the evening. I led the party under Henslow's orders.'[31] Other measures included a 'Wife's Society', 'Coal Club', 'Medical Club', 'Children's Clothing Club', and 'Loan Club', all instituted with a view to encouraging the villagers in practices of mutual charity and habits of self-dependence. Again, Darwin, who was Treasurer and Guardian of the Benefit Club in his village of Down, turned to Henslow for advice on numerous points of organization.[32]

It was in this context that the teaching of botany was undertaken. Initially an extra-curricular activity for volunteers, the early lessons were at irregular intervals and without benefit of any aids other than the plant specimens and writing slates. What commenced 'more as an amusement' than a serious study matured into the most significant element in the curriculum, comprising lessons each Monday afternoon based on an 'educational exercise' and an 'instructional lecture'. Plant stands holding rows of small vials sufficient for almost 300 labelled specimens were fixed to the lower part of one classroom wall. Suspended above was a chart summarizing the classes, divisions and sections into which the plants were to be classified. There were few concessions on the issue of a technical vocabulary; the use of precise scientific expressions was regarded as essential to the accurate description of plants and ability to spell correctly a certain number of botanical terms was an important factor governing progress through the three botany classes. Few pupils failed to get classed because of difficulties over terminology, an achievement which supported Henslow's view that once the scientific idea embodied in a technical term was appreciated, there was no problem about recollecting that term. Individual floral dissections were carried out on specially designed deal boards with the aid of penknives, forceps and hand lenses, the results being entered in a standard form on slates, previously ruled.

When the 'educational exercises' had been completed, the 'instructional lecture' was delivered, based on dried specimens selected from the school herbarium. This part of the course was divided into thirty-six meetings over the year, during which time the complete contents of the herbarium passed under review. The geographical distribution, structural peculiarities, and historical, scriptural and economic connections were all considered. Unquestionably the 'instructional digressions', as Henslow termed them, added much to the course. 'We always wind up', he wrote, 'by tasting something or other which has been flavoured by a product (or perhaps is the product itself) belonging either to an order under review, or to some other more or less closely allied to it!'[33]

E

THE PRINTED SCHEME FOR MONDAY LESSONS.
VILLAGE SCHOOL BOTANY.

Children wishing to learn Botany will be placed in the Third Class, when they shall have learnt to spell correctly the following words :—

CLASS. (I. Exercise.)	DIVISION. (II. Exercise.)	SECTION. (IV. Exercise.)
1. Dicotyledons.	1. Angiospermous.	1. Thalamifloral. 2. Calycifloral. 3. Corollifloral. 4. Incomplete.
	2. Gymnospermous.	(V. Exercise.)
(III. Exercise.)	1. Petaloid.	1. Superior. 2. Inferior.
2. Monocotyledons.	2. Glumaceous.	
3. Acotyledons.		

Children in the Third Class, who have learnt how to fill in the first column of the Floral Schedule, and to spell correctly the following words, will be raised to the Second Class :—

Pistils and Carpels } of Ovary (with Ovules), Style, and Stigma.
Stamens, of Filament and Anther (with Pollen).
Corolla, of Petals } or Perianth, of Leaves.
Calyx, of Sepals }

Children of the Second Class who have learnt how to fill in the second column of the Floral Schedule, and to spell correctly the following words, will be raised to the First Class :—

C. Mono-di-, &c., to poly-phyllous, -sepalous, -petalous, -gynous.
Mon-di-, &c., to poly-androus, -adelphous, Di-, tetra-, dynamous, Syngenesious.

V.	C.	V.	C.	V.	C.
	An- A-			10. Dec-	
1. Mon-	o-	5. Pent-		11. Endec-	
2. Di-	—	6. Hex-		12. Dodec-	a-
3. Tri-	—	7. Hept-	a-	20. Icos-	
4. Tetr-	n-	8. Oct-		∞. Poly-	—
		9. Enne-			

Children of the First Class will learn to fill in the third column of the Floral Schedule, and to spell correctly the following words :—

Hypogynous, Perigynous, Epigynous,
Epipetalous.
Hypogynous, Perigynous, Gynandrous.

Monday Botanical Lessons at 3 P.M., at the School, to include,

1st.—Inspection of a few species, consecutively, in the order on the plant-list. Anything of interest in their structure or properties will then be noticed.
2nd.—Hard word exercises. Two or three words named one Monday are to be correctly spelt the next Monday.
3rd.—Specimens examined, and the parts of the flower laid in regular order upon the dissecting-boards. The Floral Schedule to be traced upon the slates, and filled up as far as possible. Marks to be allowed according to the following scale :—

No.	COHESION, PROPORTION.	ADHESION (INSERTION).	CLASSIFICATION.
P./C. 1 / 3	a-, mono-, &c., gynous 2	Superior or Inferior 2	Class 1 Division 2 Section 3 Order 4 Genus 3 Species 2
St. 1	an-, mon-, &c., androus 2 mon-, &c., adelphous 3 Di-, tetra-, dynamous 3 Syngenesious 2	Hypo-, &c., gynous 4 Epipetalous 3 Gynandrous 3	
f. 1			
a-			
C.P. 1	a-, mono-, &c., petalous 2	Hypo-, &c., gynous 4	
C.S. 1	a-, mono-, &c., sepalous 2	Inferior or Superior 2	
or P.L. 1	a-, mono-, &c., phyllous 2		

4th.—Questions respecting Root ; Stems and Buds ; Leaf and Stipules ; Inflorescence and Bracts ; Flower and Ovules ; Fruit ; Seed and Embryo.

Regulations respecting Botanical Prizes and Excursions.

Prizes awarded according to the joint number of marks obtained at Monday Lessons, from Schedule Labels filled in at home, and for species first found in flower during the season.

Botanical Excursions attended only by those who obtain a sufficient number of marks at Monday Lessons. Two Pic-nic Excursions during the summer, within the precincts of the parish, open to children in each of the three Classes. Other Excursions within the parish are open only to those of the Second and First Classes. An Excursion to a distance from the parish for those of the First Class only who obtain the requisite marks.

The First Class may attend (at the proper season) at the Rectory on Sundays, after Divine Service in the afternoon. Objects of Natural History, in the Animal, Vegetable, and Mineral Kingdoms, will then be exhibited, and such accounts given of them as may tend to improve our means of better appreciating the wisdom, power, and goodness of the Creator.

A copy of the above scheme is given to every child, however young, who is ambitious of being classed as a volunteer Botanist.

Example of a Floral Schedule filled up.

				Cl. Dicotyledons.
P./C. 1 / 2	Monogynous,	Superior,		Div. Angiospermous.
St. 0	Tetradynamous, Hexandrous,	Hypogynous,		Sec. Thalamifloral.
C.P. 4	Tetrapetalous,	Hypogynous,		Ord. Brassicanthu.
C.S. 4	Tetrasepalous,	Inferior.		Gen. Wallflower.
HARRIET SEWEL, No. 7.				Sp. Common.

Table 3

Floral Schedule as used in Henslow's village school at Hitcham

Because boys could readily obtain agricultural employment at an early age and hence tended to remain in school for a shorter time, the success of botany teaching at Hitcham was more marked with the girl pupils.[34] When, in June 1855, Darwin wrote requesting specimens of plants which he could not obtain locally because of the dryness, Henslow recruited the assistance of his botanical scholars. In response to Darwin's lists, a regular supply of the seeds of various Suffolk plants was despatched to Down. 'What wonderful, really wonderful little girls yours are in the Botanical line', rhapsodized Darwin in acknowledgement of yet another consignment later in the summer.[35]

Henslow's school was built around 1840, but it was not until some seventeen years later that he first sought grant for it from the Committee of Council on Education and entered it into union with the National Society for Promoting the Education of the Poor in the Principles of the Established Church. Before this time it would appear to have been maintained out of parish charities, largely from his own purse. As such, and unlike Dawes' school at King's Somborne, it was not subject to inspection; in consequence, Henslow's contribution to the teaching of botany did not receive official recognition from the Education Office until 1859 when the Rev. M. Mitchell, responsible for the inspection of schools in Norfolk, Suffolk and Essex, included in his annual report a description of the botany lessons.[36] Furthermore, Henslow did not himself publish any substantial account of the teaching of botany at Hitcham until encouraged to do so by others.

The explanation of the late attention which his educational work attracted is to be found in developments which took place outside the field of elementary education. On his return to England in 1850, after a second extended period of scientific exploration overseas, Joseph D. Hooker found botanical research in a far from satisfactory state. 'Botany is going down rapidly it appears to me,' he wrote in 1852. 'I don't find one single Botanist started up since I went abroad; many are dead. Something it appears to me may be done by a combined movement in the Universities; is it a time?'[37] Hooker's diagnosis that the teaching of botany was failing to attract students was one thing; the means to achieve an improvement was another. His own positive aversion to teaching led him to stand outside the educational institutions of the day. His position was that of a research worker supported by his half-pay as a Naval Surgeon whilst he completed the botanical work arising from an earlier voyage to the Antarctic; there was also a limited grant from the Department of Woods and Forests to finance the investigation of the Indian collections from his second voyage.[38] Not until 1855 did he achieve a permanent post as assistant to his father, the Director of the Gardens at Kew. In the circumstances there were two courses open to him in his efforts to improve the status of botany among the sciences. The first was to exploit the various examinerships which came his way as an educational lever to produce the needed changes. The second was to assist in the organization of an effective pressure group composed of those who shared his views.

Through the examination for the Apothecaries' Company Medal, open to all England, and through the botany papers set to candidates for the medical service under the East India Company, Hooker attempted to encourage students to study plants rather than books. 'Everyone but Henslow thinks my questions dreadful . . . ,' he wrote to Huxley in 1854. 'You must remember that they (the candidates) had 8 hours; and that my object was to give questions requiring thought rather than *memory*.'[39] Hooker had married Frances Henslow in 1850 and frequently consulted his father-in-law on matters relating to the teaching of botany. 'I wish very much you could afford half an hour to think over the subject of Botany as a branch of education and a means of mental culture specially adapted to the early education of Medical men,' he requested Henslow in 1855. 'I . . . want to drive it into the heads of Medical men and students; that it is not with the hope that the Botanical knowledge obtained will ever be of the slightest direct advantage to the man in practice that it should be taught, but because . . . the mental training of a good elementary

Botanical or Nat. Hist. course is the best means of becom-
ing skilful in diagnosis of diseases and of developing his
ideas.'[40] The system of competitive examinations for the
Medical Officers of the Indian Army, in the origin of which
Hooker played a leading part, was later extended to the
British Army and to the Navy.

The influence of these attempted examination reforms
was, understandably, limited. The more significant achievements resulted from his endeavours to co-ordinate the activities of those who shared his views on the most appropriate
methods of teaching science. For a period between his
Antarctic and Indian expeditions, Hooker had been employed as fossil botanist to the Geological Survey, during
which time his colleagues had included Edward Forbes and
Lyon Playfair, palaeontologist and chemist to the Survey
respectively. On his return to England, it was natural that
he should look to them as possible allies. Forbes moved
north to the chair of natural history at Edinburgh in 1854,
but not before a productive crossing of his path with that
of Henslow.

Among Henslow's many regional activities was the
support he lent to the Ipswich Museum founded in 1848 'for
giving Instruction to the Working Classes of Ipswich in
various branches of Science, and more especially in Natural
History'.[41] In 1850, Henslow was elected President of the
Museum, the effective organization of which was a matter
of considerable interest to him. The occasion of his installa-
tion was marked by a lecture from Forbes, who also had
given much thought to the function of museums.[42] A year
later, following the meeting of the British Association for
the Advancement of Science at Ipswich, a committee was
established, with Henslow as chairman and both Forbes and
Hooker as members, to advise 'On a Typical Series of
Objects in Natural History, adapted to Local Museums'.
The report was published by the Association in 1855.
Although Forbes was lost to the cause of improved science
teaching by his untimely death shortly after his translation
to Edinburgh, the Museum question served to bring Henslow's educational activities to the notice of a wide circle,

including the officials of the recently established Department of Science and Art. Created in 1853 under the Board
of Trade with the object of encouraging industrial instruction, the new department consolidated a number of established institutions such as the Government School of Mines,
the Museum of Practical Geology and the Geological
Survey. The contribution of museums to the diffusion of
scientific knowledge was a subject central to the concerns
of a department which was later to administer the South
Kensington collections. Lyon Playfair, Hooker's former colleague, was now Secretary to the Science Division of the
new department; his fellow Secretary, Henry Cole, responsible for the Art Division, had a major responsibility for the
British contribution to the Paris Exhibition in 1855, at which
Henslow exhibited a set of Carpological Illustrations which
was much admired by the Paris botanists.[43]

In this way Henslow's contribution to the teaching of
botany at Hitcham became known to the officials of the
Department of Science and Art before it was recognized by
the government office with a prime responsibility for elementary education. Under the heading of aids to science teaching which it was supporting, the third Report of the
Department of Science and Art, dated June 1856, referred
to a set of nine coloured diagrams on structural and systematic botany which Henslow had nearly completed.[44] These
were intended to teach beginners how certain important
technical terms were employed and were prepared by Walter
Fitch who worked with the Hookers at Kew. 'Fitch has just
completed a most magnificent set of 9 Elephant-folio plates
with illustrations and analysis of about 50 Nat. Ords. and
genera designed by Henslow, and superintended by your
humble servant. It is done for National Schools under Board
of Trade', Hooker informed a correspondent in March
1857.[45] Shortly after this a teachers' manual was prepared
for the South Kensington Museum by Henslow; entitled
*Illustrations to be employed in Practical Lessons on Botany
adapted to Beginners of all Classes*, it consisted of descriptions of his teaching scheme, plant lists, floral schedules and
apparatus used at Hitcham. Both the diagrams and the

manual were designed with the intention of encouraging the first-hand experience of plants which Henslow and Hooker regarded as essential for the reform of botany teaching.

Another important ally of Hooker in his attempt to influence the teaching of science was the young man appointed to replace Edward Forbes as Professor of Natural History in the Government School of Mines, Thomas Henry Huxley. Huxley's background was in many ways similar to Hooker's;[46] after a medical training he had entered the navy as an assistant surgeon, being appointed to the expedition on the *Rattlesnake* which surveyed the coast of Australia and other islands. The two men became close friends and from 1864 were members of the famous X-Club, the small group of nine once described as 'the most powerful and influential scientific coterie in England'.[47]

It is clear that the subject of science teaching was one to which Hooker and Huxley gave their attention with almost conspiratorial zeal in the mid-50s. 'My own impression', confided Hooker to Huxley early in 1856, 'is that we shall make no great advance in teaching Nat. Science in this country, except by some joint effort of Botanists and Zoologists who should pave the way by propounding a strictly scientific elementary system – were this once effected we have sufficient command over the public, as examiners in London, and as confidential advisers to examiners and professors elsewhere, to ensure the cordial reception of such a system. What with Henslow's Botanical School diagrams now in progress and Museum Types we have made a fair start, and if you do not occupy the field in Zoology some pitiful botcher or other will.'[48]

For one who had little first-hand knowledge of the problems of teaching science, Hooker might be thought to have exhibited the over-confidence of youth in the freedom with which he bestowed advice on needed changes. To some extent the sanction for his views was his limited experience as an examiner; he relied also on information derived from Henslow; but most important of all was his profound understanding of the nature of his subject. The discipline of botanical inquiry was the prime determinant of his curriculum prescription. Systematic botany, 'the exposition of the laws upon which plants are formed as well as classified naturally,' should be the main goal of the beginner, with its potential for exercising reasoning faculties and encouraging pupils to think for themselves. A moderate amount of subject matter, thoroughly treated, 'teaching through mind and eye and hand', was his advice to his friend Harvey, newly appointed in 1856 to the chair of botany in Dublin. 'I have been talking a good deal about lecturing with Huxley, who has come to absolutely identical conclusions, and is going to alter his course accordingly at the Govt School of Mines', he revealed to Harvey the following year. 'This *entre nous* at present. He and I have often talked over the subject, and he is quite of my opinion that the present mode of teaching is worse than useless.'[49]

The recognition as an eminently successful pioneer of botany teaching which was granted to Henslow in the closing years of his life can thus be accounted for in terms of the emergence of a strong movement to reform the teaching of 'the sciences of observation' in the 1850s. Leadership of this movement was assumed by Hooker and Huxley, representing the sciences of botany and zoology respectively and Henslow's relationship to the former was an important factor in making more widely known his achievements in botany teaching at Hitcham. However, the effective diffusion of Henslow's curriculum innovation, like that of Dawes, depended upon a variety of factors by far the most important of which was the existence of a body of teachers equipped with appropriate knowledge and skills.[50] The main source of supply of teachers for elementary schools, the training colleges maintained by the various religious providing bodies, lay outside the sphere of influence of the Department of Science and Art and the teaching of botany on the lines laid down by Henslow made little progress in the type of school in which it had been evolved. Somewhat ironically – although in confirmation of Henslow's view that practical botany was suitable for the education of all classes – greater advances were made in the public and endowed secondary schools, particularly after the reports of the

Clarendon Commission in 1864 and the Taunton Commission four years later.

In this connection, the case of Rugby School is of significance. Shortly after the appointment of the Rev. J. M. Wilson as science master in January, 1859, Frederick Temple, the Headmaster of Rugby, sought Lyon Playfair's advice on the fitting up of a school chemical laboratory. It was arranged that Wilson should study under Playfair's supervision at Edinburgh University during the Christmas vacation and by 1860 a small chemistry laboratory was in regular use at Rugby.[51] Four years later, following the recommendations of the Public School Commissioners, Temple resolved to make science a compulsory subject for all boys below the upper school, a decision which entailed the teaching of science to more than 250 boys in the autumn of 1864. Although a new member of staff was recruited to be responsible for chemistry and physics, it did not prove possible to secure his services until the following year. In these circumstances, Wilson and his colleague, F. E. Kitchener, were advised by Temple to make botany the subject which was first introduced throughout the middle school, not least because it could be taught practically without waiting for the special accommodation which other sciences required and which was not then available. Following an approach to Hooker, Wilson and Kitchener spent the long vacation at Barmouth learning botany under the tuition of Henslow's son, George, then aged twenty-nine and recently appointed headmaster of Hampton Lucy Grammar School, Warwick.[52]

Both Wilson and Temple were influential figures in the future development of botany as a school subject. Together with Huxley and Tyndall, Wilson was a member of a small committee which was established by the British Association for the Advancement of Science to consider the best means of promoting scientific instruction in schools. Their report of 1867, issued as a white paper and reprinted in the Report of the Taunton Commission, placed botany on a par with physics and chemistry as a school subject capable of providing a training in the methods of science.[53] For his part, Temple was a leading member of the Taunton Commission which was charged to inquire into the endowed and grammar schools. The secretary to the Commissioners records that substantial parts of the final report and recommendations were drafted by Temple whose influence can be discerned in the approval given to botany as the most suitable science for young boys, with experimental physics and chemistry following at a later stage.[54]

It was in schools such as Rugby that the most durable memorial to Henslow's educational work was to be found during the last third of the nineteenth century and, ironically, for one who was acutely aware of the tyranny of books in the field of science teaching, it took the form of an elementary text on botany. For some years before his death he had been preparing a work intended as an aid to those who wished to introduce the teaching of botany into schools such as Hitcham; the scope is indicated by his proposed title, *Practical Lessons in Systematic and Economic Botany, Educational and Instructional, for the use of Beginners in Village Schools and Upwards*.[55] The work was six years in preparation; Darwin encouraged him in his task and Hooker provided frank criticism of the contents and presentation;[56] completion was prevented by Henslow's death in 1861. Eventually Hooker and George Henslow placed the manuscript in the hands of Daniel Oliver, Keeper of the Herbarium and Library at Kew and Professor of Botany in University College, London, who pruned the systematic section of much of Henslow's 'instructional material' and prefaced it with some introductory chapters on structural and physiological botany. The resulting *Lessons in Elementary Botany* enjoyed much success; in the words of a reviewer, 'No one could have thought that so much thoroughly correct botany could have been so simply and happily taught in so small a volume.'[57] By the early seventies the book was widely used in public and 'first grade' schools as evidence collected by Norman Lockyer, secretary to the Devonshire Commissioners, revealed; in elementary schools it was a different story and the same commissioners heard little from their witnesses to suggest that Henslow's example at Hitcham had inspired imitation elsewhere.[58]

Chapter 4

Henry Moseley: engineer of reform

The extent to which particular grass-root innovations such as those at King's Somborne and Hitcham were able to exert a general influence on the curriculum of elementary schools was dependent in large measure on the support provided by the regulations of the Committee of Council on Education. Established in 1839 under the Lord President of the Privy Council, the Committee was the national body responsible for the administration of parliamentary grant in aid of education. Its guiding principle was that the voluntary character of elementary and training schools should be maintained; grant was offered not as a substitute for local effort, but as an encouragement and supplement to it. Nevertheless, the association of grant with specific objectives and the introduction of a system of inspection to ensure that prescribed conditions were being fulfilled enabled the Committee to give direction to the development of elementary education. It is necessary, therefore, to turn now from an examination of curriculum developments in particular schools to a consideration of influences within the Education Office in Whitehall.

Initially state aid to education was restricted to the single purpose of building schools, but the regulations were soon extended to include the purchase of books and equipment, an agreed fraction of the expenditure on approved items being recoverable by a school. The Committee was also concerned to encourage the supply of suitably trained teachers to staff elementary schools and a system was created whereby pupil-teachers, after an apprenticeship in a school, might qualify by examination for a Queen's scholarship to a train-

ing college. At the end of a period of training, a further
examination led to certification which entitled the successful
candidates to proficiency grants towards their stipends. To
the extent that the Committee of Council sanctioned the
subjects of examination and the levels of attainment which
were acceptable, there was direct control of the quality of
the most important of educational resources, the teacher.
'The training colleges', wrote Kay-Shuttleworth, '. . . practically regulate the standard and methods of instruction' in
schools.[1] By virtue of the administrative influence which the
Education Department exerted on the Colleges, secular
education at the elementary level could be controlled by the
civil power.

James Phillips Kay (later Kay-Shuttleworth) was appointed
secretary to the newly established Committee of Council on
Education in the summer of 1839 and continued to serve
in that capacity until overwork and ill-health forced his
resignation some ten years later. His considerable influence
on the work of the Committee during its early years, particularly in relation to school inspection, the establishment
of the pupil-teacher system and the training of teachers, is
too well known to require detailed comment here.[2] For the
present study his significance lies in the uniformly hospit-
able attitude which he demonstrated towards the introduction of scientific knowledge into the school curriculum.

Kay-Shuttleworth's early interests in scientific experimentation have already been noted.[3] At Edinburgh University,
where he studied medicine with considerably more success
than his contemporary Charles Darwin, he made a name as
a speaker in the Royal Medical Society, before which body
on one occasion he defended the educational claims of
science against those of classics.[4] Experience during his
subsequent years as a physician in Manchester, working
among impoverished labourers and factory workers, broad-
ened his interests to include the general condition and welfare
of the poor. Following his appointment in 1835 as a Poor
Law Commissioner, the education of pauper children in workhouse schools became a subject of special concern to him.

It was to Scotland, and to Wood and Stow in particular,

that Kay-Shuttleworth turned for enlightenment on the problems of organizing these schools. Following visits to Edinburgh and Glasgow a number of Scottish-trained teachers were persuaded to accept posts in English schools with notably successful results.[5] The curricula of continental schools and of various industrial schools in this country were also carefully studied. Convinced that existing sources could not provide the supply of trained teachers upon which educational progress depended, Kay-Shuttleworth directed the attention of his political masters to this issue in the autumn of 1839. The curriculum for a training school which he then proposed included the study of English, Mathematics, Industrial Science; Social Geography and History; Colonial Geography; notions in Natural History; notions in Natural Philosophy; Agricultural Chemistry; general laws of fluids and uniform bodies; the elements of parish law; Book-keeping; Vocal Music; Industrial Pursuits; Gymnastics; and Pedagogy.[6] Overburdened it might have been, but there was no antipathy here towards the inclusion of scientific and useful knowledge in the curriculum.

In fact, the scheme was the blueprint for the training college at Battersea which Kay-Shuttleworth and his colleague, Tufnell, established as a private venture once official approval had been secured. In its early days, Kay-Shuttleworth resided in the new college himself so that he might more closely supervise its development. Of the three original tutors whom he appointed, two – William Horne and Walter McLeod – were trained in Scotland, whilst the third, Thomas Tate, a remarkable pioneer of science and mathematics teaching, was a self-educated Northumbrian whose knowledge had been acquired from those sources associated with the autodidactic tradition in science.[7]

Kay-Shuttleworth's further contribution to the movement for teaching the science of common things will be considered in a later chapter. It is sufficient here to establish that the first occupant of the vitally important administration position of Secretary to the Committee of Council on Education was not only professionally interested in science as a branch of learning, but saw it as having a distinctive educational contribution to make. This was the case not only in schools for the labouring poor and paupers, but generally. Towards the close of his life he gave valuable service alongside Huxley, Lubbock, Sharpey and Stokes, as one of the nine Devonshire Commissioners appointed to inquire into Scientific Instruction and the Advancement of Science, an important contribution to which his biographer regrettably devotes a single brief paragraph. He was a significant influence also on particular institutions. The reputation as a strong centre of science teaching enjoyed by Giggleswick School in the late nineteenth century was not unconnected with Kay-Shuttleworth's service, initially as one of the new governors appointed in 1864 by order of the Charity Commissioners, and later as Chairman of the Governors.[8]

What he advocated in public, he practised in private. The education of his eldest son, Ughtred, included chemistry lessons which appear to have been arranged at the family home, Gawthorpe Hall. From Harrow, Ughtred was later to consult his father on the desirability of keeping up the study of physiology. 'I want you to decide whether I had not better (this being my first and therefore most difficult quarter) go in for the Natural Science (examination) next quarter not this, when I shall have the advantage of preparing it with you in the holidays', he wrote.[9] The study of chemistry, at least, bore fruit in that a manual of inorganic chemistry, *First Principles of Modern Chemistry*, by Ughtred Kay-Shuttleworth, was published in 1868.

It was not long before the growth of work in the Education Office revealed the inadequacy of the original provision for the inspection of schools in receipt of parliamentary grant. By November 1843 the Lords of the Committee of Council on Education were obliged to recommend the appointment of additional inspections[10] and Kay-Shuttleworth seized the opportunity to secure the services of an inspector with scientific qualifications. Two years earlier, following a highly critical report on the Greenwich Hospital Schools, he had pressed the case for the transfer of responsibility for these schools from the Navy to the Committee of Council, at the same time recruiting to his office an inspector with knowledge of science and mathematics particularly in their applications to gunnery, navigation, shipbuilding and naval construction. The drastic reforms at Greenwich in fact took a different course and Kay-Shuttleworth's recommended candidate for the post of inspector, the Rev. Henry Moseley, F.R.S., could not be appointed.[11] The expansion approved in the autumn of 1843 provided a new opportunity, however, and Moseley became the first of Her Majesty's Inspectors of Schools to possess a scientific and mathematical background.

Educational work was no new experience for Moseley, although he had little acquaintance with the type of school with which the Committee of Council was concerned. His father, Dr William Willis Moseley, had kept a large private school at Newcastle under Lyme and Moseley had been educated at the grammar school of the town until aged fifteen or sixteen, after which he had spent some time at a school in the manufacturing town of Abbeville in northern France and at a naval school at Portsmouth.[12] It is probable that his deep interest in naval architecture stemmed from this period; apart from the influence of Portsmouth, Abbeville, straddling the Somme and close to the Channel, included ship-building among its industries. His period in France also introduced him to the work of continental mathematicians. In 1821 he entered St John's College, Cambridge, matriculating the following year, and graduating in 1826 as seventh wrangler. Dawes and Henslow were his seniors; during his five years in residence it seems likely that he would have met the latter, both as a fellow Johnian and also as secretary of the Cambridge Philosophical Society to which Moseley later submitted papers. Unlike them, however, he did not remain at Cambridge; he was ordained, becoming curate at West Monkton, near Taunton, where he was able to continue his mathematical studies and complete his first book, *A Treatise on Hydrostatics and Hydrodynamics* (Cambridge, 1830). In January 1831 he was elected to the chair of Natural and Experimental Philosophy, including Astronomy, in the newly created and still unopened King's College, London.

At an early date it was recognized that the scope of his chair was unrealistically wide, and a division of labour was achieved when Charles Wheatstone was appointed as professor of experimental philosophy in 1834, Moseley retaining the chair of natural philosophy and astronomy.[13] Even so, problems remained. There were few precedents to serve as guides on the most appropriate mode of teaching natural philosophy in a university course. The central pedagogical issue was the extent to which mathematics should be introduced. When, in 1833, the young J. D. Forbes, strongly supported by Cambridge mathematicians such as Whewell, Airy and Peacock, was appointed in preference to Sir David Brewster to the prestigious chair of natural philosophy at Edinburgh, Moseley consulted him on this point. 'Any doubt as to the propriety of viewing Mixed Mathematics as belonging to a Natural Philosophy class is at this moment peculiarly untenable', Forbes replied. 'For the whole progress of *General Physics* is happily so fast tending to a subjection to Mathematical Laws of that department of science, that in no very long time, Magnetism, Electricity and Light may be expected to be as fully the objects of dynamical reasoning, as Gravitation is at the present moment.'[14] With this judgement Moseley undoubtedly had much sympathy; he was a distinguished student of the Cambridge school himself and there is evidence from his own writings that he fully recognized the powerful contribution which mathematics, and the analytical methods of continental mathematicians in particular, could make to the advancement of scientific knowledge. In his own book on hydrostatics and hydrodynamics he had made considerable use of calculus. Yet, like Brewster, he was sensitive to the pedagogical danger of 'substituting symbols for operations of the mind . . . and for the very objects of discussion,'[15] with a consequent increase in the risk of losing relevance to real-life situations.

His dilemma was sharpened both by his own predilection towards the applications of scientific knowledge to useful ends and by pressures from contemporary society. The historian of King's College has pointed out that the years during which Moseley held his chair were ones of great engineering activity throughout the land; 'new macadamized roads, new canals, new factories, new buildings, new coal- and iron-mines, above all, new railways, were in ubiquitous process of construction. The demand for trained mechanics, surveyors, architects and designers was vast, far exceeding the supply.'[16] In response to this situation, a class in civil engineering was inaugurated in King's College in 1838, Moseley being responsible for the course in mechanics. By 1844 the department had grown to one of General Instruction in the Applied Sciences, but not before it had experienced an almost annual change of title, reflecting the enlarging scope and fluctuating bias of its studies.[17] In such a context, as his own texts on *Mechanics applied to the Arts* and *Mechanical Principles of Engineering and Architecture* make clear, the emphasis needed to be on the practical applications of scientific principles, with formal mathematical proofs appended for more specialized study. Neither the previous knowledge of the majority of his students nor the vocational ends they had in mind encouraged the more abstract and mathematical treatment of scientific problems which Forbes was advocating at Edinburgh.

Moseley's increasing association with applied science and engineering was a factor which led to his involvement in at least two extra-mural activities, both relevant to his later work with the Committee of Council. The establishment in Cornwall of a school for teaching those branches of science most applicable to mining had been under discussion for a number of years. In 1839, largely through the efforts of Sir Charles Lemon, F.R.S., the member of parliament for West Cornwall, a school of this type was opened at Truro; after satisfactory attendance at an introductory course, pupils embarked upon a three-month period of concentrated study of mathematics, mechanics and chemistry in their relations to mining. With his colleague T. G. Hall, Professor of Mathematics at King's College, Moseley played an important part in the planning and conduct of this course. Twelve years later he carried out what was perhaps the most thorough curriculum evaluation which had been under-

F

taken at that time by tracing the subsequent history of each of the boys who had followed the original course at Truro.[18]

The other activity brought him even closer to the orbit of Kay-Shuttleworth. With the establishment of Battersea Training School, Moseley was consulted as an authority on science teaching not only by Thomas Tate, the master in charge of this aspect of the Battersea programme, but also by the Rev. John Allen, a former colleague of Moseley at King's, whose duties as an inspector of schools included reporting on the new development in teacher training. Without the benefit of assistance from Moseley, Allen confessed, he would have been at a loss to carry out a competent examination of the important section of the curriculum for which Tate was responsible.[19]

It was clear that there was a need within the Education Office for an inspector who could authoritatively monitor curriculum developments in the field of science and mathematics, particularly in relation to the training of teachers. Significantly, an applied scientist was selected to fill the post. Moseley's appointment provided Kay-Shuttleworth with a resource of outstanding potential whilst there is evidence to suggest that Moseley himself was in no way disconsolate at having to relinquish his chair. The minutes of the Council of King's College record that he had sought a testimonial some years previously when a post at the Greenwich Naval School had become vacant, but on that occasion had been denied his request because Council had 'come to a determination not to grant testimonials in any case'.[20] His move to the Education Office was approved by the Archbishop of Canterbury who had the power to veto and terminate such appointments, as well as suggest suitable persons. In January 1844 Moseley embarked upon his new duties.

Initially, Kay-Shuttleworth tutored his science inspector with meticulous care and Moseley later acknowledged the Secretary to the Committee of Council as a major benefactor in relation to his educational work.[21] The elaborate instructions for inspectors of schools, previously drawn up in 1839, were now supplemented by suggestions of texts for reading, practical advice on school organization and replies to specific queries arising from the weekly journals which inspectors were required to submit. For his part, Moseley learnt rapidly; his reports, informed and perceptive from the first, testified to a discernment in relation to educational matters which quickly established him as an impressive authority in his own right. Particularly in relation to the curriculum of training schools and to the material resources for elementary education his views were reflected in a series of decisions taken by the Committee of Council.

Within the framework of his theological and sociological assumptions, Moseley's contribution during his eleven years in the Education Office was one of singular industry and inventiveness. As an orthodox churchman he never departed from the belief that the ultimate goals of elementary education were religious and moral ones; as a conscientious civil servant, and unlike Dawes, he regarded the class barriers of the stratified society in which he worked as pre-ordained and permanent. Yet on questions such as the organization of elementary education, the educational value of various branches of knowledge and the curriculum appropriate to the labouring poor he was an uncomfortably challenging, yet constructive, critic of prevailing practices. The monitorial system, in which the influence of a teacher was exerted vicariously through the intervention of older pupils, was an early target for his pen. 'To *educate* children', he wrote, 'the (direct) action of an enlightened teacher upon them is required, with an individual application to each individual mind. There must be the separate contact of the mind of the master with the mind of the child; the separate study of it; the separate ministering to its wants, checking its waywardness, propping up, and guiding, and encouraging its first efforts; building it up, and establishing it . . . I claim . . . as a privilege of the child, and as a paramount duty of the master, that his own individual culture of the child's mind, his own direct and personal labour upon it, should begin from the moment when the child first enters the school, and never be interrupted until it leaves it.'[22]

Moseley was arguing here for a more effective distribution of the resources available to elementary education. His analysis of pupil activities distinguished between individual and silent occupations such as writing, drawing and 'slate arithmetic'; group practice in skills such as reading which could be carried out under the supervision of monitors or pupil-teachers; and oral instruction of classes involving the direct influence of a teacher.[23] This last element in his tripartite scheme, the essential agency by which a child might be encouraged to reflect and reason, was regarded by Moseley as fundamental to the organization he proposed. Its main drawback was that it offered limited opportunities for the child to think as an independent agent, to seek knowledge for himself and overcome difficulties without the aid of a teacher. To this end it was necessary to devise situations involving self-instruction, an activity which depended upon the availability of suitable books. 'It is in the well-balanced union of the two methods of oral instruction by the master and self-instruction by the child,' wrote Moseley, 'the former being pursued in the school and the latter prescribed by the master but pursued during the child's leisure hours at home, that the secret of elementary education appears to consist.'[24]

The question of school books adapted to the purpose of elementary education was one to which Moseley turned repeatedly in his early reports. Partly on grounds of economy (its cost being considerably less than that of any secular book of comparable size) the work most frequently used in the teaching of reading was the Bible. However, whilst pupils might be able to read mechanically from the Scriptures, inspection revealed a widespread lack of comprehension of the subject matter. Further, in Moseley's experience, 'a child taught to read only in the Scriptures, appears, in some measure, to have lost the faculty of reading when any other book is placed in its hands'. If the inspectors' test of reading ability had employed a secular text instead of the Bible, the results would have been even less satisfactory than reported.[25]

For Moseley it was essential that pupils should be familiar with the resources of written language if their minds were to be enlightened, their manners humanized, and their leisure hours usefully and pleasantly occupied by the perusal of books.[26] It followed that more appropriate textual aids were needed than those generally employed in schools, but in laying down the specification which such works had to satisfy, he rejected the view that reading could be taught as a mechanical skill independent of an understanding of subject matter. A plurality of objectives was associated with the reading lesson, including the imparting of useful information and the development of rational modes of thought. By a carefully graduated progression, reading lesson books would simultaneously extend the linguistic competence of pupils, exercise their powers of reasoning and enlarge their general knowledge.

The lack in children of the working classes of everyday knowledge, with its correlates, a paucity of ideas and a poverty of diction, was the characteristic of elementary education which struck Moseley most forcibly after his first tour of inspection of schools in the Midlands.[27] Unless elementary schools could compensate for these common elements of knowledge which, in the case of children of 'the more educated classes', were derived from their homes, pupils would at best be half-educated and a chasm would remain between the minds of the educated and the uneducated. In a striking passage which foreshadowed the distinction drawn a century later between restricted and elaborated codes, Moseley described the learning problems of a child from a working-class home:[28] 'Words familiar to the ears of our children, and recognized by them in their true meaning when they are first taught to read them, are strange to the children of a labourer, and unintelligible; and those more complicated modes of expression which are proper to elaborate forms of thought, and which exercise the reasoning faculties of our children from an early period, conceal effectively from the apprehension of the children of the poor the idea in the construction.' Indeed, an education which was derived predominantly from a middle-class literary culture might well have the consequences of inhibiting the growth of rationality in the children of the labouring poor.

In this way, Moseley was brought to focus his attention on the content of the curriculum of elementary schools. 'School houses may be built and teachers maintained', he wrote, 'and yet the education of the people may remain to be provided for.'[29] Little progress would be achieved until the curriculum was better adapted to the needs of children in elementary schools. Yet the providers of education were singularly ill-qualified for the design task in hand. 'The inner life of the classes below us in society is never penetrated by us. We are profoundly ignorant of the springs of public opinion, the elements of thought, and the principles of action among them – those things which we recognize at once as constituting our own social life, in all the great moral features which give to it its form and substance.'[30] It was a grave error to suppose that, for the education of the poor man's child, nothing more was required than was needed for the education of middle- and upper-class children. In reality, the task was an infinitely more difficult one. The ineffectiveness of so much of elementary education hitherto was due to the practice of breaking off a fragment from upper class education – its mechanical and technical part – and giving it to the poor man's child in charity. 'To give to such a child the mechanical power to read, without teaching it to comprehend the language of books', Moseley argued, 'is to give it a resource which is not likely to be used, and which will probably be soon lost. And when we have taught the child to understand the language of books, to leave it without instruction in respect of all those collateral elements of knowledge which are necessary to the full intelligence of that which we read in respect of any one element, is to leave the child in an ignorance almost as entire as though the language of the book remained unknown to it.'[31]

Moseley was in no sense arguing for an attempt to impart a superficial acquaintance with a wide spectrum of secular knowledge. Indeed, he had previously expressed the view that 'a thorough mastery of one branch of knowledge constitutes in itself an education'.[32] The fundamental problem in designing a curriculum for the schools of the people was to identify those branches of knowledge with the greatest potential for promoting moral and intellectual improvement. To these ends and with these children not all subjects were of equal worth. By 1845 Moseley had begun to establish his scale of knowledge values; the case for geography, particularly in its local aspects, was considered with approval;[33] arithmetic, if looked upon as the logic of the people and developed with relevance to the intellectual culture of the working class child, was also an essential ingredient;[34] but no branch of secular instruction was likely to be more effective in elevating the character of the labouring man than a knowledge of those principles of science which had an application to his welfare and future occupations.[35] Armed in this way, the child had a resource of immense value for his future struggle with the material elements of existence. He would be equipped to avoid the degradation of mindless labour, whilst acquaintance with the laws of nature would place in his hands one link of a chain which led up to God.

By 1847, the various strands of Moseley's developing educational thought had conjoined to yield a coherent theory of elementary education embracing the content of the curriculum, methods of instruction, textual aids and the training of teachers. Administrative decisions had already been taken by the Committee of Council in concordance with his views. In 1846 the pupil-teacher system had been inaugurated and the following year grant was extended to aid the purchase of reading-lesson and text books for use in elementary schools and training colleges.[36] Nevertheless, between the idealized scheme and the concrete reality of most National Schools there remained a gulf of wide dimensions. It was understandable therefore that, when in the spring of 1847, transfer to a new school district brought King's Somborne to his notice, Moseley should vigorously uphold this as a remarkable manifestation of his educational views. Here was an education based on respect for the culture of the labouring classes; an attempt had been made to imbue the reading books and oral lessons with secular knowledge selected in terms of its relevance to village children. The result, as measured by the physical, mental and moral attainments, was outstanding. The curriculum of

King's Somborne 'deals with reason rather than with facts, and with things rather than with words,' Moseley explained, in analysing the reasons for Dawes' success. 'Intended for a class of persons who are to delve out an existence from the material objects which surrounds them, it assumes the properties of these objects to be legitimate subjects of interest to them, and of reflection.'[37] It followed that in such a scheme 'the science of common things' should occupy a central place.

The contrast with Henslow's views could scarcely have been sharper. For Henslow the educational value of science lay primarily in the process of scientific inquiry and in the disciplining of mental faculties For Moseley, as for Dawes, the emphasis was on the utility and application of the product. Compared with the knowledge which resulted from scientific inquiry, the inductive aspects of science had little to contribute to the education of the labouring poor. Particularly through the study of subjects such as mechanics and chemistry a child was enabled not only to satisfy his natural curiosity about the world around him, but was equipped to transform it, to achieve practical ends which he deemed worthwhile. Labour undertaken in this spirit, in which there was an association of thinking and acting, was pleasurable, in contrast to mindless work, directed to no useful end. It was Moseley's matured view that 'To develop this character of the *maker* in the child, as contrasted with the *worker*, is the function of physical science in elementary education.'[38]

From a difference in objectives, differences in teaching methods and content stemmed. For Henslow, individual experimental work was an entailed means of achieving his prescribed end; and rather than utility, practical considerations of cost and availability of resources determined the choice of subject matter. For Dawes and Moseley no such intimacy with the techniques of scientific investigation was required; scientific knowledge was something to be understood and used without the necessity of undergoing the discipline of inquiry. It was legitimate to acquire scientific knowledge from books and the purpose of 'experiments' was to make more vivid and concrete the abstract verbal account. In consequence experiments could be performed as demonstrations by the teacher, with limited pupil involvement. The 'conversational lecture', an oral lesson based upon experiments, was the appropriate instructional mode. As to subject matter, relevance to the material needs of the learners was the prime consideration.

There is no evidence to suggest that Moseley was aware of Henslow's school before the early fifties or that his advocacy of the King's Somborne curriculum was an act of deliberate choice between two competing paradigms of science education. His first communication with Henslow would appear to have been late in 1852 over the question of diagrams used in the teaching of botany at Cambridge and Hitcham.[39] At that time Moseley was already deeply involved in the promotion of the movement for teaching 'the science of common things' whilst Henslow's experiment in teaching botany to village children was still in a rudimentary stage. Despite mutual invitations, circumstances prevented the two men from meeting and Henslow's contribution to science teaching remained unnoted by the Education Office until the end of the decade. Even if knowledge of Henslow's work at Hitcham had come earlier to the inspectorate it is doubtful if Moseley's course of action would have been different. The congruence between his educational beliefs and the practical experience of Dawes was striking to a degree. Furthermore, his opinions on the most appropriate elementary school curriculum had much in common with those of powerful influences such as Kay-Shuttleworth. To have changed direction would have been to risk slowing down the progress of elementary education at a time when the prospects for advance seemed unusually favourable. Theoretical considerations and practical expediency conspired to the same end. Until the appointment of Frederick Temple as his successor in July 1855 Moseley worked tirelessly to secure the conditions necessary for the introduction of science as a basic component of the elementary school curriculum.

If at times the arguments he employed in support of the

educational value of science seem tinged with a spurious and contrived pragmatism, it is necessary to bear in mind the latent distrust of science amongst many who would read his reports. In such a context religious and moral categories could never safely be neglected in discussion of the outcomes of school science teaching. In so far as a knowledge of science enabled a connection to be forged between thinking and doing, so transforming labour into a pleasurable activity, it was seen as promoting the designs of Providence and sweetening the daily toil of the worker. It could even be that strikes and industrial unrest would be diminished if labour was so informed with understanding. Yet if in his public utterances on education Moseley justified the teaching of science in terms of its stabilizing influence on the structure of a hierarchical society, he also saw science as the great transformer of the material condition of the nation.

His views were most forcefully expressed to Sir Charles Trevelyan who sought Moseley's comments on proposals for the reorganization of the civil service early in 1854. The Trevelyan–Northcote report, together with Jowett's appendix giving details of a scheme of examination, had received a wide circulation. For appointments in the higher grades of the service, Jowett proposed an examination comprising four 'schools', any two of which might be chosen by a candidate:

1. Classical literature;
2. Mathematics with practical applications and natural sciences;
3. Political economy, law, moral philosophy;
4. Modern languages and modern history.

Of this classification Moseley was severely critical. Mathematics, he stressed, was a very different study from a natural science. But worse than this, 'To place all that goes by the name of science in one (so called) school out of four . . . is not . . . to accept *the present* of human knowledge, or to look to *the future*, but to hark back into *the past*.' The public mind was now educating itself according to a scientific rather than a literary type and the examination ought to reflect this. Otherwise there would be a danger that one type of education would come to be represented in the administration of public affairs. 'The idiosyncrasy of *one class* of mind will pass upon it, and (to use an engineering phrase) it will eventually be shunted upon the rails of one class of thinkers.' Moseley's remedy was the addition of three further 'schools' in 'experimental science', 'mechanical science' and 'the sciences of observation'. Without this exten- sion, many scientists who had exercised a major influence on the material welfare of the country would have been excluded by Jowett's scheme which also failed to provide any open- ing for engineers – 'a class of men who seem to be taking the world into their own hands'.[40]

In effect, Moseley was challenging the conception of a liberal education implicit in Jowett's proposals. Experience had shown that, although a scientist might devote himself almost exclusively to one department of knowledge from early life, 'yet, through the means of that *one study,* his mind (educated by that *one phase* of it) has received a *large* and *liberal* development as to other forms of knowledge'.[41] Science, considered in its social nexus, was a powerful instrument of general education which the proposals for examination had seriously under-valued.

Moseley's was a lone voice in relation to the primacy of scientific subjects in the upper-grade examination. Of the proposals for an examination for the lower grades of post, he was less critical. Here Jowett, influenced no doubt by his knowledge of Dawes' work at King's Somborne, had included a 'useful knowledge' paper of questions about common things. With apparent inconsistency for one who elsewhere had conceived elementary education as fitting the labourer more harmoniously to his allotted tasks, Moseley aligned himself with Dawes and Jowett in approving the opportunities for social improvement which the scheme of examination offered. But social mobility was never to be an end in itself; it was to be encouraged only in so far as it contributed to the ultimate religious and moral objectives of education, and to the creation of a climate of opinion more strongly in support of elementary schools.

By most of his contemporaries Moseley was regarded as a vigorous and uncompromising champion of the educational value of the physical sciences. He nevertheless maintained an unwavering allegiance to his church and to the established order of society. Nowhere was this seen more clearly than in his reactions to the radical curriculum developed at Chester Diocesan Training College by its principal, the Rev. Arthur Rigg.[42] A fellow Cambridge mathematician, Rigg had taught science at the Royal Institution, Liverpool, before being appointed in 1839 to direct the work of the newly projected training college at Chester. When Moseley carried out his first inspection in the spring of 1844 he found an emphasis on industrial occupations and their underlying scientific principles which was far in excess of anything attempted elsewhere. Some bias in this direction was to be expected of the college, placed as it was 'in the immediate neighbourhood of the vast population of Manchester and Liverpool, and destined to provide for the educational wants of a diocese including within its limits the greatest manufacturing districts of the kingdom'. On its own, a stress on applied science and workshop skills had much to commend it, but coupled with a wide disparity in the abilities and characters of the students, it left Moseley disturbed. At one extreme he found men of considerable intellect and cultivation; others, more limited, had fostered their intelligence under conditions of extraordinary difficulty. (One student, a former cotton spinner, had learnt algebra and geometry from a book propped up on his machine, reading in the interval of the return of the jenny.) But there were also those whose academic attainments were minimal, whose presence was more a consequence of an inability to pursue any other career with success, and who could never be transformed into accomplished teachers on any conventional model within the relatively short period of time at Chester. These men, in Moseley's opinion, were quite unsuited for appointment to elementary schools and could derive little benefit from the course.[43]

Following a further visit to Chester in November 1845, Moseley returned to the question of the principles on which

Rigg's curriculum had been constructed. He agreed that in any attempt to educate the poor it was no use appealing to the moral advantages of instruction or the ennobling tendencies of knowledge. Such arguments would be ineffective when dealing with people whose energies were dissipated in a perpetual struggle with the physical difficulties of existence. To serve them effectually and to secure their co-operation, their own views on what was best for their children must be respected. In so far as Chester was giving to its students a practical knowledge of the pursuits of the labouring classes, it was placing them in a position of vantage. There could be a fruitful communication between the parents of the children and the schoolmaster. The danger lay in the fact that, far from his education weaning the Chester student from the labouring classes from which he had come, it was strengthening his links with it. Neither in dress, manners nor speech was the 'worker schoolmaster' assuming any distinctive or separated character except in matters of moral restraint and behavioural propriety which it was appropriate that any labouring man should cultivate.[44]

Moseley did not challenge the premise – that the elementary schoolmaster should respect the values and attitudes of the labouring poor; nor did he dispute that scientific knowledge, particularly in its application to industrial processes, should form an important part of the curriculum; but he could not accept that the schoolmaster should be assimilated into the culture of those he served. 'This theory of a schoolmaster is diametrically opposed to that on which the system of every other training college . . . is founded. The tendency of every other is elevating. This would . . . tether (the student) fast to that state of life from which he started.' Worse still, it would dissociate the schoolmaster from the class above him. A breach between the class of elementary schoolmasters and the clergy could not be contemplated other than with 'unmingled apprehension'. Control of elementary education would pass from the church and schoolmasters might become converted 'into active emissaries of misrule'.[45] At Chester it appeared that the applied science and craft component of the curriculum had acquired too great an ascendancy.

If Moseley's ambivalence was exposed by Chester, at least it can be said of him that he was no bigot, tediously obsessed with the neglect of science in education and insensitive to the implications of his views. The logic of his curriculum argument was tempered by considerations derived from his religious and social beliefs. Within these limits he laboured unsparingly throughout his life for the cause of science education. After his translation to Bristol as resident canon in the cathedral there, he played a leading part in the establishment of the Bristol Trade School, a pioneering institution renowned for its scientific curriculum.[46] The Council of Military Education and the Institution of Naval Architects also benefited notably from his services, particularly in relation to schemes of examination in scientific subjects.[47]

Moseley's own scientific work was inevitably punctuated by the heavy demands on his time made by public service. Nevertheless he continued to carry out modest investigations until shortly before his death in 1872, submitting a paper to the Royal Society in the previous year. Sadly, the rapid advance of mathematical physics had left him ill-equipped to compete with a new generation of researchers and those who refereed his later papers were unable to recommend publication.[48] Ironically, one of his critics was J. D. Forbes. Such talent for original scientific inquiry as had been bestowed on the Moseley strain was to emerge more strongly at a later date: his son, Henry Nottidge Moseley, F.R.S. (1844–91), became Linacre Professor of Human and Comparative Anatomy at Oxford; his grandson, Henry Gwyn Jeffreys Moseley (1887–1915), one of Rutherford's most distinguished students, was the young physicist 'of brilliant promise and achievement' whose death in action in the Gallipoli campaign 'was everywhere recognized as an irreparable loss to science'.[49]

Chapter 5

The Movement for Teaching the Science of Common Things

Dissociated support for the teaching of science in elementary schools crystallized into a well-defined movement in the early 1850s. In its application to an understanding of 'common things', scientific knowledge became recognized as singularly well adapted to the needs of working-class children. To ensure its inclusion in the curriculum it seemed necessary to supply three resources; appropriately designed and inexpensive scientific apparatus; secular reading lesson books containing interesting scientific information; and, most importantly, suitably trained teachers without whom the stream of scientific knowledge would be cut off from the young.

Aid for the purchase of school equipment had been introduced in 1843 shortly after the establishment of the Committee of Council on Education. Whereas the schedule of apparatus which accompanied Kay-Shuttleworth's statement of the conditions of grant dealt primarily with basic classroom furniture such as desks, blackboards, easels and reading frames, it listed also such items as diagrams for teaching mechanics and natural history, cabinets of specimens for object lessons and sets of chemical apparatus for teaching agricultural chemistry.[1] It is not possible to determine precisely the extent to which schools purchased specific pieces of apparatus because statements of expenditure rarely differentiated between the various items listed in the schedule. During the late forties it seems most probable that only limited assistance was sought for the teaching of science. A number of schools, including King's Somborne,[2] obtained grant for the purchase of scientific apparatus but the major portion of the expenditure under the heading of apparatus clearly went towards the provision of items of furniture.

By 1849 the rapidly increasing calls on the parliamentary grant for education led the Committee of Council to seek economies as a result of which the apparatus grant was withdrawn.[3] For a number of reasons, however, aid for the purchase of scientific equipment became a matter which necessitated exceptional treatment. Not only did the Colonial Office raise the general question with the Committee of Council, but a specific application for grant was received in October 1851 from Cheltenham training school.[4] So far as the Colonial Office was concerned, interest in science teaching arose from the fact that a stage had been reached when colonial powers were being induced to encourage native education. Thus, the Court of Directors of the East India Company were to issue in 1854 a dispatch which stressed the importance of primary instruction for the masses; in their view it was 'a sacred duty to confer upon the natives of India those vast moral and material blessings which flow from the general diffusion of useful knowledge'.[5] In such an enterprise science teaching had an important part to play. The Cheltenham application for grant in order to purchase scientific apparatus was a timely intervention from the training school front. It is tempting to account for it in terms of the influence of Dawes, recently removed to the deanery of nearby Hereford. Certainly at a later date he was to play a part in the educational affairs of Cheltenham College, a proprietary school with a notable department of modern studies,[6] but there is no evidence to suggest his association at the earlier date with the work of the training school. No doubt Moseley, as inspector of church training schools, encouraged the application, but the prime mover would appear to have been the principal of the Cheltenham training school, the Rev. C. H. Bromby.

Here was yet another member of the small but influentially positioned group of clerics who saw the teaching of science as essential for the moral and religious salvation of the children of the poor. A Cambridge contemporary of

Rigg, although, unlike him, a classics graduate, Bromby became principal of the Cheltenham training school on its opening in 1847. His educational beliefs were in many respects close to those of Dawes and Moseley. Despite, or perhaps because of, his educational background, he challenged the primacy of classics in the school curriculum; it is questionable, he wrote, 'whether the facility of throwing six miserable feet into an iambic is the ultimate intention of human existence'. Instead, more recognition needed to be given to the fact that many children had a greater faculty 'for the study of things than for the study of words'. Educational practice should provide opportunities for them to 'trace the wonders of a merciful Creator in His own works – in the structure of a flower – in the beautiful laws of chemical physics – in the animal anatomy, or in the harmony of astronomical science'.[7] Both in the curriculum of the Cheltenham training school and in his lectures to working men in the local Mechanics' Institute, Bromby proclaimed the advantages to be derived from a study of the elements of applied sciences, particularly chemistry. It was to these ends that his application was made for grant to aid the purchase of scientific apparatus. As an educational thinker, unquestionably of lesser stature than either Dawes or Moseley, and, as a scientist, with no pretensions to be other than a rank amateur, Bromby nevertheless played a significant part in promoting the flow of needed resources for science teaching.

Within a fortnight of receiving the Cheltenham application, Lingen, as Secretary to the Committee of Council on Education, had written to Moseley instructing him to prepare a schedule of scientific apparatus which could be recommended for adoption in training schools.[4] Additionally, information was sought on a course of study and text books with which the apparatus might be used. A second, less elaborate schedule of apparatus for use in elementary schools was also commissioned, economy and simplicity to be the hall marks of apparatus under both headings. For their part, 'their Lordships' were proposing to grant two-thirds of the cost of purchasing a set of approved apparatus. A noted firm of scientific apparatus manufacturers, Messrs Griffin of Baker Street, had already been in correspondence with the Committee with an offer of assistance. In Griffin's view a great reduction in the cost of scientific apparatus would result from the increased demand which was anticipated.

Moseley's inquiries, which amounted to a national survey of apparatus for teaching science, extended over the whole of the following year, at the end of which period he was able to report the availability of three sets of apparatus approved for use in elementary schools and costing £10, £15 and £20 respectively, together with more elaborate sets for training schools, costing £100, £125 and £150.[8] Each of these was manufactured by three London firms, Griffin & Co., Knight & Co., and Horne, Thornthwaite & Co. His report also included a long list of miscellaneous apparatus and science teaching aids available from a wide range of suppliers including the Chester Diocesan Training School, the National Society's Repository, and the Working Man's Educational Union.

The complete survey, occupying sixty pages of the Minutes of the Committee of Council,[9] throws a fascinating light on the range and quality of the aids to science teaching available in the mid-nineteenth century. Griffin, for example, offered a small compound microscope, magnifying seventy-five diameters, together with a collection of forty-two mounted slides and other items for £1 5s 3d. The same firm produced a magic lantern for ten shillings with an associated set of astronomical slides. The basic set of thirty-nine items of chemical apparatus and materials for the experiments in Johnston's *Catechism of Agricultural Chemistry* cost £1 5s 0d. Scientific diagrams, lecture illustrations, sectional models and apparatus for experiments in the various branches of natural philosophy were available, if not in profusion, at least in a quantity sufficient to suggest that the progress of science teaching need not be hindered by lack of suitable material aids.

Moseley's commission had included more than the compilation of an inventory, however. The 'regular and methodical application of science to the purposes of instruction', as prescribed by 'their Lordships', required the association of apparatus with a well-conceived scheme of study. Fragmentary and unconnected attainments in science were of little value. Furthermore, apparatus would only be used effectively by teachers who themselves understood the scientific principles involved, and under the conditions prevailing in schools and training colleges neither teachers nor pupils could be expected to acquire mastery over the full range of the physical and biological sciences. It was clear that guidance had to be offered on the branches of science which were best suited to the purposes of elementary instruction.

In following Dawes[10] and assigning to chemistry a position of primacy when the sciences were considered from an educational viewpoint, Moseley was influenced by a variety of considerations, including the ready availability of inexpensive apparatus and of elementary texts well adapted to teaching. But more than this, the science of chemistry was 'to a greater extent than any other a science of common things'. In Moseley's view 'Agriculture, horticulture, the economy of food and fuel, cleanliness, ventilation, etc. are, under the highest forms, but the applications of it'. Of all the sciences, chemistry had the most direct relevance to the needs of pupils in both rural and urban situations. Furthermore, he wrote, 'it is a characteristic of the science of chemistry that, with whatever is to be reasoned upon and understood, there is associated always something to be done'.[11] It was his conviction that chemical knowledge conveyed to its possessors the power to impregnate labour with thought and to acquire a degree of mastery over the material conditions of life.

The composition of the sets of apparatus approved for purposes of grant reflected Moseley's judgement on the educational value of chemical knowledge. Whilst Griffin's £20 'selection' for use in elementary schools included some items for the teaching of hydrostatics, pneumatics, electricity and magnetism, the larger quantity of chemical apparatus and materials was chosen with special reference to the teaching of agricultural chemistry. A similar 'mixed' cabinet was produced by Horne, Thornthwaite & Co., whilst the corresponding set of Knight & Co. consisted entirely of chemical apparatus and materials.[12] For work in training schools, a broader range of apparatus was provided, the chemical items being adapted to the extended courses outlined in certain approved texts such as Fownes' *Manual of Elementary Chemistry* and Wilson's *Chemistry*.[13] The latter work was recommended by Moseley as the text on which schoolmasters should be examined in order to provide evidence of proficiency in science when applications for grant were made.

The decision to re-establish government grant in aid of the purchase of scientific apparatus so soon after the withdrawal of the general apparatus grant to schools requires a word of explanation. Unquestionably the major influence was the recognition, following the Great Exhibition of 1851, that, by comparison with other nations, England lagged in the provision of scientific instruction to the great mass of its industrial population. On the opening of the new session of Parliament in November 1852 reference was made in the speech from the throne to the need for a comprehensive scheme whereby scientific instruction might be supplied in a more systematic manner than hitherto.[14] The result was the addition, in the following March, of a department of science to the department of practical art already in existence under the Board of Trade. As explained in earlier chapters,[15] the new Department of Science and Art consolidated a number of separate institutions including the Government School of Mines and of Science applied to the Arts, the Museum of Practical Geology, and the Geological Survey. The unified metropolitan bodies were conceived as the centre of a network of provincial institutions, created and sustained in large measure by local efforts, which would propagate sound industrial knowledge to the manufacturing population of the country. The new system was to be complementary to the work of existing schools. In the words of its designers, the Commissioners for the Exhibition of 1851, 'by confining our attention to technical instruction, and not extending it to general education in science and art, we shall be adding to, without interfering with, the means of instruction already existing in schools and colleges. As a preliminary knowledge of the principles of science and art would be required by the students entering the institution proposed by us, the effect would be to give an impetus to general education, which could not fail to be of material advantage to those bodies.'[16]

Aid for the purchase of scientific apparatus by training and elementary schools was, therefore, a measure which consorted well with the larger plan for the establishment of a national system of industrial instruction. Furthermore, because the Department of Science and Art undertook to provide models, diagrams and apparatus for purchase at reduced rates by provincial schools, Moseley's survey of scientific equipment was of particular interest to the new science division.

A detailed examination of the relationship between the work of the Science and Art Department and that of the Education Department is the subject of a later chapter in this book. At this stage it is sufficient to register that science education in the early fifties developed under dual administrative control, with both departments having an interest in fostering developments in elementary education. The Secretary and Inspector of the science division of the Department of Science and Art, Dr Lyon Playfair, endorsed the view that a sound foundation of interest in science needed to be laid in elementary schools if subsequent instruction was to flourish. As he recorded in this first annual report in 1854, 'The chief attention of the Department has . . . been, and will continue to be, for some time, devoted to this object (i.e. fostering a taste for science by infusing it into primary education) rather than to the creation of separate higher institutions.'[17] The omens seemed to favour a period of fruitful collaboration directed towards the establishment of science as an essential component of general education. The Committee of Council agreed to place on its lists those models, diagrams and pieces of apparatus which the Department of Science and Art had commissioned and which were likely to be of interest to primary and training schools.[18]

Reciprocating, the Museum of Practical Geology offered space for the display of the specimen cabinets of scientific apparatus prepared as a result of Moseley's survey;[19] and it was to Playfair that Moseley wrote for assistance in connection with the first examination in chemistry of schoolmasters who sought apparatus grants under the new regulations.[20] Yet there was no question of a fusion of action. To identify the new department too closely with the cause of elementary education would have been to risk embroiling it in religious squabbles. Playfair had chastening first-hand experience that educational pronouncements of an apparently innocuous character could bring embarrassing consequences,[21] whilst Moseley was too seasoned a campaigner to provoke unnecessary disputes. 'I must ask you this entirely as a private favour', he confided in Playfair on the question of the chemistry examination, 'because I am sure that it will not do to mingle up the *official* duties of two departments. Yours is secondary and ours *primary* education. We shall do our work best by acting cordially and helpfully but separately.'[20]

One further development needs to be examined before leaving the subject of apparatus for teaching 'the science of common things'. Both Playfair and Moseley were closely associated with the work of the Society of Arts, a body whose long-standing concern for industrial education had been sharpened not only by the international comparisons of 1851, but also by comments from the three hundred or more scientific, literary and mechanics' institutes which had recently been brought into union with the Society. In June 1853, at the second annual conference between representatives of these institutes and the Council of the Society, the question of provision of books and apparatus for science teaching featured prominently on the agenda.[22] Richard Dawes, whose educational work on behalf of the labouring classes had led to his election to the Council of the Society, expressed the view of many delegates when he attributed the failure of mechanics' institutes to a lack of previous elementary education.[23] It was clear that the scope of the Society's interest in education needed to extend into the field of elementary instruction. As another speaker put it, if they wanted the fire to burn, they must light it at the bottom.

The outcome of these discussions was a decision to celebrate the Society's centenary the following year by holding an international Educational Exhibition which it was hoped would do for education what the Great Exhibition had done for manufacturers. Harry Chester, assistant secretary to the Committee of Council on Education and prime mover in the matter of the Educational Exhibition, was appointed chairman of the Council of the Society for 1853–4.[24] Together with Playfair, also a Council member, he was elected to membership of a small committee of four charged with the task of organizing the exhibition. A detailed account of the chequered history of the planning and preparation of the exhibition has appeared elsewhere[25] and need not be repeated here other than to say that the Society was obliged to enlarge substantially the scale of its exercise before this could be brought to fruition. The basic problem was that of avoiding any risk of conflict with the various religious bodies and other providers of education. There was a constant danger that industrial or technical instruction would be equated with 'godless instruction' and great care needed to be exercised in order that the Society's excursion into the educational field did not provoke antagonism. A cumbersome and representative committee of some 170 members had to be brought into being at short notice. The needs of the institutes, in whose comments the exhibition had its origins, became overlaid by the wider consideration of ensuring effective collaboration between factions normally in contention. A remarkable degree of harmony was achieved, although from the grass root level there came embittered comment that 'original apparatus newly invented by practical and skilful teachers' had been displaced by products sponsored by official bodies and commercial organizations. In its excessive eagerness to secure the co-operation of the great educational societies the Society of Arts had 'sacrificed the claims of justice'. It was asserted that the 'real producers' of school apparatus were forced to exhibit in side galleries, on a staircase, 'and worst of all in a wretched loft . . . quite beyond the reach of any but the most expert climber'.[26]

Much of the preparatory work for the exhibition had been undertaken by four small sub-committees, on two of which both Dawes and Moseley served. The objects to be exhibited were arranged in six classes: section one included laboratory designs; section three was concerned with scientific and other apparatus; books and diagrams were displayed in another section.[27] Financially the exhibition was not a success and there is evidence that the attendances disappointed the expectations of the organizers.[28] Nevertheless, the display of available scientific apparatus from home and overseas sources would appear to have provided a stimulus to the growth of science teaching. The situation in the training schools at the time of the exhibition was described by Moseley in the final report before his replacement in the inspectorate. In his opinion, 'if the scientific apparatus possessed by all the training school for schoolmasters in this country were collected together it would not be found to equal in quantity – and would be far inferior in quality to – that which was exhibited at the Educational Exhibition . . . as the apparatus of one single model school for children in Norway'.[29] The figures for government grant for scientific apparatus over the subsequent three years would suggest that the shot had gone home.

Expenditure from education grant in providing scientific
apparatus[30]

Before 31. xii. 1853	18– 0– 0	
	1854	65– 6– 8
	1855	429–11– 8
	1856	757–10–11
	1857	2,345–15–11

It will be recalled that for Dawes and Moseley, in contrast to Henslow, scientific apparatus was required in elementary schools less for individual practical work by pupils than for the performance of demonstration experiments in the context of conversational or oral lessons. Furthermore, in the instructional system which they advocated, secular reading books played an essential part as sources of scientific knowledge. The availability of suitable reading material was as crucial to the success of the movement for teaching the science of common things as the supply of scientific apparatus. Contemporaneously with their efforts to bring scientific apparatus within the reach of elementary schools, it was necessary, therefore, for the friends of popular education to improve the situation in relation to reading lesson books.

Grant in aid of the purchase of school books had been introduced in December 1847, shortly before ill-health terminated Kay-Shuttleworth's period of office as secretary to the Committee of Council on Education. Those books 'which had received the most extensive sanction from public opinion' were listed in two schedules, one for use with pupils, the other for teachers and pupil teachers. The Committee of Council was at pains to make clear that it did not assume any responsibility for the quality of these works beyond the extent that it was possible to ascertain and register accurately the opinion of the public. It was not the business of the state to assume the role of evaluator in relation to school texts; the list was compiled in the light of information about the adoption of books in schools under inspection. If subsequent experience showed that there was no demand for a book on the list, the schedule would be modified accordingly. All books listed were eligible for grant and it was the responsibility of school managers to select from the schedules those works which they wished to introduce into their schools. By virtue of the increased sales which it was forecast would result from the introduction of grant, a substantial reduction on the retail price of all books had been successfully negotiated with publishers, one of whom – Messrs Longman & Co. – was appointed by the Committee as agent responsible for the distribution of material to the schools.[31]

Reference has already been made to the use in Dawes' schools of reading lesson books prepared by the Commissioners of National Education in Ireland. No doubt influenced by knowledge of the extraordinary successes achieved at King's Somborne, and by Moseley's enthusiastic advocacy of Dawes' methods, it was arranged that the Irish Commissioners should supply their books to the Committee of Council for distribution to British schools. In consequence, as Lingen stated some years later, 'The public . . . had the advantage of obtaining a series of school books, admitted to be equal, and generally considered to be superior, to any others that are published, at a price far below the charge commonly made for such books.'[32] It is recorded that, in 1848, sales of Irish books by the Committee of Council averaged about £300 a month.[33] Taking the mean price of a reading lesson book as 6d (the price of the five Irish readers was 1d, 4d, 8d, 9d, and 11d) it would appear that some 144,000 books were sold during the year.

The outstanding sales of the Irish books and their mode of distribution provoked British publishers to petition the government, arguing that the principles of free trade were being contravened. The ensuing controversy, which has been described by Donald H. Akenson, led to a revision of the arrangements for the sale of Irish lesson books in this country. In 1852 it was decreed that the Irish works could not be made available directly to schools seeking grant from the Committee of Council. Instead the Commissioners' books were to be published by private firms who were chosen for the contract by open bidding.[34]

Irrespective of the change, the popularity of the Irish books remained high. Of 902,926 copies of reading lesson books ordered by managers of schools in Great Britain within the period September 1856 to May 1859, 480,724 – or more than one-half – were copies of books in the Irish series.[35] In the same period no other series of readers reached 100,000 copies. Containing much scientific information the works provided a partial answer to the need for secular texts to support the teaching of elementary applied science. It was the opinion of James Tilleard, Tate's co-editor of the *Educational Expositor*, that, 'If the scientific lessons in these books were well illustrated by teachers, by means of simple experiments, and made the nucleus for additional informa- tion *not* to be found in the reading book, much would already be done towards the teaching of science.'[36] Unfortunately few teachers were equipped to supplement the readers in the manner indicated by Tilleard. Whilst they represented a great advance at the time of their original publication in the 1830s, the Irish books retained substantial defects. The vocabulary was often unnecessarily abstract and recondite; little attempt had been made to revise the works in relation to the advance of science and technology. 'We would fain find in them some notice of railroads, electric telegraphs, and other inventions,' a contemporary critic complained.[37] Most important of all, the content of the readers defined a curriculum which was notable for its irrelevance to everyday life. Although elementary chemistry, physics and natural history were preferred to classical mythology and biblical history, the works were not designed to serve the ends of the movement for teaching the science of common things. Little attempt was made to present scientific knowledge as having any practical value to the children of the labouring poor.

To remedy this defect Kay-Shuttleworth and others attempted to bring into being a new series of reading books whose content would reflect their views on the forms of knowledge most useful to children in elementary schools. In the early months of 1853 a document prepared by Kay-Shuttleworth and containing a 'clear and comprehensive table of common things which should be known' was circulated for comment to a number of influential figures including Lyon Playfair, the Bishop of London, Lord Ashburton, and one or two potential authors such as Harriet Martineau.[38]

It is clear that Kay-Shuttleworth took a comprehensive view of the knowledge requirements of working-class children. In addition to a section entitled 'Explanation of Natural Phenomena', the synopsis included headings such as 'Home and Health', 'Sanitation and Nursing' and 'The Nature and Use of Some Imported Products'. The response from his correspondents was uniformly encouraging. Playfair's support was tempered only by comments on the difficulties likely to confront a learner because of the interdisciplinary organization of subject matter. In his view it would be better to classify the subject matter into departments, a step which would in any case be necessary if suitable authors were to be recruited. 'No one elementary book can be written upon the general grouping such as in your paper', he informed Kay-Shuttleworth, 'but excellent books might be written on the classified division'.[39]

C. J. Blomfield, the Bishop of London, likewise approved of the curriculum which Kay-Shuttleworth proposed, especially if 'the manual application of this knowledge – the *use* of tools, machines etc.' could be included. On a practical point of implementation he advised against including too detailed an outline of subject matter under specific headings such as 'Explanation of Natural Phenomena'. 'It will frighten some', he warned, 'and give to others an opportunity to cavil.'[40] But as to the general design of the project, the consensus was expressed by Harriet Martineau. 'There can I think be no manner of doubt of the necessity of such a course of instruction, if we are to call these children educated.'[41]

The approval of representatives of science, non-conformity and the established church having been secured, it would be pleasant to record that Kay-Shuttleworth's plans were brought speedily to fruition. Unfortunately the problem of finding suitable authors was not easily solved. The original intention had been to hold a competition with prizes for those manuscripts selected for publication. Both Playfair and Martineau advised strongly against this course of action, urging that no writer of established reputation would risk time and labour on such an exercise and that experienced authors were vital for the success of the enterprise. Playfair, particularly, was active in attempting to enlist the co-operation of distinguished scientists who might write primers suitable for use in elementary schools. Thus, John Tyndall, the newly appointed Professor of Natural Philosophy at the Royal Institution was approached in October 1853 with a view to preparing an introductory physics reader.[42] Tyndall's preoccupation with scientific research had already led him to reject a proposal that he should

Table 4

Advertisement for Hughes' Reading-Lesson-Books

deliver a course of lectures in the Government School of Mines. Despite Playfair's assurance that the Committee of Council on Education would support the work and that the exercise would be lucrative, Tyndall initially declined. Some time later he was to yield to persuasion and completed a set of eighteen lessons on natural philosophy which were published in a series of reading lesson books edited by Edward Hughes, headmaster of the Royal Naval Lower School, Greenwich. Playfair, himself, was advertised as one of the distinguished panel of authors contributing to Hughes' readers, the first of which, on its appearance in 1855, was hailed as a landmark. 'It is almost the first of its kind', a reviewer in the *Philosophical Magazine* claimed, 'in which the principle has been recognized that only the ablest men can expound the elements of a science successfully, and that the task is in every respect worthy of their valuable time.'[43] Unfortunately not all contributors were able to demonstrate the 'rare felicity of illustration' which characterized Tyndall's lessons; in addition, a measure of literacy was presupposed which resulted in the readers being classified as 'advanced'. Their use was further restricted by considerations of cost; in contrast to the Irish readers which in the late 50s sold at prices ranging from $\frac{1}{2}$d to $7\frac{1}{4}$d, the readers in Hughes' series cost 2s 8d each.

If the response from potential authors within the scientific community was characterized by a measure of reluctance, no such inhibitions were encountered when Playfair approached publishers. In reply to an inquiry, Robert Chambers of Edinburgh declared himself more than willing 'to set immediately about the preparation of a series of small books', drawing attention at the same time to a number of successful works already available including his own *Introduction to the Sciences*.[44] By the early part of 1854 Chambers had submitted a draft manuscript which Playfair circulated to his collaborators. All were critical, though none more harshly so than Kay-Shuttleworth. 'I consider Chambers' prospectus quite puerile' he wrote angrily to Playfair. '(His views) are so foolish that I feel it is necessary some one should rescue the whole subject from becoming . . .

ridiculous.'[45] Despite these strictures *The Book of Common Things* was published by Chambers and was included in the Committee of Council's list of works eligible for grant. Too much was left to the background knowledge and resourcefulness of the teacher, however, for the work to be more than a token contribution to the movement for teaching the science of common things.

It should be made clear that there was in fact no shortage during the 1850s of reading lesson and other books dealing with scientific knowledge. Typical of the reading books was the small volume entitled *Natural Philosophy for Beginners* and its companion, the more advanced collection of *Readings in Science*, which had been prepared under the direction of the Committee of General Literature and Education appointed by the Society for the Promotion of Christian Knowledge. The *Daily Lesson Book No. 4* of the British and Foreign School Society likewise included a complete series of lessons on the various branches of natural philosophy. As to other works, between 1856 and 1859 the Committee of Council's list contained the titles of 18 geology, 21 botany, 32 zoology, 28 chemistry, 58 natural philosophy, 32 mechanics and 34 popular astronomy books.[46] Indeed, natural philosophy was one of the few fields in which the popular Irish school books were outsold by British works. Yet this cornucopia was singularly barren in relation to the educational needs of the labouring poor as diagnosed by Dawes and Moseley. Walter McLeod, one of Kay-Shuttleworth's original appointments at Battersea, included a certain amount of information on 'common things' in one of his series of basic readers and his erstwhile colleague, the prolific Tate, wrote *The Little Philosopher; or, the Science of Familiar Things* which came, perhaps, as close as any book to Kay-Shuttleworth's conception of what was needed.[47]

From less discerning pens the emphasis on 'a knowledge of common things' encouraged contributions to a literary vein of popular compilations of factual information exemplified by John Timbs' *Things Not Generally Known*, and Dr Brewer's *Guide to the Scientific Knowledge of Things*

Familiar. Frequently catechetical in style, they presented science in discrete, unstructured snippets designed for the amusement and edification of the curious. Enjoying wide popularity – 113,000 copies of Brewer's *Guide* were printed between 1848 and the thirty-first edition in 1873[48] – they made their way into a considerable number of schools. In contrast to the type of book which Kay-Shuttleworth sought, however, such works lacked the approval of men of science. As T. H. Huxley remarked, when a witness before the Devonshire Commissioners mistakenly associated Brewer's *Guide* with the movement for teaching the science of common things, in such works 'there was no means to lead the mind of a child to what might be called purely scientific considerations; the design of that education was pure information, no attention was made to use the information, that was the cardinal defect'.[49]

A more reputable product of the alliance between science and the friends of popular education, whilst not strictly a science reader, was the book entitled *Lessons on the Phenomena of Industrial Life and the Conditions of Industrial Success*, published under Dawes' name in 1854. Playfair had early sought Dawes' advice in connection with Kay-Shuttleworth's proposal to publish reading lesson books. Understandably there was an enthusiastic response, tempered only by Dawes' perceptive assessment of the critical stage which the movement had reached. 'I think much depends in the next year or two upon those who are taking the lead in this educational movement', he wrote to Playfair in February 1854, 'and it is most important that we should pull well together and that we should be discreet no less than zealous in our efforts.'[50] Discretion indeed was needed for the undertaking proposed by Playfair, which was that Dawes should lend his name to a work to be written by William Ellis, one of the leading proponents of secular education. As Ellis later recounted of the book, 'The Dean hopes to obtain admission for it into the Church Training Schools, and if such an Ogre as I am were known to be its author, the circulation of the work might be narrowed, and the Dean's influence weakened, both of which it is desirable to avoid.'[51]

Ellis and Dawes were, in fact, old allies who had discovered much common ground in their discussions within the Society of Arts on the subject of schools for the labouring poor. In the event Ellis' manuscript proved more suited to the needs of teachers and pupil teachers than for children learning to read and was not published as a classbook for schools. It was agreed that all profits from the work should be used for the award of prizes to schoolmasters who excelled in teaching the science of common things.[52]

Prize schemes represent another strand in the activities of those who promoted the teaching of elementary science. At the time when Kay-Shuttleworth consulted him on the subject of the knowledge requirements of working-class children, Lord Ashburton, Dawes' neighbour in his King's Somborne days, was working towards the institution of a system of special awards open to students in training schools, and to teachers, for attainment in 'the knowledge of common things'. By the end of 1853 he had obtained Lingen's agreement to the use of Committee of Council school inspectors as examiners in connection with his scheme which was formally announced on 16 December at a meeting of elementary schoolmasters at Winchester.[53] Ashburton disclaimed any originality on his part in stressing the importance of a knowledge of the science of common things, acknowledging that he wished to see extended to every village school what had been found to succeed so admirably at King's Somborne. His prize scheme, which was restricted to students at the Winchester training school and to schoolmasters of inspected church schools in Hampshire and Wiltshire, had the support of the diocesan authorities as well as the Committee of Council. Comparable schemes in other regions were projected. Dawes announced one for Herefordshire,[53] Miss Burdett Coutts established one for women teachers at Whitelands Training School,[54] and both Lord Landsdowne and Lord Granville indicated their intention to offer similar prizes in their own localities.[55] 'I hazard the prediction that you will hear a great deal more of it; that COMMON THINGS will pass into a phrase of education,' the Rev. W. H. Brookfield asserted when, as the inspector responsible for the adminis-

H

tration of Ashburton's scheme, he introduced the subject to his audience of teachers.[56] Dawes' *Suggestive Hints* and Joyce's *Scientific Dialogues* were recommended books for those wishing to prepare themselves. The scheme achieved useful, and at times outstanding, results according to the testimony of Dr W. B. Carpenter, Registrar of the University of London and Vice-President of the Royal Society, when he appeared before the Select Committee on Scientific Instruction in 1868. Carpenter had examined candidates for the Ashburton prizes and had been impressed by the high quality of the answers.[57]

Apparatus, texts and prize schemes were important factors in the attempt to bring about a major curriculum change. In the limit, however, the key to progress was to be found not in the material aids to education but in the teachers who would employ them. The generation of a supply of school-masters proficient in science and skilled in pedagogy was crucial to the success of the movement. There were formidable difficulties here. In Dawes' estimate not one in a hundred of the stock of elementary school teachers at the turn of the half century was equipped for the task,[58] whilst Moseley's experience led him to doubt whether the whole of the training schools could furnish a master possessing enough scientific knowledge.[59] The opportunity for change occurred in the summer of 1853 when the newly appointed Committee of Council of Aberdeen's government, under Lord Granville, undertook a review of the regulations governing teacher training. One criticism which had been made of the existing system was that it had been marked by a tendency on the part of the students to attempt more than could be done well; in consequence, attainments were superficial. With a view to raising the standard of work in the training schools, particularly in relation to the subjects taught in elementary schools, the Committee resolved to establish grant in order to augment the salaries of certain lecturers. These were to be men able to provide satisfactory evidence both of academic ability in the basic subjects of the elementary school curriculum and of skill in adapting these subjects to the purposes of instruction. One consequence of this decision was, of course, the need to prescribe those branches of knowledge most suited to the education of the poor and Moseley's influence can be detected in the inclusion of physical science, geography and applied mathematics among the five subjects listed, the others being history and English literature.[60]

As a corollary to the supplementary minute of August 1853, under which the new arrangements were established, Moseley was charged by Lord Granville to draw up a scheme of examination common to all male students in training schools and to teachers seeking certification. This was a considerable and pioneering undertaking, which resulted in an exercise 'on a larger scale . . . than any other examination before held in this country'.[61] Moseley seized the opportunity to consolidate physical science as one of the basic subjects of elementary education; as he pointed out, although it was not usually so considered, it was so in practice as anyone who cared to look into the reading lesson books could see. 'A large proportion of the lessons in those books are on questions of physical science; the teaching of which can have no reality, and will indeed lead . . . to grave misapprehensions and blunders, unless the mind of the master be prepared for the explanation of them to the children by a systematic course of instruction in such subjects.'[62] It followed that all students in training schools should study science. Moseley was at pains to emphasize that no addition was being proposed to the subjects in which students had been examined previously. 'Industrial Mechanics' was a study of long standing in the curriculum of several of the training schools. Under the revised arrangements, however, it became a prescribed subject of examination for all at the end of the first year. At the end of the second year, the examination was to include Physical Science, covering hydrostatics, pneumatics, electricity, heat, optics and inorganic chemistry. However, it was not the intention that the teaching of these branches of science should be limited to students who remained in the training schools for a second year. Principals were advised that 'it may often be judged expedient . . . to teach to the students in the first year sub-

jects not prescribed for examination by Her Majesty's
Inspectors until the end of the second year'.[63] In other words,
all students were expected to follow a broad foundation
course in physical science, one element of which, mechanics,
was to be examined at the end of the first year. Ambitiously,
a third-year scheme was also devised in which a measure of
specialization was possible, experimental science being one
of five possible courses.

The new design went beyond anything that Moseley had
previously advocated. On a number of occasions he had
expressed his views on the subjects of examination for the
certification of schoolmasters, but had invariably distinguished 'the sciences' from 'the subjects proper to elementary
instruction'. His earlier preference had been for a classification of examination subjects under five 'great and obvious
divisions':

1. The subjects proper to elementary instruction.
2. The exact sciences.
3. Literature.
4. The experimental sciences.
5. The natural sciences.[64]

The new arrangement, whereby science was assimilated
into the category of subjects to be taught in elementary
schools, was an administrative development which promised
to achieve more effectively the objectives of the movement
for teaching the science of common things. As was the case
with the regulations governing grant in aid of the purchase
of scientific apparatus, the encouragement given to the improvement of attainments in scientific knowledge on the part
of training school students was not unconnected with the
larger plan to promote a national system of industrial
instruction. It was essential that the rudiments of science
should have been acquired before secondary education for
artisans and others was attempted. Some indication of the
success of the measure can be obtained by looking at
examination results. In their assessment of the students, the
inspectors employed a six-point scale ranging from 'failure',
through 'imperfect', 'moderate', 'fair' and 'good' to 'excel-

lent'. Of the 330 first-year male candidates from the fourteen Church of England training schools in 1856–7, 142 obtained grades of 'fair', or better, in the examination in Mechanics. Of the 206 second-year candidates, 166 obtained grades of 'fair', or better, in Physical Science.[65]

By the mid-fifties many of the conditions necessary for the introduction of science into the elementary school curriculum appeared to have been satisfied. Apparatus had been produced, the supply of trained teachers was growing and an administrative structure had been devised to support and encourage the development. Events seemed poised for a significant advance. As the Duke of Argyll pointed out in his presidential address to the Annual Meeting of the British Association for the Advancement of Science in 1855, it was possible for the influence of the state to be exerted most beneficially on behalf of science through the educational rules and principles of administration of the Privy Council.[66]

Chapter 6

A Conflict of Studies

That plans so carefully laid and apparently well supported should fail to achieve their purpose is a striking indication of the manifold determinants of curriculum change. It has been customary to ascribe the exclusion of science from the elementary school curriculum to the constricting effect of the Revised Code of 1862.[1] Unquestionably the new regulations which followed the report of the Newcastle Commissioners were a severe discouragement to the teaching of science, as indeed they were to the teaching of most subjects other than the three Rs. By the time of their introduction, however, the fate of the movement for 'the science of common things' had already been decided. As early as July 1856 the outcome was clear to Moseley. 'We are now nearly at a dead stop . . .', he wrote from his new home in Bristol to Kay-Shuttleworth. 'I doubt if much real progress is being made. The friends of the education of the working classes have a sense of being at last beaten – of having come to an impassable obstacle.'[2] Premature in recording so definite a terminus to the activities of the movement, Moseley's appraisal was nonetheless an accurate reading of events. It contrasted poignantly with Lord Granville's buoyant prediction, two summers previously, of a rapid growth in the amount of science taught in schools, consequent upon the introduction of new teacher training regulations.[3]

In the present chapter, and that which follows, an attempt will be made to account for this failure to establish science as a basic component of the elementary school curriculum. The diverse strands of evidence cannot be contained within the framework of any unitary explanation in terms, for example, of parsonic opposition to science teaching. Nor is it merely a question of identifying the variety of circumstances external to the movement which conspired to frustrate its ends. It is necessary to inquire further and to examine the extent to which the movement itself was afflicted with internal conflicts and division of purpose. In addition, the failure of the curriculum innovation proposed by Dawes and Moseley can be attributed in part to the activities of others with an interest in establishing science as a component of general education. The intrinsic strains within the movement and the reactions of scientists, in particular, to this pioneering attempt at curriculum development are examined in what follows. The extent to which the outcomes of science teaching were seen to be in conflict with the objectives of other promoters of elementary education for the poor is the subject of a later chapter.

It will be clear from what has gone before that those who advocated the teaching of applied physical science in elementary schools were in no sense a formally constituted pressure group. Unlike the members of the National Association for the Promotion of Technical and Secondary Education later in the century, they were not united by any explicit statement of aims. Nor were they all external to the centres of decision making. It was rather the case that individuals, independently and from a variety of standpoints, had converged upon what appeared to be a common view of the most appropriate curriculum for elementary schools. Within the legislature Lord Granville, President of the Committee of Council in both Aberdeen's coalition and Palmerston's first government, lent active support to the development. In the administrative departments of state, Kay-Shuttleworth (until his retirement), Moseley and – for a time at least – Lyon Playfair, likewise worked to implement the change. Their efforts were supported by Lord Ashburton, who, whilst not occupying a position in the governments of the day, was nevertheless a significant influence in the land. Within the training colleges, two principals, Bromby of Cheltenham and Rigg of Chester, were notable proponents of science teaching along the lines which Dawes had described in his *Suggestive Hints*. At Battersea, two of Kay-

Shuttleworth's early appointments to lectureships, Walter McLeod and Thomas Tate, had advanced the same cause through their teaching and text-book writing. On leaving Battersea, Tate taught science at the government training school at Kneller Hall during the principalship of Frederick Temple; and when, in December 1854, he occupied the chair at the first annual meeting of the United Association of Schoolmasters, the theme of science teaching was prominent throughout the conference. The opening address was delivered by Bromby, followed on the second day by a contribution on 'The Teaching of Common Things' from a practising schoolmaster. The spirited discussion which ensued, seemed to indicate as strong support for the movement at the classroom level as existed in Whitehall and the colleges.[4]

In so far as the recipients of elementary education might be said to have had a voice, they too would appear to have concurred. In the judgement of many historians of education there was little pressure from below for elementary education during the period under consideration; a social demand for education could scarcely be said to exist. Whilst this may be true in relation to the literary and religious curriculum provided in the majority of elementary schools, the consumer response changed markedly when a different commodity was offered. As James Hole, the experienced Secretary of the Yorkshire Union of Mechanics' Institutes noted, 'if the proper article be provided, the working man will pay, not the whole cost perhaps, but a fair proportion of it'.[5] That there needed to be a strong scientific component in 'the proper article' is suggested by the remarkable successes of Dawes' schools at King's Somborne and, later, Hereford, and by the extraordinarily large and constant attendances at the science lectures for working men given in the Government School of Mines.[6] It is true that some voices, including that of Frederick Engels, saw the study of natural science as deflecting working men from consideration of the urgent political and constitutional issues which directly affected their own interests.[7] In general, however, there was powerful support for views such as those of

William Lovett in whose *Address on Education* and *Chartism*, and indeed in whose own teaching, prominence was given to the educational value of science. Lovett himself prepared several elementary text books on scientific topics for use in schools.[8] The same opinion was reflected when, in 1856, five thousand working men of the London Polytechnic, the London Mechanics' and other institutions petitioned the President of the Committee of Council on Education. 'Your memorialists would respectfully suggest that the elements of the natural sciences, political economy, physics, chemistry and drawing, should be taught in our elementary schools. For the want of such instruction men fall into serious social errors; and labour, instead of being an enlightened and intelligent application of principles, is but too often a dull round of monotonous drudgery.'[9]

Despite the impressive range of this consensus, there were elements of agreement which were more apparent than real. As has already been seen, Moseley could not follow Rigg when the latter took their principle of curriculum design to its logical conclusion and threatened not only the status of literary studies but also the control which the church exercised over the elementary schools.[10] There was agreement about ends only in so far as these were seen as leaving the established order undisturbed. On the question of means there was also a difference of opinion. The increasing involvement of the state in the education of the poor was part of a wider movement towards collectivism and centralization. Occasional set-backs such as that encountered in 1854 with the abolition of the Board of Health, may be seen as the Benthamism of *laissez-faire* triumphing over the Benthamism of bureaucratic organization. *The Times* applauded this particular measure in a leader. 'We prefer to take our chance of cholera and the rest, rather than be bullied into health.'[11] In terms of this opposition between 'collectivism' and '*laissez-faire*', men such as Lord Granville, Kay-Shuttleworth and Moseley may be seen as liberals, prepared to achieve a desirable end by a modest *ad hoc* increase in central control. A knowledge of science was to become an obligatory requirement in the scheme of examination of all training college students. In contrast, there is evidence that for some supporters of the movement, notably the Peelite Lord Ashburton, this was going too far. Prize schemes as an incentive were one thing; the burden of initiative and effort still lay on the individual student or teacher. The 'improvement by the Government itself of the Training Schools' was another. In the summer of 1853 when Kay-Shuttleworth requested Ashburton to use his influence with Lord Granville to forward the larger measure, he met with polite prevarication.[12] By the end of the year, Ashburton had announced his own scheme at a meeting of elementary schoolmasters at Winchester,[13] much to the chagrin of Kay-Shuttleworth. 'Lord Ashburton's views have so surprised me and disappointed me', he complained to Playfair.[14] In the event his mortification was short-lived, for some few months later Moseley was able to secure the approval of the Committee of Council for the new scheme of examination for the male training colleges. This was carefully presented as the consolidation of existing practices, following extensive consultations with the college principals.[15] Ashburton's non-co-operation nevertheless served to highlight a potential source of dissension in the movement; it was also a timely reminder of the strength of opposition to any measures deemed likely to inhibit voluntary local effort.

Although the movement commanded general support from serving teachers there was disgruntled comment from a number of voices, particularly on the issue of misappropriation of the central pedagogical idea. Thomas Tate was not slow to remind his readers that 'the science of common things' had been the subject of lessons given by him some twenty years or more before the present wave of interest. 'Noble lords and learned doctors, and newspaper editors, have lately discovered the importance of teaching the science of common things in our schools' he chafed, deprecating the fact that 'some of them, no doubt, will have their names emblazoned in our blue books as the great renovators of popular education'.[16] Those who had been at the classroom frontiers, pioneering new curriculum developments, were entitled to feel aggrieved if, without acknowledgment, what they took to be their system was 'heralded before the public with a great flourish of trumpets, as if it were really a new thing!' Walter McLeod agreed with Tate in his judgement that Locke, Pestalozzi, and the advocates of object lessons, were the true begetters of the movement, the progress of which could be traced through the work of reformers such as Wilderspin and Stow to the present day. 'But it had happened in this case as it had happened before,' was his vexed complaint. 'Those who had laboured most had been passed over, and those who had made the greatest noise got the greatest credit.'[17] Interestingly, Lord Ashburton, whilst upholding King's Somborne as the model for imitation, also related developments there to his own experience when, as a young man of seventeen, he had visited Geneva in the interval between leaving Eton and going to Oxford. It was during this period, he informed the schoolmasters at Winchester, that 'Faculties were called into play which lay till then undeveloped, and I found my mind ripen more rapidly during those few months than in years previous; and now, advancing in age, I still continue to add more and more to my knowledge by the application of the general principles of common things which I there learned.'[18]

The origin of Dawes' educational ideas has been considered in an earlier chapter where it was pointed out that little evidence exists to suggest a debt to educational reformers from the continent.[19] Dawes did not employ the term 'object lesson' to describe his 'improved secular instruction' although the term was in common use in the educational literature of his day; nor did he invoke faculty psychology in order to prescribe the objectives of education.

The accuracy of Tate's judgement on the origin of the movement is not a significant issue. The dispute over priority is, however, of importance. Those who were familiar with the history of educational ideas – and this group included a number of the most active and progressive school teachers and college lecturers – tended to assimilate Dawes' innovation into an existing tradition which regarded the development of mental faculties as the main task of elementary education. In so far as 'intellectual powers and moral feelings' were to be cultivated 'through the instrumentality of things or subjects which might be known and understood by the child' there were resemblances.[20] But differences arose from the fact that Dawes' practice was unconstrained by theoretical views about a hierarchy of faculties which determined the range of subjects to be studied and the teaching methods to be employed. Sociological rather than psychological considerations marked his system. A consequence of this contrast in viewpoints was that different perceptions of the objectives of the movement existed in the minds of its supporters.[21] Distortions and debasements of the original model were frequently to be observed in the classrooms of schools purporting to teach the science of common things, so much so that Moseley was driven to comment on this matter in his penultimate report. He described a lesson, typical of many that he had observed.[22]

'A teacher proposing to give an oral lesson on coal . . . holds up a piece of it before his class, and having secured their attention, he probably asks them to which kingdom it belongs, animal, vegetable, or mineral – a question in no case of much importance, and to be answered, in the case of coal, doubtfully. Having, however, extracted the answer which he intended to get from the children, he induces them by many ingenious devices, much circumlocution, and an extravagant expenditure of the time of the school, to say that it is a *solid*, that it is *heavy*, that it is *opaque*, that it is *black*, that it is *friable*, and that it is *combustible*. And then the time has probably transpired, and the lesson on the science of common things, assumed to be so useful to a child, is completed.'

This bore little relation to the experimental investigations which Dawes had described in *Suggestive Hints* and which included the destructive distillation of coal, the production of coal gas, the rough calculation of the quantity of carbon dioxide produced during combustion and a simple version of the carbon cycle. Without an adequate knowledge of science on the part of the teacher, lessons on the science of common things degenerated into barren exercises in 'observation' and 'classification'. Little new and useful knowledge was imparted and 'the foundations of intelligence, enterprise, activity, and industry in the common affairs of life' remained unlaid.[23]

In one further respect the movement was inherently vulnerable. Whilst according primacy of place to science when secular knowledge was considered from an educational standpoint, it had nevertheless evolved without official support or sanction from the scientific community of the day. It is true that, at an individual level, Dawes enjoyed cordial relations with at least two front-rank investigators, Edward Frankland and John Tyndall, and that Moseley had previously occupied the chair of natural philosophy at King's College. But neither man was a participating member of any formal association of scientists, much less an invisible college of researchers. The promoters of the movement for teaching the science of common things were external to the main streams of scientific activity. Furthermore, the masters who were needed to teach science in the schools were to acquire their understanding of the subject without benefit of direct apprenticeship to a seasoned investigator, but through the mediation of a training college lecturer, himself unlikely to possess experience of original research. In their turn, the schoolmasters would transmit scientific knowledge to their pupils.

An obvious danger in this situation was that, dissociated from its living source, and put to service by those with no experience of, and commitment to, original inquiry, science might be misconstrued with results prejudicial to its own reputation. In the hands of men like Dawes and Moseley little damage would be done, but the widespread introduction of scientific knowledge into the school curriculum, unmonitored by scientists themselves, might have unfortunate consequences for the advancement of science. This was particularly the case with elementary education for the people. Since the establishment of the Committee of Council, educational advance had been achieved against a background of almost continuous dispute amongst the religious providing bodies. To associate science with this field and to bring it into relationship with the Education Office would be to link it to a public which was, in Lingen's words, 'not a political one, but a religious one, and a religious one in fragments'.[24] Furthermore, the effect of scientific knowledge upon religious belief was a matter of widespread concern, the culmination of which might be seen as the clash between Samuel Wilberforce and Thomas Huxley on the subject of evolution at the end of the decade. No group was more sensitive to this potential antipathy to science than the Commissioners for the 1851 Exhibition, at whose instigation the Department of Science and Art had been created in 1853. Within the new department, as previously noted, the geologists and naturalists of the Government School of Mines, the Museum of Practical Geology and the Geological Survey were particularly vulnerable.[25] The failure to ensure their support was to prove a costly tactical error on the part of the movement for teaching the science of common things.

Of the major scientific institutions in the 1850s the Department of Science and Art occupied a cardinal position in relation to the introduction of scientific knowledge into the curriculum of common schools. Other bodies, such as the British Association for the Advancement of Science and the Royal Society, whilst acknowledging the need to make science an integral part of education, tended at this stage to restrict their concern to the public schools, the universities and adult education. Thus, in 1854, under the leadership of Lord Wrottesley, an amateur astronomer of some distinction and a perceptive statesman of science, the British Association undertook a survey of opinion among scientists on the most effective measures which could be adopted by the government to improve the position of science and its cultivators in the nation. The ensuing report provided evidence of widespread agreement on the need for science to be more thoroughly incorporated into education. The principal targets for reform, however, were seen as being the universities and their supporting schools. On the basis of this survey, the Council of the Royal Society drew up twelve resolutions which were transmitted by Wrottesley to the government early in 1857. Four of these related to educational measures, but none was concerned with science at the primary level.[26] It is clear that the introduction of science into elementary schools was not seen by scientists as an urgent matter likely to 'improve the position of science or its cultivators'. Implicit in the resolutions was a distinction between the teaching of science for the benefit of science and the teaching of science for the personal development of the learner.

The activities of the British Association were not marked by a serious concern for the introduction of science into elementary education until the time of the Education Act of 1870. After this date the Association acted as an important pressure group for the re-establishment of science as a subject of elementary instruction.[27] In the 1850s, however, beyond an occasional reference in a presidential address, the teaching of science in schools for the labouring poor was not an issue which either the British Association or the Royal Society appeared to regard as falling within its field of interest.

To a considerable extent, the same was true of another metropolitan centre of research activity, the Royal Institution. In contrast to the British Association and the Royal Society 'teaching by courses of philosophical lectures and experiments' was a declared objective of the Royal Institution.[28] As early as 1799 its architect and original clerk of works, Thomas Webster, had proposed the foundation of a school of mechanics for artisans, being prompted in this action by the observation that his workmen were frequently unable to understand what was required of them. Unfortunately Webster's scheme encountered opposition, some of which would appear to have been political in its origins, reflecting fears engendered by events across the Channel. In his own words, 'this project for improving mechanics, well intended as it was, which promised to be so useful, and which had already gained for the Institution "golden opinions" was doomed to be crushed by the timidity (for I shall forbear to speak more harshly) of a few. I was asked rudely (by an individual I shall not name) what I meant by instructing the *lower classes* in science. I was told likewise it was resolved upon, that the plan must be dropped *as quietly as possible.* It was thought to have a dangerous political tendency. I was told that if I persisted I would become a *marked man.*'[29]

Subsequent developments in science teaching within the Royal Institution, at the hands of Brande, Davy and Faraday, tended to be with audiences drawn from a less politically controversial sector of society. It was not until 1854, when the managers of the Institution organized an important series of lectures on 'Science and Education', that a wider audience of scientific knowledge was seriously contemplated in Albermarle Street. 'Bence Jones is full of a project for getting seven great guns to lecture upon education after Easter. He talks also of working men's lectures', Tyndall recorded in his Journal early in February 1854.[30] When the education lectures were eventually delivered later in the year, five of the seven included in their title a reference to the importance of their subject 'as a branch of education for all classes'.

It will be necessary to return to a consideration of these lectures shortly, but before doing so a word is required on the relationship of the Department of Science and Art to the movement for teaching the science of common things. The Department's expressed concern for primary education has already been noted in an earlier chapter where reference was made to Lyon Playfair's contributions to the production of new reading lesson books and scientific apparatus for teaching purposes.[31] Initially, it would appear that Moseley's proposals for the consolidation of applied physical science in the curriculum of elementary schools had drawn a favourable response from the new department. Playfair was, of course, a key figure in this matter. Translated from the chair of applied chemistry in the School of Mines to the post of Secretary of the Science Division, he enjoyed an established scientific reputation. In addition, he was not unfamiliar with the corridors of power. He had served with notable success on a number of commissions of inquiry, had been an indispensable aide to the Prince Consort in the organization of the Great Exhibition of 1851 and was frequently consulted by government departments on scientific questions.[32]

The support of the principal scientific civil servant in the land seemed to augur well for the movement. Yet by the time of his department's fourth report, for the year ending December 1856, Playfair had significantly modified his views on the most appropriate type of science to be incorporated into elementary schools. The passage in the report is worth quoting in full.

'The Training Schools throughout the country have hitherto chiefly cultivated the physical rather than the natural sciences, and when the school master introduces science into his primary school, he generally selects mechanics, physics, or chemistry, as the subjects of study. But the sciences of observation, such as zoology, botany, and physiology, are more suitable to the children of primary schools, than the abstract physical sciences referred to, which are better adapted for secondary schools. The study of the sciences of observation would naturally aid and be aided by instruction in drawing, and would implant that love of nature which is required to insure the success of the intermediate schools and scientific institutions throughout the country. If these views are correct, it will be for your Lordship to consider whether it would not be desirable to induce an increased study of the sciences of observation in the Training Colleges. Some of the physical sciences, such as chemistry and experimental physics, are required to explain several of the most common phenomena of life, and, in this point of view, may be studied with advantage even in a primary school; while, as their abstractions are relieved by illustrations, they compel observation; but, as a whole, they do not appear to be so well suited to educe a love of nature in the minds of children as a knowledge of the plants, animals, and stones seen in their daily walks.'[33]

This represented a marked change in the intended objectives of science teaching in elementary schools. For Dawes and Moseley the prime aim has been the intellectual development of children by the use of scientific knowledge to provide opportunities for the exercise of reason and the testing of speculation. Improvements in the moral and religious

I

condition of the children of the poor were assumed to follow as a matter of course, once self-confidence and integrity of thought had been achieved. By giving a prominent place in the curriculum to applied sciences such as mechanics and agricultural chemistry, education could be related to a culture which was familiar to the labouring classes; furthermore, the restricted linguistic experiences of so many elementary school children need no longer be an insuperable obstacle to the growth of rationality. In contrast, the view now being expressed by Playfair involved the displacement of objectives to the affective domain. The principal aim was 'that love of nature' which was deemed necessary to ensure the success of subsequent stages of scientific instruction for which the Department of Science and Art had a special responsibility. In so far as intellectual development was recognized as an objective of science teaching, the emphasis was on a training in observation, for which end the natural history sciences were regarded as the most appropriate studies.

The source of Playfair's revised views is not difficult to uncover. What he now advocated was an accurate reflection of opinions on the educational value of science which had been expressed on numerous occasions by his former colleagues in the Government School of Mines. At the opening of the School in November 1851, the Director, Sir Henry de la Beche, and each of the six members of staff responsible for a course of instruction had delivered an introductory lecture.[34] That of Edward Forbes on 'The Relations of Natural History to Geology and the Arts' dealt at length with the contribution of a study of natural history to education. Whilst much attention was given in schools to the training of the memory and the reasoning powers, the basic faculty of observation 'upon the correct exercise of which the value of the others in a great measure must depend' was, in Forbes' opinion, almost entirely neglected. Instead of building upon the natural tendency of young children to observe and classify natural objects, the prevailing curriculum bound and cramped the youthful intellect 'into traditional and fantastic shapes'.[35] This was a matter of immediate practical concern for schools of applied science, such as the Government School of Mines. It was not the business of such institutions to teach the rudiments of science which students should have acquired elsewhere, prior to admission.

Forbes' thesis was reiterated by his colleague, Robert Hunt, in his introductory lecture to the course on Mechanical Science. For Hunt, all the great applications of science confirmed the proposition that human progress was directly dependent 'upon careful observation, and the habit of recording, in a systematic manner, the facts'.[36] As Keeper of Mining Records, Hunt's judgement was possibly influenced by the requirements of that office. Additionally, however, his experience over twenty years with classes in mechanics' institutes had brought home to him the difficulty of achieving the right level in such lectures. It was all too easy to shoot arrows over the heads of the audience. In his opinion, the most appropriate type of science class was one involving field-excursions and country walks, with the members of the class recording their observations. 'To listen to a lecture from a man of ability is good' he asserted, 'to read with attention is good – but to observe is infinitely better than either.'[37]

At the time when these inaugural lectures were delivered, the Department of Science and Art had not yet come into being and Playfair was on the staff of the Jermyn Street institution, responsible for the course on Chemistry applied to the Arts and Agriculture. His own introductory lecture eschewed any consideration of the process of scientific discovery and of the disciplinary value of science as an instrument of education. Instead, he chose as his subject the way in which abstract scientific knowledge, cultivated without any thought for its utility, nevertheless yielded applications which were unexpected – unimagined even – by its practitioners. It followed that the pursuit of scientific knowledge should not be trammelled by questions such as *'Cui bono?'* Science was 'too lofty for measurement by the yard stick of utility'.[38] At the same time it was vitally important to keep under constant consideration its practical relations to life because 'the overflowings of science' could 'enter into and animate industry'. Indeed, future industrial progress depended to such an extent upon the advance of science that it was vital to secure the incorporation of science into the educational system. It was Playfair's judgement that, 'As surely as darkness follows the setting of the sun, so surely will England recede as a manufacturing nation, unless her industrial population become much more conversant with science than they now are.'[39]

Implicit in Playfair's lecture and explicit in the contributions of Forbes and Hunt were fundamental criticisms of the position adopted by Dawes and Moseley. For the latter, utility for the learner was the supreme criterion by which scientific knowledge was to be assessed. Its value in primary education was in direct proportion to its applicability to the events and circumstances which constituted life for the labouring poor. On this educational scale, the most important sciences were chemistry and mechanics; in contrast, when education was seen as an exercise involving the training of mental faculties, natural history commended itself as an elementary study.

By the time of Playfair's appointment to the Department of Science and Art in the spring of 1853, the movement for teaching the science of common things had made substantial progress. In the circumstances it would appear that Playfair saw collaboration with the Education Office as the only sensible course of action. His own position as joint secretary and inspector for science was assailed by problems. Despite protests, his fellow secretary and inspector for art matters, Henry Cole, had been obliged to yield on the question of the title of the new department, it being agreed that 'Science' should stand before 'Art'.[40] Yet in terms of achievement, as measured by teachers trained and provincial schools established, science could show nothing comparable to the Department of Practical Art and the provincial schools of design with which Cole had been associated previously. To make matters worse, the Government School of Mines, which it was intended should be developed as the metropolitan nucleus for a network of provincial science schools, failed to collaborate in the realization of these plans. Its director, Sir Henry de la Beche, had given an unwilling consent to Playfair's move to the Department of Science and Art; with the transfer to the Board of Trade of his cherished empire – the Geological Survey, the Museum of Practical Geology and the School of Mines – he was clearly loath to deal with a former subordinate.[41] In consequence it was agreed that he should have direct access to the President of the Board, leaving Playfair powerless to effect any changes in the School. By July of 1853, the situation appeared so unpromising that Playfair composed a letter to the Prince Consort, informing him that little could be expected from the science division of the new department, where he, Playfair, had been cast in the role of 'a mere clerk in the administration'.[42] It is not clear whether this letter was actually dispatched, but simultaneously a discussion took place between Playfair and Lord Granville, President of the Committee of Council on Education, in which the difficulties were fully ventilated.[43] It seems probable that the decision to concentrate the energies of the science division on the establishment of science in primary education dates from this meeting.

If, in the cause of short-term progress, Playfair felt obliged to suppress his doubts about the teaching of applied physical science in elementary schools, and indeed to make a virtue of necessity by supporting the innovation with some vigour, others had no such compulsion. Two important series of lectures, both concerned with the theme of science and education, served to bring the issues into sharp relief and to register forcefully the position of the government scientists of the Geological Survey and the School of Mines. Reference has already been made to the Royal Institution lectures delivered in the early summer of 1854. In one sense, the broadside from the 'seven big guns' was notably successful in establishing the claims of science as an instrument of education. The opening contribution from Whewell dealt with the case for introducing a new element into liberal education whereby the mind would be familiarized with inductive reasoning through 'the exact and solid study' of a science. The process was to be characterized by the acquisition of a knowledge of things, involving experimentation, as opposed to a knowledge of the names of things. Only in this way, maintained Whewell, could 'the mind escape from the thraldom and illusion which reigns in the world of mere words'.[44] Neither Whewell, nor Faraday who followed him, entered into the details of subjects of study or the practical issues of instruction in schools. Faraday's 'Observations on Mental Education' were largely concerned with the contribution which a study of science could make to the development of an educated judgement – the antithesis, in his view, of the careless, the over-confident, the presumptuous and the hasty. Each of the five lectures which followed was delivered by a persuasive advocate for the study of a particular subject – Latham for language, Daubeny for chemistry, Tyndall for physics, Paget for physiology and Hodgson for economic science. The implicit theme was the relative merits of the languages and the sciences as instruments of education, though Hodgson was typical of the speakers in arrogating no superiority for his subject as a means of mental discipline.[45] There was little point in adopting a competitive stance when the qualities of mind being trained were so different. Science, in Faraday's graphic phrase, flowed 'in channels utterly different in their course and end to those of literature'.[46] Tyndall likewise rejected the notion that there was an antagonism between science and philology. 'Is there no mind in England', he pleaded, 'large enough to see the value of both, and to secure for each of them fair play?'[47] Yet despite this statesman-like rejection of Bence Jones' injunction to 'extol science at the expense of language' and have 'a knock at our existing systems of education',[48] the Royal Institution lecturers were concerned in the main with issues characteristic of a limited sector of education. Their implied focus was the curriculum of middle- and upper-class schools. No one had seriously advocated the teaching of classical languages in elementary schools for the poor. Furthermore, in so far as they touched upon the selection of appropriate scientific knowledge for the elementary school curriculum, the lectures complicated rather than simplified the issue. In addition to physics and chemistry, physiology also was now seen as having a strong claim on a place in an abbreviated and already crowded timetable. Paget was by no means alone in regarding his subject as basic to the instruction of the poor, being supported in his view by many of those associated with the public health movement. Secularists such as George Combe, William Ellis and William Lovett had all advanced the claims of physiology and in 1853 the Privy Council had received a petition, over the signatures of sixty-five leading physicians and surgeons, entitled 'Medical Opinion on the importance of teaching Physiology and the Laws of Health in Common Schools'.[49] One consequence of this pressure was the production by Playfair's department of a series of physiological diagrams suitable for teaching purposes;[50] in addition, an increased allowance of pay was sanctioned for those who held a certificate of ability to teach the subject. In the context of *laissez-faire* this may be seen as a proper response by an administrative department of state to a publicly expressed want. It is also an indication that the Department's support for the views of Dawes and Moseley on elementary instruction in science was by no means unqualified.

Apart from an approving reference by Daubeny to Dawes' incorporation of chemical knowledge in the curriculum of elementary schools,[51] there was little direct reference in the Royal Institution lectures to the movement for teaching the science of common things. In the series delivered later in the summer, in connection with the Educational Exhibition of the Society of Arts, matters were different. Here state-aided education was the centre of concern and the lecture committee, under the chairmanship of Charles Babbage and including both Dawes and Moseley as members, had organized a programme of over sixty contributions on this topic.[52] The place of science in general education was a prominent theme in what was, without doubt, the most comprehensive and authoritative set of public lectures on education which had ever been held in England. Whewell again was enlisted to deliver the opening address; Dawes spoke on the teaching of the science of common things; and the leading experts of the day were marshalled to lecture on the learning of basic skills such as reading and writing, as well as on the teaching of subjects such as mathematics, music, history, geography, and the various sciences.

If it served no other purpose, the lecture programme of the 1854 Educational Exhibition succeeded in polarizing views on the teaching of science in elementary schools. On the one hand there were the advocates of applied physical science, the members in fact of the movement for teaching the science of common things. On the other hand there were those who urged that science should be taught without regard to its applications; the emphasis should be on the analogue of the 'pure, graceful and thoughtful in literature' with its correlative civilizing and elevating effects.[53] Among the important proponents of this view were scientists from the Government School of Mines. Robert Hunt, in particular, argued that a study of science for its own sake was an exercise which tended 'to the refinement and elevation of every human feeling'. In addition, he raised the objection that the continued educational emphasis on science as useful knowledge would prove harmful to the progress of science.

'I fear that the reaction in favour of a scientific education is likely to lead us into many errors', he warned, 'and I conceive that we have an illustration of these errors in the excellent educational exhibition gathered together in this hall.'

'In its general character this exhibition is essentially practical; it is a great exemplar of the feeling which has grown out of the Great Exhibition – *that science in its useful application to the purposes of life, is the aim and end of education.* I would not for one moment deny the value of practical science as a branch of education, but I must contend that the idea of measuring the value of science by its practical utility is degrading it from the high position it should occupy. Yet this is the characteristic feature of the science teaching which will, we have to fear, be adopted. . . . If we once yield to this, farewell to all advancement of knowledge. That which is already known may be most usefully applied, but no new truths will dawn upon the darkened horizon within which we shall confine ourselves.'[54]

To counter-balance this critical and lugubrious view, Hunt outlined a scheme for teaching the elements of physics by the use of inexpensive apparatus and familiar playthings. His emphasis was on an understanding of principles such as the impenetrability of matter and the conservation of momentum, without reference to applications. The immediate aim was 'to awaken curiosity, produce new ideas, and lead to observation'. In his opinion, pure science could be taught without expensive equipment and models, 'and the annoyance of seeing this useless when it is supplied, because the use of the tool is not familiar to the workman'.[55] Moreover, by abandoning utility as the supreme criterion for the selection of knowledge, a nobler being was produced. Taught in this way, science was morally improving because an understanding of the physical principles which controlled the material world enriched the conception of 'our Almighty Ruler'. In short, as a subject of elementary instruction, pure science was cheap, spiritually elevating and consonant with the pursuit of scientific truth. An emphasis on applied science, in contrast, was expensive, inculcated mercenary ends and endangered the advancement of science.

Hunt's standing in the field of nineteenth-century science education is in no way comparable to that of some of his colleagues such as Tyndall, Playfair and Huxley; nonetheless he was a figure of significance whose pronouncements on the teaching of science were respected. His inaugural lecture at the opening of the School of Mines had been singled out, with that of Playfair, for commendation by Edward Forbes[56] and Playfair had strongly supported Hunt for the important post of Secretary to the Society of Arts when this had become vacant in the spring of 1853. 'Of all men I know', he wrote to Cole, 'he is the most capable for it, having the art of pleasing everybody.'[57] In June of 1854,

Hunt had been elected to a fellowship of the Royal Society. By virtue of his experience as a successful researcher and teacher, his opinions were imbued with an authority which was widely recognized.

Untenable though his position may seem today, the views which Hunt expressed commanded much support in the mid-nineteenth century. The importance of research for its own sake, without regard to applications, had been the subject of Playfair's opening lecture in the School of Mines. Whewell's caveat on the prevailing emphasis on applied science, in his review of Herschel's *Preliminary Discourse*, has already been noted, as has Darwin's defence of research which was 'wholly unapplied'.[58] The application of increased funds to the encouragement of abstract science was a central point in the Royal Society's submission to the government in January 1857.[59] In asserting the claims of pure science, in the context of education, Hunt was reflecting the views of many of his fellow researchers.

His other point, the attribution of moral and devotional outcomes to the study of science, was a familiar theme in protestant thought.[60] Because the Book of Nature and the Book of Scripture were works by the same author, the study of either was supposed to enhance religious belief. What Paget earlier in the year had referred to as 'the ever-pending conflict of intellect and faith',[61] the possibility of a contradiction between the natural and the revealed, was not seriously contemplated by Hunt, for whom the record of natural science was 'a great didactic poem'.[62] It followed that the task of the science teacher was to lead the mind 'through nature up to nature's God'. Of course, there was no antithesis here with the views of Moseley, who had himself written a work on *Astro-theology* in which the truths of astronomy were taught in 'a reverential, if not devotional, spirit'.[63] Moseley, likewise, would not have dissented from the proposition that a study of science could excite sublime feelings of awe and wonder. On this point the difference between the two was one of emphasis; for Hunt, the moral and devotional outcomes were both the supreme and proximate ends of science teaching; for Moseley, the stress was on a range of intervening and subordinate aims, such as the application of scientific knowledge to the solution of problems arising from the material environment of the poor.

Up to this point Hunt's advocacy of pure science in the school curriculum had been largely in general terms; the issue of content remained unresolved. It is true that in the Educational Exhibition lecture to which reference has been made his illustrations had been drawn from his own subject, physics. However, four days later, in a subsequent lecture, he borrowed extensively from Edward Forbes in presenting a case for the teaching of the sciences of observation, particularly natural history.[64] The importance of a study of natural history was, in fact, to emerge as one of the most strongly delineated themes in the series. The opening notes were sounded by another Fellow of the Royal Society, William Carpenter, who systematically outlined the educational benefits which could result. Because natural history trained all the reasoning faculties and was also a subject with poetic, moral and religious bearings 'it might be made to act beneficially on a larger proportion of man's faculties than any other single object of pursuit'. Anticipating the objection that dwellers in large towns were cut off from the museum of nature, Carpenter recommended the use of aids such as the microscope to enable them to make biological observations, throwing out the suggestion that, if the Society of Arts wished to help the progress of education, it might advantageously promote the manufacture of an inexpensive microscope of better quality than those currently available.[65]

Carpenter's was a temperate statement of an alternative to 'the science of common things' which was beginning to command increasing support. It was left to one of Hunt's colleagues to crystallize the content issue by advancing a powerful and specific argument for the teaching of biology, in preference to other sciences, so paving the way for Playfair's revision of judgement on the most suitable branches of science to include in the elementary school curriculum. At the same time there is a conjunction to record. The scientific opposition to the teaching of applied physical science now merged with the movement for the improved status of the natural history sciences, botany in particular, which has been noted in an earlier chapter when considering the work of J. S. Henslow.[66] Hunt's colleague, the newly appointed successor to Edward Forbes, was none other than the young T. H. Huxley who, in the 1854 Educational Exhibition series of lectures, made his debut as a speaker on educational matters.[67]

It was in this lecture that Huxley gave his celebrated definition of scientific method as a mere extension of the mental processes used in everyday life. 'Science', he contended, 'is nothing but trained and organized common sense, differing from the latter, only as a veteran may differ from a raw recruit.'[68] Mill, rather than Whewell, was the source of his philosophy of science in which scientific ideas had the status of direct derivatives from sensory experience. Influenced by Kant, Whewell took a different view; in scientific discovery, the mind supplied a new conception in terms of which previously disordered facts were bound together. Scientific ideas could not be reduced to the logical outcome of observed differences and agreements between phenomena.[69]

In aligning himself with Mill, Huxley had both biological and educational ends in mind. Much of his lecture was given over to an examination of the standing of his subject as a branch of knowledge. Because the methods of biology were precisely those of all other sciences, it followed that biology could not be regarded as an inferior and inexact science. For Huxley, not only did it bear favourable comparison with other sciences – it was, for example, '*the* experimental science *par excellence* of all sciences' – but also its central position in the spectrum of human knowledge placed it in a more intimate relation with humanity than the physico-chemical sciences. Furthermore, when considered from an educational standpoint, biology was no whit inferior to other scientific studies as an instrument of mental training. Indeed, argued Huxley, it provided unrivalled opportunities for the exercise of the faculties of observation and comparison. Practical benefits accrued to its students also. It had an obvious relevance to the laws of health; but, at least as important, it could exert a powerful influence over the finer feelings of man by encouraging him to seek out the beauties of natural objects.[70]

Huxley's contribution to the resurgence of the natural history sciences is a subject which lies outside the scope of the present chapter. Of immediate significance, however, are the grounds on which he championed biology as an instrument of education. His primary justification was in terms of the training of general faculties of mind and in so assimilating his espousal to the mainstream of argument by which classics and mathematics were sanctioned as core subjects in the curriculum, it might appear that Huxley was being strategically astute. His position, however, was founded upon the equation of science with rational empiricism and the association of the methods of biology with those of common sense. This was a different point of departure from that of Dawes and Moseley; furthermore it represented a view of science which was by no means shared by all his fellow workers. In terms of it, Huxley was able to inflate the educational claims for a study of science in a manner denied, for example, to Whewell. For the latter, the process of induction, in which the mind acquired 'a new and distinct view or hit upon a right supposition', could not be taught.[71] Some appreciation of the inductive process by means of which scientific knowledge had been obtained was, of course, a basic element in any liberal education; it might be achieved either by the solid study of some portion of an established science or by the study of history of science, an excellent remedy, in Whewell's opinion, for the logician's oversimplified view of science.[72] Yet the outcome of such learning was not to be assessed in terms of general abilities to 'observe', 'compare', 'classify' and 'generalize'. The appropriate evaluation was more limited in scope, being concerned with the extent to which the learner could demonstrate an understanding of the technical vocabulary of science.[73] Science was studied in order that the learner might understand the natural world as it was understood by scientists.

In contrast, the central point in Huxley's espousal of biology as a branch of education was its value as a means of disciplining certain general faculties of mind. By invoking the concept of mental training he was able to state his case in terms familiar to those who regarded classics and mathematics as the staples of the curriculum. At the same time, he built his argument upon a foundation which was to become progressively weaker as evidence accumulated against the doctrine of formal training.[74] The rigorous discrediting of faculty psychology had to await the results of empirical researches at the turn of the century, but even around the time of Huxley's lecture there were distinguished scientific voices which seriously questioned the training argument. Faraday, for example, with typical perspicacity, informed the Public School Commissioners in 1864 that 'The phrase "training of the mind" has to me a very indefinite meaning. I would like a profound scholar to indicate to me what he understands by the training of the mind; in a literary sense, including mathematics. What is their effect on the mind? What is the kind of result that is called the training of the mind? or what does the mind learn by that training? It learns things I have no doubt. . . . But does it learn that training of the mind which enables a man to give a reason in natural things for an effect which happens from certain causes? . . . It does not suggest the least thing in these matters.'[75]

This specificity of intellectual attributes arising from particular studies, to which Faraday alluded, was, of course, a principle implicit in the curriculum prescription of Dawes and Moseley. It was precisely because of their differential outcomes that certain branches of knowledge were more appropriate than others in the curriculum of common schools. Their study provided the kind of training which was deemed most useful to the children of the poor. Paradoxically, by virtue of an unpretentious concentration on the development of rational modes of thought within a limited scientific context, coupled with an emphasis on the applicability of scientific principles to the understanding of a wide range of events and occurrences, more of the necessary conditions for transfer of learning were being satisfied by the scheme of Dawes and Moseley than by that of Huxley.

A secondary, but telling, point in Huxley's argument for the teaching of biology was its unique association with socially acceptable affective objectives such as 'a love of nature' and 'the ability to derive pleasure from the countryside'.[76] In an age when, as a later Huxley was to point out, 'a tour of Westmorland was as good as a visit to Jerusalem',[77] such civilizing outcomes were bound to appeal. Of course the prospect of individual contentment and social harmony, fostered by the informed contemplation of the beauties of nature, was a highly romanticized view of the consequences of studying biology. It was also one to which the applied physical sciences could not easily aspire. An awareness of religious misgivings about the natural history sciences would seem to have encouraged the Jermyn Street practitioners to over-emphasize the respectability of their studies.

With the advantage of hindsight it is easy to be critical of the arguments employed by Huxley and his colleagues in the Royal School of Mines. Yet for a contemporary such as Playfair, embroiled in the difficult task of promoting science in education, and particularly at a time when his department was being drawn into closer administrative relations with the Education Office in Whitehall,[78] such considerations as Huxley advanced must have weighed heavily. The result, as has been noted, was the transfer of Playfair's support from the movement for teaching the science of common things to the rising cause of the natural history sciences. Henslow, rather than Dawes, appeared to hold the key to future curriculum developments in science.

Chapter 7

The Politics of
the Curriculum

Questions about the social functions of elementary education and the content of the school curriculum were forced irresistibly upon teachers and administrators in the mid-1850s. At the classroom level, the harassed practitioner was beset with solicitations to add new studies to his course; in addition to the claims of the science of common things and of natural history, those of music, drawing, physiology and economics were all being pressed. There was an urgent need for what Robert Lowe later termed 'the science of ponderation' whereby, in his words, 'we shall put into the scales all the different objects of human knowledge and decide upon their relative importance'.[1] Inevitably, educators were obliged to clarify their purpose when this accumulation of new knowledge came to bear upon a curriculum previously shaped by the requirements of scriptural literacy. The short period of time for which the majority of children were in attendance at schools only served to accentuate the problem.

At the national level, the publication in 1854 of the educational statistics of the 1851 Census marked a turning point for many providers and administrators of elementary education. A quantitative picture was now available from which it was clear that the early age at which children were removed from school, a factor widely regarded as the greatest obstacle to progress in elementary education, was not due to 'work and wages' alone. After allowing for those in employment, three million children between the ages of five and twelve should have been in schools. Yet the Census figures showed that almost a third of these were absent.[2]

Other reasons than the state of the labour market had to be sought to account for the empty places in elementary schools. The 'grand cause', according to the Census report, was the slight esteem which parents had for the education being offered. It was hardly a matter for surprise that the working class, 'seeing that the purely mental training which their children pass through in the present class of schools can rarely exercise an influence upon their future temporal prosperity, and having for some generations past been tutored not to look *beyond their station*, should esteem a thorough education of this character to be not worth the time and money needful for its acquisition.'³ As long as the curriculum remained untuned to the values and attitudes of the consumers, elementary education was likely to prove unattractive.

Simultaneously there was a recognition that the improvement of the social condition of the great mass of the people was too complex a problem to be solved by educational means alone. Popular education was only one of many needed instruments of amelioration; co-ordinately and *pari passu* more effective means of improving the physical conditions of life were required.⁴ Indeed, without these, much educational effort would be vitiated. 'However carefully the tree of knowledge may be planted,' Horace Mann affirmed in his Census report, 'and however diligently tended, it can never grow to fruitfulness or beauty in an uncongenial air.'⁵ The financial implications of this viewpoint were not overlooked; more economical means of achieving social improvement might exist than the investment of ever-increasing resources in the field of education. The previous disposition had been to overburden elementary schools with aspirations; there was now need for a more modest and realistic appraisal of what could be achieved, an exercise which was in no way discouraged by the climate of financial stringency which marked the aftermath of the Crimean War.

Re-examination of the objectives of elementary education brought into sharp focus a central dilemma for curriculum planners of the mid-nineteenth century. The principles of curriculum design advocated by educators such as Dawes

K

and Moseley were undoubtedly successful when evaluated in terms of the immediate response of children to the schooling offered. They were, however, open to a substantial criticism; a curriculum founded upon knowledge which had been selected because of its immediate utility in the lives of the pupils might imprison children for ever in the confines of their own environment. Such an education, reinforcing, rather than extending, the experiences of learners, could hinder, if not totally frustrate, social mobility. A ghetto curriculum, with undesirable hermetic qualities, might result; as with the radical course of study at Chester Training College, the student would be tethered fast to the state of life from which he started.[6]

It has been suggested by certain writers that the concern of the Victorians with the education of the poor can best be understood as a concern about authority, power and the assertion of control.[7] Those who regulated the curriculum of elementary schools were in a position to determine 'the patterns of thought, sentiment and behaviour of the working class'. Schools for the people were deemed effective to the extent that their pupils emerged 'respectful, cheerful, hard-working, loyal, pacific and religious'.[8] On this view, the prime social function of elementary schools was a political one whereby children were initiated into the accepted norms of behaviour in society, and the existing political and social order was sustained. To the extent that the curriculum prescription of Dawes and Moseley was specific to a social group and took for granted – even reinforced – the existing stratification of society, it might be said to satisfy this political requirement. Yet its specificity was also its principal weakness from a political standpoint. As Daubeny remarked in a telling passage of his Royal Institution Lecture, 'the exclusion from the curriculum of any study which is admitted as an integral part of the training given to the people at large, must tend to the isolation of the class (above) . . . and consequently weaken its connexion with those below it'. The inclusion of a subject such as chemistry in the curriculum of schools for the lower and middle classes made it imperative, in Daubeny's view, to impose it upon the upper; 'under the circumstances of the present age, and in this country more especially, the maintenance of a superior position, and of superior moral influence, involves the necessity of superior mental culture'. In the case of a priest, for example, a legitimate influence over the laity could only be maintained 'by the ascendancy of his character, and by the extent of his information with respect to subjects on which the people with whom he mixes are able to estimate his superiority'.[9] Cross-examined by the Public School Commissioners eight years later, Sir Charles Lyell was to make an identical series of points. The introduction of science into schools for the middle classes, for example, put into their hands 'a certain amount of power' which was, at that stage, denied to the upper classes.[10] The existing order would not be maintained if new knowledge was distributed unevenly.

The alternative to a curriculum designed in terms of the specific requirements of a social group was a common curriculum with identical objectives for all classes of learner. In this way the danger of disconnecting the ruling and subordinate classes might be avoided; a normative corpus of knowledge could be readily controlled; and, from the learner's point of view, the conditions on which upward social mobility could be achieved were made abundantly clear. Such a curriculum, conceived in terms of the right disciplining of mental faculties, had many attractions for those who saw popular education as an instrument for achieving political and social stability. Additionally, it consorted well with what might be called the cultural role of education whereby the transmission of aproved values and accredited intellectual skills was emphasized.[11] By way of comparison, the community-related curriculum of Dawes and Moseley sanctioned new knowledge and a non-literary mode of learning which was both novel, in the sense of being unestablished in university education, and potentially threatening to prevailing intellectual styles.

Education had at least one other function to fulfil beyond its political and cultural ones. As conceived by the Royal Commissioners for the 1851 Exhibition it had an important economic role to play by supplying the occupational skills needed in an industrial society.[12] To some extent the inclusion of applied scientific knowledge in the curriculum contributed to this end, although it was never the intention of Dawes and Moseley that industrial training should be a part of elementary education. Rather, a knowledge of particular occupations with which a child might be familiar was made a basis for the exercise of reasoning powers and the understanding of scientific principles. Advocates of the common curriculum went further in claiming to eschew any reference to particular walks of life. The aim was to be a general training, applicable to any situation. It was not the business of elementary education to anticipate, or prejudice, the selection of a particular line of employment. 'We must give to all, as far as possible, that which will be needed by all, and on which the narrower employments of after-life may properly be built,' a contemporary exponent maintained. 'Let us refuse to be seduced into any purely technical education.'[13]

A significant analysis of the function of elementary education and of the relative importance of various subjects of study was given in an address to schoolmasters, in 1854, by Joshua Fitch, shortly before he assumed the principalship of the British and Foreign School Society Training College, Borough Road. Fitch was later to be appointed by Lord Granville to the inspectorate, in which service he exerted a considerable influence on the development of elementary education in the later decades of the century.[14] At the time of his lecture he was a young man of thirty, newly appointed to the staff of Borough Road. 'How do we evaluate where education has been effective, when a former pupil returns to school?' he asked his audience. Obviously, one did not set a sum or a sentence to parse. Rather, argued Fitch, we ask the young man about his position and prospects, and we find out if his associations and pleasures are innocent or not. 'Is he expecting an increased income soon; has he invented a little contrivance for economizing his work? Is he fond of reading? Is he loyal and respectful to yourself and the school?' By these tests the efficacy of schooling could be judged. The details of grammar and ciphering may have been forgotten, but if questions such as the above could be answered in the affirmative, all was well.[15]

As to the means to these ends, Fitch was equally clear. 'The principle on which the university course may be vindicated, is precisely that which justifies the ordinary practice of our schools' was his view. A knowledge of common things, as recently advocated by Lord Ashburton and others, was altogether too restrictive; it should be obtained, not in schools, but through 'actual practical acquaintance with life'. In contrast, 'a man whose mind has been subjected to the sort of training which obstruser subjects give, is better qualified to meet the experience of life in a right spirit, to receive it discreetly, and to use it effectively'. In concrete terms, this meant a curriculum composed of reading and writing – the main instruments by which all future knowledge was to be attained; arithmetic – 'the mathematics of the elementary school'; English grammar – the classics of the poor; with a little geography and history. These six subjects, Fitch recommended, ought to 'share among them the bulk of our teaching power'.[16] Singing, the quality of which often seemed to indicate the moral tone of a school, was more 'an elegant accomplishment' than 'a necessary branch of education' and ought to be regarded as a treat which was given out of school hours. Drawing, despite the fact that, for a great manufacturing nation, we were unquestionably poor at design, was 'not an indispensable part of the education of every child; nor yet a part of that course through which even the majority should be expected to pass'. As to 'a knowledge of common things', which Fitch equated with the acquisition of 'the practical knowledge of facts which every man possesses', this was to be obtained from country walks, star gazing, and domestic experiences. 'Is a school designed to supersede these teachers?' he remonstrated. The disciplining of mental faculties was the schoolmaster's task. 'If children go into the world ignorant of common things, it is not for the want of technical instruction about them; but either because their daily life has been

confined to a narrow and unlovely world, their homes are
wretched, and God's fairest works kept far out of their
sight (circumstances over which we have but small control),
or else because their powers of observation and of thought-
fulness have been insufficiently developed; and this is a
defect which I believe would be more truly corrected by
the good and sound teaching of arithmetic, geography,
grammar, history and the Holy Scriptures, than by all the
catechisms and manuals of miscellaneous information ever
written.'[17]

It would be difficult to find a curriculum which contrasted
more severely with the liberal views of Dawes and Moseley
than the reactionary programme outlined by Fitch. Elementary schools were conceived primarily as instruments of
social control. After religious instruction, the foremost task
was to discipline the pupils in reading and writing, skills
which, according to Fitch, 'must always be laboriously
taught'; there was no escaping 'the necessity for this
mechanical drudgery'. Science, as a distinctive mode of
acquiring knowledge, might scarcely have existed. A
common, literary-orientated, curriculum, assuming un-
limited transfer of training, was to prevail. As for those
children from deprived home backgrounds, most appeared
to be abandoned as lost souls already. In other cases, where
the disjunction between home and school was not totally
irremediable, a single chance of salvation was offered
through the strict regimen of mental discipline.

It might be argued that Fitch was doing no more than
accept the realities of the classroom situation in adopting
this reversionary stance. An examination of his extensive
comments on the specific issue of teaching the science of
common things lends some support to this view. Whilst
conceding that a study of the scientific principles underlying the facts of common life was a legitimate part of
school work and had a justifiable claim on a fraction of
'our thirty hours a week', his remarks on this subject were
largely directed at the unsystematic teaching of 'general
knowledge'. 'If the spirit of the age demands of us that we
should abandon our time-honoured discipline in grammar,

in arithmetic, and in scriptural knowledge', he proclaimed, 'in order to make room for superficial teaching about gas and steam engines, and textile manufactures and sanitary regulations, then I think we should have moral courage to say of the age, "We think the demand unreasonable, and founded on a wrong principle, and we will not comply with it".'[18] Few would have disagreed; but Fitch was here tilting at a straw man of his own creation. No one had seriously advocated what he criticized. Such substance as his argument contained lay in the fact that the stated aims of the movement for teaching the science of common things were frequently debased in the classroom. Moseley's observations on this situation have already been noted[19] and he would have agreed with Fitch in condemning much that had been taught as science in the past. Furthermore, both men acknowledged the crucial role of the teacher-training colleges in achieving future progress. Beyond this point their paths diverged. Whereas Moseley strove to establish science in the education of all prospective teachers, Fitch, and others like him, saw the mid-fifties as a period for retrenchment and consolidation on traditional lines.

Moseley's replacement as inspector with special responsibility for the Church Training Colleges was formally announced in July of 1855.[20] The new incumbent, Frederick Temple, a future headmaster of Rugby and Primate of all England, was an Oxford contemporary of Lingen and a significant link in the Balliol connection with the Education Office which was at that time being forged.[21] Temple was neither a stranger to science nor inimical to it as a school subject. After the closure of Kneller Hall, the government teacher training establishment of which he was principal from 1850 to December 1855, and before taking up his duties as Moseley's successor, he had been engaged on the revision of the official lists of scientific apparatus for which government grant was available. His assistant in this task was Thomas Tate, who had been science tutor, under Temple, at Kneller Hall.[22] Subsequently Temple encouraged the teaching of science at Rugby where he made it a compulsory subject for all boys below the upper school.[23] At the same time it is clear that he did not share his predecessor's judgement on the central importance of science in the school curriculum. Despite its value as a discipline for the intellect, science, in Temple's view, had intrinsic limitations as a branch of education. 'When I say that the study of literature humanizes', he told the Public School Commissioners, 'I mean that it cultivates that part of our nature by which we are brought into contact with men and with moral agents.' In contrast, science could never rise 'to touch the sense of personality or responsibility, the sense of being yourself a person and having to deal with other persons'.[24]

The assertion that the study of literature and the study of science yielded different outcomes, would have brought no protest from scientists such as Faraday and Tyndall. Where Temple differed was in maintaining the clear superiority of literary studies. 'If we are to choose a study which shall pre-eminently fit a man for life', he maintained, 'it will be that which shall best enable him to enter into the thoughts, the feelings, the motives of his fellows.'[25] With these ends in view, science was assigned a lowly place in the scale of subject values. It might yield power over the material forces of the universe, but it left untouched 'the greater forces of the human heart'. As a later writer blandiloquently remarked, 'it makes a botanist, a geologist, . . . an engineer, but it does not make a man'.[26]

The relative merits of literary and scientific studies was by no means an unfamiliar issue and Temple's views had a distinguished ancestry. Renaissance humanism, for example, in placing an emphasis on the moral aspects of man's character, had accorded primacy to rhetorical and philological studies. The mastery of natural philosophy was of far less importance than that of moral philosophy. Whilst it was laudable to investigate the secrets of nature, wrote Matteo Palmieri in the fifteenth century, 'we hold them still of the minutest interest in the supreme task of solving the problem how to live'.[27] In the second half of the nineteenth century, whilst it was perhaps more difficult to sustain this particular point, similar arguments prevailed. A characteristic of much English romantic thought was the notion of an antithesis between imagination and reason; furthermore, on the prevalent Millian view, scientific method was seen as a calculus of discovery which superseded imaginative insight. It followed that science could only play a subordinate role in an education the prime aim of which was to humanize the masses.

Temple's first tour of duty as inspector of the Church of England Male Training Colleges occupied the summer and autumn of 1856.[28] The following January a circular letter was sent to all college principals, over the signature of Lingen, advising them of significant changes in the syllabus of studies.[29] At one stroke all that Moseley had striven for, in an effort to establish science as a core subject of the curriculum, was undone. The weighting of subjects, as indicated by the scale of marks supplied in the circular, was a severe discouragement to any college wishing to enter first-year students for the examination in Mechanics. In the scheme for the second year, Physical Science was demoted to one of four optional subjects, the others being the prestigious Latin, Higher Mathematics and English Literature. As the circular explained, the Committee of Council had been guided by two considerations in assigning marks to the different studies; first, the powers of mind indicated by proficiency in each; and, second, the direct practical utility of each subject for purposes of elementary education.

In his annual report Temple later commented on a tendency which the colleges had shown to attempt more than could be accomplished satisfactorily;[30] the point was reiterated in the Committee's guidance to principals. It was to be distinctly understood that proficiency in a few subjects was valued more highly than mediocrity in many. The list of examinable subjects was long only so that colleges might exercise a degree of freedom in the selection of subjects for their courses. Superficial study would be penalized; thus, in no case would two papers marked 'moderate' receive as many marks as would have been given to one of them marked 'good'.

The direction of change was clear. By the time of the

Table 5

Subjects of study: first year	Marks awarded to students who achieved the grade of		Subjects in which failure resulted in a candidate not being classed
	'Good'	'Excellent'	
Religious Knowledge	100	125	*
Arithmetic	60	75	*
Grammar & English Language	60	75	*
School Management	60	75	*
Reading	60	75	*
Spelling	—	—	*
Penmanship	60	75	*
History	60	75	
Geography	60	75	
Geometry	60	75	
Mechanics	50	$62\frac{1}{2}$	
Algebra or Latin	50	$62\frac{1}{2}$	
Drawing	50	$62\frac{1}{2}$	
Music	50	$62\frac{1}{2}$	

To achieve a First Class a student needed 600 marks
To achieve a Second Class a student needed 450 marks
To achieve a Third Class a student needed 300 marks

[Adapted from: Committee of Council on Education, *Minutes 1856–7* (London 1857), p. 9]

certificate examinations in 1859 Mechanics had disappeared from the list of subjects examined at the end of the first year of study, and the number of second-year students offering Physical Science had dwindled to seventy-five, concentrated in four colleges where resources for this work had previously been established.[31] The most vital asset for the success of the movement for teaching the science of common things, a supply of teachers qualified to take advantage of the scientific apparatus grant, had been drastically curtailed.

The full significance of these changes in the training of schoolmasters can only be appreciated if they are seen against the background of simultaneous developments in the Department of Science and Art. With the establishment of the new department it had been hoped that the training of science teachers would be included among the activities of the Metropolitan School of Mines in Jermyn Street. Indeed, the first report of the Department had referred, optimistically, to the prospect of co-operation with the Committee of Council on Education in the provision of special courses for teachers who showed an aptitude for science.[32] As long as this possibility remained, there was hope that science might become established as a branch of general education, if not in the form of applied physical science, then as natural history or systematic botany.

It is clear that the role of the Metropolitan School in relation to the training of teachers was a constant source of conflict between its director, Sir Henry de la Beche, and Playfair. De la Beche was unquestionably resentful and jealous of Playfair, who, in turn, saw his former chief as the major obstacle to the development of Jermyn Street as a national centre for science education.[33] It was the opinion of Henry Cole, Playfair's fellow secretary, that a revolution was necessary in Jermyn Street if the educational objectives of the Department were to be achieved;[34] so long as de la Beche held office the prospect of even modest change was slight. 'Playfair thought de la Beche would resign with a pension of £300 and a K.C.B.,' Cole recorded hopefully in his diary in November 1853,[35] but Sir Henry retained his directorate, yielding little, until his death in 1855. For a while it appeared that a new director, more sympathetic to the cause of science teaching, might then be appointed. Playfair himself wished to achieve a separation of research from educational activities and, for the School, urged the claims of John Phillips, the assistant general secretary of the British Association for the Advancement of Science and Reader in Geology at Oxford. 'He . . . is an enthusiastic Educationalist, acquainted with the mining proprietors, is an excellent lecturer, and a most amiable man,' he reported to Cole.[36] But a week later his hopes were dashed. 'Sir Roderick Murchison is the new Director,' Cole was informed. 'All my proposed reforms and division of the Geological Survey from the School overruled.'[37]

From the scientific community, support for Murchison was overwhelming, a recommendation for his appointment, over the signature of Wrottesley, as President of the Royal Society, and bearing the names of most of the leading researchers of the day, having been presented to the government.[38] Faraday and Darwin, both normally averse to signing ordinary testimonials, had attached their names to the document. Furthermore, it was known that Murchison was acceptable to the science professors at Jermyn Street. For his part, Murchison insisted that the post he wished to hold was that of Director General of the Geological and Mining Survey including control of the Museum and responsibility for the work of the Jermyn Street professors. 'I make this remark', he wrote to Playfair, referring to the scope of his new post, 'because from what dropped when you spoke to me, it appeared as if the Appointment might be remodelled or made into a new one.'[39]

The conclusion cannot be avoided that de la Beche and Murchison interpreted their roles in strictly scientific terms and remained predominantly concerned with the advancement of geology.[40] Their prime allegiance was to the research and specialized training institution and they successfully resisted the attempt to broaden its functions. Although the second annual Report of the Department of Science and Art promised new and more effective arrangements for the training of science teachers in the Metropolitan School of Science (as the School of Mines had been restyled) there was little to show in the way of results.[41] Some training college students from the London region attended at the School for special lectures, but their work there contrasted sharply with their college studies which were characterized by opportunities for teaching practice as well as by a severe discipline and regular examinations. Evening science lectures were instituted in 1854, the first course by Hofmann on chemistry being attended by 253 persons including sixty schoolmasters. The following year the course was given by Huxley, with seventeen teachers in attendance. Thereafter the evening science lectures for schoolmasters were not renewed.[42] By 1857, the year in which the transfer of the Department of Science and Art from the Board of Trade to the Committee of Council on Education became effective, all hopes of establishing a central training school for science teachers had been abandoned. As an alternative, an arrangement was made whereby selected students could proceed to Chester Training College for further study in preparation for the Department's certificates of competency.[43]

In fairness to the eminent scientists who lectured in the School of Mines, it must be said that they were heavily overworked with numerous commitments outside the School. Whilst they were willing for pupil teachers and college students to attend their science lectures, the provision of specially designed courses of training for science teachers was something beyond the resources of the School.[44] However, the basic difficulty would seem to have been a reluctance to depart from established roles and enter a field which was insecure and even antipathetic to science. Murchison, in particular, viewed with alarm the transfer of the Department of Science and Art from the Board of Trade to the Privy Council. The Jermyn Street establishment would then be under the jurisdiction of those who 'both by their training and position, must be to a great extent disqualified from assigning their due importance to the practical branches of science. Such persons', he protested to Lord Stanley, then President of the Board of Trade, 'may object to a course of study which, as now pursued, is irrespective of religious teaching. Experience has shown in how sickly a manner practical science is allowed to raise its head under the direction of those persons whose pursuits are alien to it.'[45]

Murchison's letter was of no avail: the union was formally effected by an Order in Council dated 25 February 1856, although it was not until January of the following year that the new Education Board held its first meeting. Whilst the concern of de la Beche and Murchison for the welfare of their cherished Survey is understandable, the failure of the Metropolitan School to make a significant contribution to the training of science teachers at this crucial stage left no alternative but to rely upon the supply from the government aided training colleges. As has already been seen, the turn of events in the Church colleges, following

Moseley's replacement in the inspectorate, destroyed any chance of increasing the limited stock of teachers competent to introduce science into the schools for the people.

In one further respect Playfair's efforts to further the teaching of elementary science were frustrated by the Director of the School. Literally days before the opening of the Educational Exhibition of the Society of Arts in July 1854, de la Beche convened a meeting with Cardwell, President of the Board of Trade, in order to discuss the question of diagrams and other teaching aids which had been produced at the instigation of the Department.[46] Playfair was not invited to attend and, unusually, the meeting was held in Jermyn Street instead of Cardwell's office. It was agreed that no imprint of the Department could be used in connection with publications and diagrams without the express sanction of 'my Lords' of the Board of Trade; furthermore, proofs of all materials were to be submitted in future so that the Board might approve or veto publication. In effect, this meant that de la Beche, or his nominee, would scrutinize all proposed diagrams and apparatus; only with his agreement would future aids be produced. A specific order was issued that no diagrams were to be exhibited at the Educational Exhibition other than those which had been specially authorized. As Norman MacLeod, the Department official who attended the meeting, informed Playfair, 'This will I fear prevent any of your diagrams being exhibited.'[47]

No doubt part of de la Beche's concern was with the scientific accuracy of any diagrams and publications which might be associated with the Department of Science and Art, but, beyond this, one can again detect a reluctance to associate science with a field as controversial as elementary education. It was possible, for example, that certain geological and physiological diagrams might be found offensive to religious susceptibilities. In addition, the Society of Arts was afflicted by tensions which could have worked to the disadvantage of the Department. The central issue here was the fate of the surplus from the 1851 Exhibition, a sum of £186,436. The Mechanics' Institutes and other bodies in union with the Society were pressing for a distribution to the provinces. In contrast, the Prince Consort and the 1851 Commissioners favoured a metropolitan development in which the School of Mines had a significant part to play.[48] 'A hot day yesterday in the Council of the Society of Arts' Playfair was to record some short time later, when the chairmanship of the Society changed on an anti-Commission, anti-Marlborough House vote.[49]

De la Beche's conservative and protective stance is the more understandable when it is recalled that he had nursed the Survey and the Museum of Practical Geology from small beginnings into significant government establishments. As the Prince Consort remarked in a memorandum written at the time of de la Beche's death, these institutions had been raised by Sir Henry 'almost as it were under disguised colours, at a time when little interest was felt generally in the subject, this being at the time the only recognition in this country of the claims of science to be directly fostered by the Government'.[50] To expose so rare and precious a plant in the turbulent arena of religious and political controversy might be to blight it mortally. Unfortunately the price of survival on de la Beche's terms was high when considered from the standpoint of science education.

The more important factors which contributed to the failure of the movement for teaching the science of common things have now been surveyed. To summarize: the movement had intrinsic weaknesses arising both from its informal organization and from the different perceptions of its objectives which various members held. Among scientists there was a division of opinion as to how best their subject might be incorporated into the curriculum, with one particularly influential group of researchers being strongly opposed to the teaching of applied science in the context of general education. It was maintained that not only would an emphasis on applications limit the educational potential of experimental philosophy, but the consequences of such an approach would be prejudicial to the future welfare of scientific inquiry.

More generally, there was a conviction on the part of certain educators that science as a branch of education had inherent limitations because it did not touch on human values; although it might contribute to the training of intellectual skills, it could not compare with literary studies as a humanizing agent. Moreover, an emphasis on the teaching of science might have outcomes which were in conflict with the stated or implicit objectives of the recognized providers of education for the poor; not only might religious and moral beliefs be weakened, but the established social order might be disturbed. The principle of design underlying the community-related curriculum of Dawes and Moseley was regarded as unsound. A truly liberal education did not encourage the division of society into 'so many unconnected units, displacing and repelling one another'.[51] To quote Daubeny again, 'the idea of imparting a special direction to the primary education of youth, in accordance with their respective rank or future destination, is not only in itself unphilosophical, but also in manifest contradiction to the principle which has always guided us in our schools and colleges'.[52] As Newman – to whom Daubeny acknowledged a debt – had argued two years previously, a man should not be usurped by his occupation.[53]

Together with some other general issues the validity of this criticism of the community-related curriculum will be examined in the final chapter which follows. Before turning to this task, however, a word is necessary on certain administrative decisions which were taken in the late 1850s. Whilst not related specifically to the movement for teaching the science of common things, they nevertheless set the seal on earlier events, and proved a crucial determinant of the place of science in the school curriculum.

At the time of its establishment in 1853 there were many, including Lord Granville and Playfair, who questioned the wisdom of placing the Department of Science and Art under the Board of Trade; its rightful place was held to be under the Lord President of the Council, alongside the Education Office.[54] Opposition to this view came from those who, like Henry Cole, urged that science and religion should not be mixed.[55] As has been seen, their cautions prevailed initially. Nevertheless, the two departments had numerous points of contact; in its early years at least the Department of Science and Art shared with the Education Office a concern for science teaching in elementary schools and both were engaged in the provision of science teaching aids and the certification of science teachers. Furthermore, Cole had succeeded in reaching agreement that drawing should become a part of elementary education.[56] When in 1856 the post of Vice-President of the Committee of Council was established in order that the Education Office might be represented in the Commons, the opportunity was taken to unite the two agencies offering grant for education. The Department of Science and Art became part of the newly created Education Department under the Lord President.

Simultaneously, Playfair's influence in the affairs of the Department would appear to have been diminished and responsibility for fostering developments in science education was progressively assumed by Henry Cole. At the inception of the Department, Playfair had shared with Cole the title of Secretary and Inspector, their spheres of responsibility being science and art respectively. Additionally, Playfair held the title of Vice-Director of the School of Mines.[57] By January of 1855, for reasons which are by no means clear, an administrative rearrangement had taken place. Possibly because of de la Beche's obstructiveness in the science field, possibly because two secretaries gave the appearance of overprovision in a time of financial stringency, Playfair was created sole secretary with no inspection duties, whilst Cole was created Chief Inspector for art matters, with increased duties. It was agreed that de la Beche would sanction all minutes of the Board which embodied decisions of scientific matters, while Playfair's part in these affairs was reduced to responsibility for the accuracy of the minutes.[58] Apart from this reduction of Playfair's influence in the field of science education, the new arrangement was not a particularly effective one. Cole was a more experienced and capable administrator than Playfair and when the executive was reorganized in the early months of 1857, following the transfer to the Education Department, he was created Secretary and General

L

Manager of the Science and Art Department, with Playfair as his professional adviser on scientific matters, bearing the title of Scientific Referee and Inspector-General of
the Science Schools.[59] A year later Playfair had moved to
the chair of Chemistry at Edinburgh, leaving Cole to assume
formal responsibility for the science as well as the art work
of the Department.

In fact, Cole had begun to lay plans for the extension of
science teaching well before Playfair's departure and the
years immediately following the transfer to the Education
Department can be seen as ones in which the Department of
Science and Art and the Education Office cautiously negotiated a state of equipoise and defined their respective
spheres in the field of science education. 'I cannot help
thinking that "Science in general" belongs to "Education in
general" and would grow best in connection with it,' Cole
wrote to Lingen in the summer of 1858, 'while "Science
technical", such as Mining, or Navigation, . . . might have
special arrangements.'[60]

Political beliefs about the extent to which it was proper
for the state to intervene in educational matters played a
significant part in determining the nature of the aid offered
by the Department of Science and Art. The prevailing
doctrine of the central administrators such as Cole and
Lingen was that of *laissez-faire*; direct financial aid from
the centre was regarded as likely to weaken local effort and
undermine private enterprise. More preferable was a system
in which voluntary achievement was rewarded by prizes,
scholarships and cash payments. It was in this context that
the principle of payment by results was evolved. 'It is the
result which we wish to be attained,' Playfair informed
Tyndall, early in 1857. 'How this result is to be attained
would be left to private enterprise.' 'The State wishes a
certain knowledge of science; it is willing to pay for this.
The knowledge may be had in the School, College, or
Garret, by books, oral demonstration, or experiment – in
any way – if its *attainment is effected*, we will pay for it. . . .
If Queenwood or the Royal Institution or a National School
at Battersea, or an Artisan at Poplar produces a certain

knowledge of Science in its pupils, we will pay those pupils for proving that they have this knowledge, and we will go further and pay the Teacher so much for every pupil whom he has sent up with the required standard of knowledge. . . . This is the idea which we are trying only experimentally to find out its weak and strong points and I should be only too glad to have them pointed out by good thinkers and earnest educationalists like yourself.'[61]

This proposal to reward results had financial and curricular implications which Lingen, in particular, strenuously opposed. The principle of special bounties for particular subjects was involved; so far as elementary education was concerned, once conceded, such a principle might lead to the neglect of unsupported studies. 'Many persons (I for one)', he wrote, 'do not think that scientific instruction beyond such as a common schoolmaster can learn in the ordinary course of his training to give, the best subject to encourage under 11 years of age – and, if science be specially encouraged to please one set of people, music must soon be encouraged in like manner, to please another set – something else to please a third (social science, for instance, to please Mr Ellis) – then it will be found that the real elements of instruction are suffering neglect – and *they* again will need encouragement – and so, at last the whole scale of payment will be raised – and this process – first at one bidding and then at another – may go on indefinitely.'[62] Escalating grants and an unstable curriculum were the likely and undesirable consequences of the adoption of a system of special payments for science teaching in elementary schools. 'We were not received with open arms by the primary division,' Cole recalled at a later date.[63]

Implicit in Lingen's comment was a view of 'the real elements of instruction' close to that of Fitch and Temple. If, in order to promote scientific instruction, the government felt it necessary to employ what Lingen termed 'a system of bonus and premium', then he was resolved that this should interfere as little as possible with elementary schools. So far as the curriculum of general education was concerned, the progress of science teaching was to be determined by the extent of public demand. The balance of studies in primary education was not an issue on which the government should interfere. Should it be generally felt that a knowledge of science was of importance, then those able to teach the subject would be called forward, and rewarded, according to the state of the market.

The adoption of the principle of payment by results by Cole's department was unquestionably an important factor contributing to the elimination of science from the elementary school curriculum. The attempt to generate a supply of masters competent to teach science in elementary schools was abandoned by the primary division in January 1857[64] at the very moment when its new partner was introducing a mechanism to stimulate the growth of science teaching. Three months later, responsibility for the administration of grant for scientific apparatus was transferred from the Education Office to the Department of Science and Art.[65] From the figures below it can be seen that applications for grant declined as the supply of qualified masters decreased. The grant itself was terminated under the new regulations which followed the report of the Newcastle Commission in 1861.

Expenditure from education grant in providing scientific apparatus[66]

Before 31.xii.1853	18– 0– 0	
1854	65– 6– 8	
1855	429–11– 8	
1856	757–10–11	
1857	2,345–15–11	
1858	313–16– 7	(27 schools)
1859	461–15– 9	(38 schools)
1860	177–14–10	(16 schools)
1861	224– 8– 8	
1862	30–19–10	

By July of 1857 Cole appears to have reached an understanding with Lingen that scientific subjects should not be introduced into elementary schools until there was evidence that arithmetic was being well taught;[67] for his part, Lingen undertook to instruct his inspectors to stimulate the formation of Cole's Schools of Art. Although Cole obtained a concession in January 1858 when the regulations governing school building grant were extended to cover the erection of science rooms,[68] it was nevertheless ruled shortly afterwards that elementary schoolmasters with pupil teachers could not earn payment from the Science and Art Department for teaching science classes.[69] In this way the spheres of action of the two departments were progressively defined. By the time of the celebrated Minute of June 1859, which ushered in a comprehensive scheme of payment by results in practical geometry, physics, chemistry, geology and natural history, the Department's concern had been limited to adult artisans. 'It has become necessary to consider carefully the relations which are likely to grow up between Science instruction and Elementary instruction', the Seventh Report of the Science and Art Department stated, 'and to take care that teachers engaged in the latter shall not be attracted to become Science teachers, to the neglect of elementary instruction.'[70] Like a transplanted tissue in a living organism, science had been rejected from elementary education. Henceforth it was categorized as a subject of secondary education and it is pertinent to recall that secondary has both a temporal and a subordinate connotation.

Ironically, the device of payment on results was adopted by the primary division of the Education Department with the introduction of the Revised Code in 1862. Robert Lowe's justification of his Department's application of the principle to the basic skills of reading, writing and ciphering in elementary schools was that these represented 'an amount of knowledge which could be ascertained thoroughly by examination, and upon which we could safely base the Parliamentary grant. It was more a financial than a literary preference. Had there been any other branch of useful knowledge, the possession of which could have been ascertained with equal precision, there was nothing to prevent its admission. But there was not.'[71]

It should be noted that those from whom he had acquired the principle, notably Cole, suffered no such inhibitions in relation to both art and science. Lowe's *ex post facto* rationalization in terms of the administrative merits of his choice of studies lacks conviction. His measure was a basically conservative one which chartered a reactionary view of the elementary school curriculum and effectively constrained developments in the teaching of science for the remainder of the century.[72]

Chapter 8

Science Education: past and present

Within the last century and a quarter the social environment of science education has been radically transformed. At the time when Dawes and Moseley fought their cause science was a national enterprise of limited scale, operating at the level which Derek Price has termed 'little science'.[1] State and science had not begun to interact in any significant way and the limits of the principles of voluntaryism and *laissez-faire*, applied to the growth of scientific activity, were only just becoming clear.[2] Today, in contrast, 'big science' is not only heavily dependent upon state patronage, but has become inextricably interwoven into the economic, political and ethical problems of the age. Concomitantly, there has arisen a national system of secular education in which the importance of scientific studies is recognized at all levels.

Yet despite these major contextual changes, there remain striking similarities between many of the issues which engaged science educators in the mid-nineteenth century and those which occupy their latter-day counterparts. Indeed, when writing about the first concerted attempt to introduce science into the school curriculum, it is difficult to escape the feeling that there persist today, still unresolved, many of the crucial problems generated by this venture. Some of the more important of these are identified and discussed briefly in this final chapter. Whilst each problem is broached in the context of nineteenth-century science education, its manifestations in present-day science curriculum developments will also be examined.

THE TYRANNY OF ABSTRACTIONS

From an educational standpoint it is significant that science developed slowly on the human time-scale; compared with language, drama and the arts it is characterized by relative youth. If we take the age of mankind on the earth as 100,000 years, it is perhaps not too misleading to place the burgeoning of science within the last two hundred and fiftieth of this period. Not until the sixteenth and seventeenth centuries did the rate of acquisition of scientific knowledge begin to quicken and the practitioners of science associate into stable, enduring groups such as the Royal Society.

A necessary, although by no means sufficient, requirement for this remarkable surge of intellectual activity was the introduction into scientific thought of conceptions of which there were no directly observable instances. The idea of linear inertial motion is a classic example from the seventeenth century. The doctrine of atoms, explaining – in Perrin's phrase – 'the complications of the visible in terms of invisible simplicity'[3] is an illustration from a later period. By the use of theoretical entities or constructs which were not obviously derived from an everyday view of the world, but which were creative products of the scientific imagination, the explanatory and predictive powers of science were progressively increased. If at times the ideas might appear to confound common sense, as was the case with the heliocentric theory of Copernicus, nevertheless, for initiates, as Galileo recorded, 'reason was able . . . to commit such a rape upon their senses, as in despight thereof to make herself mistress of their credulity'.[4] Such conviction was aroused especially when, in addition to their qualitative value, the conceptions of science lent themselves to quantitative statement. The application of mathematics to the description of nature was a further vital step in the growth of modern science.[5]

The transformation to which reference is being made has been well summarized by Sir Cyril Hinshelwood in his Eddington Memorial Lecture of 1961 :

'The position of the early men of science was similar to that of the layman today. The conventions in terms of which explanations were given and questions answered could not be too far removed from the everyday world of common-place things. . . . As science progresses the nature of the mental schemes and constructions evolves and becomes more sophisticated . . . the concepts tend to become more and more recondite. It is fair to say that the mathematical symbolisms of much modern physics serve their primary purpose of representing the universe . . . only to people who are deeply versed in a special kind of language.'[6]

The use of highly abstract concepts which are connected to experimental observations by complex logical relation-ships, in conjunction with the close liaison of experimental science and mathematics, has enabled science to achieve intellectual advances of unprecedented magnitude. White-head's remark that 'the utmost abstractions are the true weapons with which to control our thought of concrete fact'[7] has been abundantly vindicated. Yet the picture is not one of total gain. In terms of an understanding of the physical world the price has been a tendency to concentrate upon relatively simple phenomena, to the exclusion of much of the complexity and imperfection which characterize real life problems.[8] In terms of a general education involving science the very steps which have increased the power of science as a mode of intellectual inquiry have generated formidable problems associated with its teaching and learning.

It will be recalled that the extent to which mathematics should be incorporated into the elementary study of natural philosophy was a problem which had exercised Moseley in connection with his own course at King's College, as it had divided his contemporaries.[9] For some, such as J. D. Forbes, there was but one road forward, common to both research and teaching – that of the continuing subjection of general physics to mathematical treatment. Wherever possible scientific problems were to be translated into the dis-embodied symbols of algebra; after manipulation of these symbols the solution could be retranslated into physical terms.[10] For others, whilst conceding the value of this process in scientific research, its application in an educa-tional context was regarded as beset with pitfalls. The

symbols might be used as substitutes for, rather than as
aids to, thought[11] and the physical significance of the process
would be lost. Moreover, a withdrawal into the realms of
abstract symbolism might lead to a weakening of the connection of science with practical affairs. Scientific principles
might be learnt and manipulated without their relevance to
real-life situations being explored.[12] Finally, the ability to
translate aspects of concrete experience into some form of
symbolic representation and then to reason on this at an
abstract level was rarely found in young persons before
adolescence. In modern terms it corresponds to the Piagetian stage of formal operational thought.[13] There would
appear to be natural limits on children's understanding of
abstract scientific ideas which it is difficult, if not impossible,
to transgress, a point implicit in Playfair's transfer of
support from the physical to the natural history sciences.[14]

Of course the tyranny of abstractions afflicts the learning
of subjects other than the sciences, but its effects have been
felt with particular severity in attempts to establish
chemistry and physics as basic components of general education. Indeed, there is some force in the argument that the
sciences, like history, are studies which require matured
minds on the part of the learners. If this were in fact the
case their potential contribution to the school curriculum
would be late and little. On psychological grounds alone,
however, there are good reasons why this view cannot be
accepted. Thus, it is impossible to say with precision when
pupils are ready to assimilate an abstract scientific concept
such as kinetic energy or dynamic equilibrium. Acquision
is rarely sharp and individual differences alone would pre-
clude a simple re-ordering of course content. In addition, the
more familiar that pupils are with content and concrete
instances, the more readily, within limits, can hypothetico-
deductive reasoning be elicited. Intuitive and concrete
operational thought are necessary precursors to formal
operational thought. Whilst scientific ideas cannot in themselves be made easier, they can be introduced in different
ways and at different depths so that pupils' understanding,
whilst limited initially, can grow progressively.[15]

This, it would appear, was what Richard Dawes was doing at King's Somborne with such conspicuous success. He made no attempt to teach science formally in the sense of having short-term objectives associated with the detailed understanding of abstract scientific ideas. Moreover, there was no intention that his scholars should be equipped to practise science. But he provided a rich variety of illustrations of scientific knowledge applied in situations which were meaningful and relevant to them. His pupils were required to act on physical materials and participate in experimental inquiries in an environment which provided opportunities for discussion between children and teacher. In short, many of the conditions which modern research would suggest are necessary for the successful acquisition of abstract scientific knowledge by children were being fulfilled.[16]

Of course, it does not follow from approval of Dawes' teaching of science in a nineteenth-century village school that the substance of his course would meet the needs of young children in schools today. Re-interpretation is necessary in terms of applications and activities which are relevant to pupils in the present age. The problems of cottage ventilation, personal hygiene, family nutrition, manual competencies and agricultural improvements are no longer central to the majority of pupils; the present-day counterparts are more likely to be found in the social problems of the age and in the leisure activities and hobbies of young people. At the same time, the need remains, as Moseley so clearly saw, for teachers whose mastery of scientific knowledge is allied to skills in its application and to sensitivity to the values which prevail in the homes of their pupils.

CONCEPTIONS OF SCIENCE AND THE OBJECTIVES OF SCIENCE TEACHING

The highly abstract nature of much of the thinking involved in the study of science is the first of the central educational problems to which reference was made at the beginning of this chapter. We turn now to a different issue, that of the educational objectives which might legitimately be ascribed to a study of science as a school subject and, in particular, the influence which different conceptions of the nature of scientific activity have had on the selection of these objectives.[17]

It has been noted earlier that Dawes and Henslow did not share a common view on the ends which science teaching should serve.[18] For Dawes, as for Moseley, scientific knowledge was useful knowledge; science was studied principally so that learners might benefit, in a practical sense, from an understanding of the natural world as scientists understood it. In this opinion they were close to Francis Bacon who, in his Preface to *The Great Instauration*, had written: 'I would address one general admonition to all; that they consider what are the true ends of knowledge, and that they seek it not either for pleasure of the mind, or for contention or for superiority to others, or for profit, or fame, or power, or any of these inferior things; but for the benefit and use of life; and that they perfect and govern it in charity.'[19]

For Henslow, with his research orientation, the unique characteristic of science as a branch of learning was the method by which knowledge was acquired; the inductive aspects of scientific activity, rather than the conclusions, were of most significance from an educational point of view. Science was studied in schools, not for its informational benefits, but because it trained the powers of observation and reasoning. With Huxley, this argument was taken to its limit. The methods of biology were associated with those of common sense and the study of science was justified in terms of the training of the general faculties of mind involved in all rational thought.[20]

Two different conceptions of science were involved in these positions. For those who followed Huxley, science was an activity which attempted to correlate publicly observable data in a rationally consistent manner; it assumed a discoverable order in events, emphasized the logical origins of its constructs, retained an openness to new data and recognized the revisionary character of its explanations. At the same time it had no preference for any particular type of data and, in consequence, the activities of the botanist, the chemist, the geologist and the physicist were fundamentally no different from those of, say, a supermarket manager today. The similarity between the work of a scientist and that of a doctor in diagnosing a disease or of a lawyer in sifting evidence had, in fact, been remarked upon by both Henslow and Hooker.[21]

The conception of science implicit in the educational prescriptions of Dawes and Moseley (and explicit in the writings of Whewell) had many features in common with that outlined above, but differed in two quite crucial respects. First, the process of scientific discovery was seen as involving conjectural elements which could not be reduced to a systematic logical operation; it followed that the creative, as opposed to the critical, aspects of the process of science could not readily be taught.[22] Neither Dawes nor Moseley invoked a faculty training argument in their espousal of science as a school subject. Deductive skills were, of course, involved in the testing and application of scientific principles, but science had no monopoly on these. Second, scientific knowledge was seen as characterized by the conceptual frameworks to which scientists were committed and by which the direction and range of their activities were determined. The choice of data was far from free; scientists were constrained by their prevailing paradigms.

From these two conceptions of science quite different claims for the learning of science were engendered. Powerful, but misleading, statements about the improvement of critical thinking and of problem-solving abilities resulted from the Henslow–Huxley view. The tendency was to overload science with educational responsibilities whilst ignoring the contribution which other studies might make towards these objectives.[23] Less inclusive claims were associated with the alternative view. Although the study of science could undoubtedly assist the development of rational modes of thought, its unique contribution was to an understanding of the scientist's conception of the natural world. The value to be placed on this restricted claim turned on the extent to which science was held to have enriched the life of man.

Those who, like Moseley, saw science as the great transformer of the material and intellectual condition of mankind
urged its inclusion as a central element of the school curriculum. Others, like Fitch and Temple, whilst acknowledging its existence, assigned to science a subordinate educational role compared with the traditional humanities.

The question of content or process, subject matter or
method of inquiry, is a recurring and still unresolved issue
in the relatively short history of school science teaching.[24]
In recent years, as a reaction to the presentation of science
as a monolithic and stable body of factual knowledge,
attempts have been made to bias the objectives of science
teaching towards a greater concern for the procedures of
scientific inquiry. Of one extreme example of curriculum
development in this vein, the elementary school programme
of the American Association for the Advancement of
Science, 'Science – a Process Approach', it is interesting to
read the comments of a perceptive critic, Myron Atkin:
'A basic flaw in the process is the apparent assumption that
science is a sort of commonsensical activity, and that the
appropriate "skills" are the primary ingredients in doing
productive work. There seems to be no explicit recognition
of the powerful role of the conceptual frames of reference
within which scientists and children operate and to which
they are firmly bound. These general views of the physical
world demand careful nurture . . . by a variety of means.'[25]

Atkin's criticism might be extended to recent attempts to
include an understanding of the nature of scientific inquiry
as an objective of secondary school science courses. The
level of sophistication in discussion about the scientific
content of new courses has not been matched when the
procedural aspects of science have come under review. In
many recent schemes there is implied a philosophically
naïve, undiversified view of scientific inquiry which shows
little advance on Huxley's commonsense empiricism.[26]

This situation is closely related to the widespread
advocacy of discovery methods of learning which characterized the curriculum reforms of the 1960s. In order to
achieve an understanding of the procedures of 'the scientist',

children were supposedly placed in the position of a scientific investigator. As the Progress Report of the Nuffield Foundation's Science Teaching Project stated in 1964, the intention was to get pupils 'to think about scientific things in the way that practising scientists do'.[27] By employing a discovery approach it was hoped that both the substance and the methods of science could be learnt simultaneously.

A general discussion of the merits and limitation of discovery learning lies outside the scope of this chapter,[28] but it must be pointed out that the acceptance of 'an understanding of the procedures of science' as an educational objective does not logically entail the adoption of discovery methods of learning. Furthermore, only on the basis of the most superficial analysis of the nature of scientific activity, could it be said that such methods enable children to think and work in ways characteristic of a successful practitioner of science.[29]

The argument can be illustrated by brief reference to one single element of scientific procedure, that of the criticism and testing of a theory. There is, of course, the Popperian point that testing needs to be severe, with falsification rather than confirmation as the end in view, and that this condition is rarely achieved in a school laboratory.[30] But, beyond this, the picture normally conveyed is that of a two-cornered fight between theory and experiment, with theory falling if the results of experiment confound a prediction. This is an over-simplified model on at least two counts. First, experimentation is rarely easy and the proposition that the results of experiments should be the final arbiter in scientific matter is debatable. Coutts Trotter's quip that the law of the uniformity of nature could never have been discovered in a science laboratory is relevant here. Indeed there is a case to be made in favour of the thesis that the results of an experiment should never be trusted until they have been checked against a good theory.[31] Second, as I. Lakatos has pointed out, the decision to reject a theory requires more than its mere confrontation with experiment; it also requires the presence of a better theory, with successes of its own to recommend it. A more appropriate model is that of a three-cornered fight involving two theories and experiments. If no suitable alternative exists, any scientific theory, even one at odds with certain points of experimental evidence, is better than none at all. It might at least provide a rational underpinning for the direction of future research.[32]

If we are really serious about wanting children to gain anything other than the most naïve and unsophisticated understanding of the procedures by which scientific knowledge grows and changes, the minimum requirement would seem to be the detailed study of two competing scientific systems, of the data from which they have been constructed, and of the factors which have determined their scientific fates. Such an undertaking might well be blocked into an existing course at an appropriate point and could provide an excellent opportunity for the history of science to fulfil the role in which Whewell cast it, as an effective remedy for over-simplified views on the nature of science.[33] But clearly other possibilities exist. Even so, it is difficult to see how both objectives, an understanding of the mature concepts and theories of science and an understanding of the processes by which scientific knowledge grows, can be achieved simultaneously. The former involves the initiation of the learner into a developed conceptual system and his task is to come to terms with an established and largely uncontroversial body of knowledge.[34] The concern, in Kuhn's phrase, is with 'normal science' and even with heuristic methods of learning it is difficult to avoid acquiring a misleading impression of science as a human activity. At an advanced level it is probably true that the dichotomy between product and process is less sharp and that the understanding of scientific conclusions is contingent upon an appreciation of their relationship to the data from which they were constructed. At the school level, the return to original sources is clearly impossible on the scale required and the acquisition of scientific knowledge is inescapably tinged with dogmatism. To the extent that this matters, we ought to attend to process as a separate objective, important in its own right, alongside content. The problem of reconciling these objectives in school science teaching has been considerably underestimated: from an educational stand-point the methodology of scientific inquiry has so far proved a Pandora's box rather than a panacea.

As a codicil to this discussion of the process aspects of science, it must be questioned whether curriculum reformers in the late 1950s and early 1960s did not over-react to the prevailing authoritarian teaching of science and make rather too much of the view that scientific knowledge was 'no more than a corrigible human creation' and 'a temporary codex, continually restructured as new data are related to old.'[35] As Alvin Weinberg has remarked, if science is all that ephemeral, if Newton's second law must indeed be classed as a temporary codex, it is somewhat surprising that science has been as useful as it has in human undertakings.[36] The distinction which Weinberg draws between 'science as search', with its inevitable progression through fragmenta-tion and specialization to ever greater degrees of abstraction and purity, and 'science as codification', the body of con-solidated scientific knowledge which, once discovered, has some degree of permanence and utility, is educationally important here. The view of science which informed the original Nuffield school science projects, and the American PSSC, CBA and CHEM study projects, was 'science as search' and in so far as these courses were concerned to put children in the position of a scientific inquirer after new knowledge, the stereotype was that of the pure scientist, supremely oblivious to the applications and wider implications of his work. Science was studied as an end in itself.

There are two comments that need to be made on this point. First, as the Newson Report confirmed, many pupils respond better to work when this is 'more realistic' and 'practical'.[37] This is not to argue for a narrowly vocational, as opposed to a liberal, education, but merely to make the familiar pedagogical point that good teaching needs to capitalize upon situations which are relevant to the learners. Second, the transition from 'little' to 'big science' has involved an increasingly complex interaction between science and technology, on the one hand, and between these activi-

M

ties and society, on the other. In recent decades science has enjoyed the patronage of society largely because of its role as a source of technology which, in turn, has been seen as a means of satisfying social demands that, until lately, have remained remarkably stable. With the awareness of new problems associated with matters such as population growth, poverty, limited natural resources and environmental quality, the social objectives which science is required to serve are being redefined and, as the OECD report on *Science, Growth and Society* pointed out, the establishment of social goals cannot be left to scientists alone.[38] In the words of Lord Zuckerman, 'The layman, the members of the public have every bit as big a part to play in the field of technological decision as have the scientists from whose basic ideas new applied science and new technology springs.'[39] The educational requirements here are twofold. We need scientists who are aware of the applications and potentialities of their work and are able to communicate effectively to a public; we need a laity with sufficient understanding of science and its influence to participate in fruitful debate.[40] At present neither the specialized education of scientists nor the general education of the public, the scientific components of which are largely modelled on 'science as search', satisfy these requirements. One crucial element in the successful resolution of this difficulty would seem to be the adoption of the applications and influences of science as a predominant theme in general education. And this in turn would entail an emphasis on the consolidated parts of scientific knowledge, for, as Weinberg remarks, these are the parts on which the applications of science largely depend.[41]

It is significant that both the earlier discussion in this chapter on children's understanding of abstract scientific ideas and the subsequent examination of the objectives of school science education should have led to a common end; the need to re-assert the utility of scientific knowledge. This is not to be achieved by garnishing existing 'pure' courses with a sprinkling of miscellaneous applications; nor by an injection of 'industrial realism' which requires pupils to display an interest in highly specialized applications which lie outside their experience; least of all, by creating a new school subject, 'applied science'. The requirement was expressed by Dawes in the title of his science teachers' guide;[42] science must be made to bear upon 'practical life', and what constitutes 'practical life' needs continual reinterpretation in the light of the dominating problems of each society and the immediate concerns of particular learners.

THE CONTRIBUTION OF SCIENCE TO THE SOCIAL AND MORAL DEVELOPMENT OF CHILDREN

We turn now to examine a quite basic objection to the inclusion of science as a central component of general education, the contention that it fails to contribute to the social and moral development of learners. This was the essence of Temple's reservation about the value of science as a humanizing agent. The study of science might train the intellect, but, unlike literature, it did not 'touch the sense of personality' or cultivate 'that part of our nature by which we are brought into contact with men and with moral agents'.[43] The scientist's approach as an unobtrusive observer, questing after objective knowledge by analysis and obstruction, was held to foster a withdrawn, stunted and mechanized vision of the world. There appeared little in the study of science to encourage the development of confidence and self-reliance in dealing with every-day problems; learners found few opportunities to exercise independent thought and judgement in realistic situations and to develop a sense of responsibility towards other people and to the community as a whole.[44]

The argument dates at least to the seventeenth century when men of wit like Addison, Pope and William King, thinking no doubt of the microscopic observations recorded in the *Micrographia* of Robert Hooke, and of similar accounts in the pages of the *Philosophical Transactions*, scoffed at minds that could 'admire nothing except fleas, lice and themselves'.[45] In the twentieth century, A. N. Whitehead, in a celebrated passage, warned of the educational danger in 'a celibacy of the intellect which is divorced from the concrete contemplation of the complete facts'.[46] Under the influence of science we had acquired professionalism in knowledge and specialization in education; the result, according to Whitehead, was that 'we neglect to strengthen habits of concrete appreciation of the individual facts in their full interplay of emergent values'.[47] More recently, Sir Frederick Dainton has remarked on the widespread view that a scientist is a man 'voluntarily withdrawn from human contact; disassociating himself from personal and societal problems . . . a man who is "objective" to an objectionable degree.'[48]

However distorted the lay view of a stereotypical scientist may be, the sustained nature of these criticisms requires some comment. First, it should be observed that Temple's judgement was based upon a view of science as a mental discipline; like any other school subject, science was taught primarily for the training it imparted. The specific applications of science were of secondary importance; systematic, not economic, botany was his first choice for a compulsory science subject at Rugby. Science in the school curriculum had to be 'pure'. Yet in so insulating science from practical affairs, in studiously ensuring its disconnection from society, it is not surprising that few issues of a social or moral nature arose.[49]

Second, whereas in the mid-nineteenth century the extent of the interaction between science and society was so limited as to be educationally insignificant, the case is vastly different today. Science has now penetrated deeply into the fabric of life, both at the level of the individual and of society; environmental problems, for example, lead directly to economic, ethical and political issues of personal and communal concern. On Temple's criterion, that the most valuable school subjects are those which relate to human problems and moral issues, science in education might be said to have at last come of age. An inward-looking and discipline-biased conception of the objectives of science education will no longer suffice. The applications of science and its social nexus must also be considered, a task which inevitably leads to the field of values and controversial issues where moral and political judgements are required.[50]

A third and final comment on the criticism that the study of science is 'non-humanizing' can best be made if Temple's reservations are framed in a different way. It has already been noted that education can be looked at from the standpoint of social control, whereby its function is the political one of initiating children into approved behavioural norms.[51] On this view, the social and moral development of children is measured by the degree of their conformity and the value of school subjects by their contribution to this end. Science presents, perhaps, a unique case here. For some of its practitioners in the nineteenth century, scientific knowledge was seen as subservient to larger ends – economic, social, moral and religious. For others, scientific knowledge was an end in itself. The logic of the latter position was not always clearly perceived by early advocates of 'pure science', amongst whom the ambivalent stance of Playfair was not uncommon;[52] whilst championing pure research, free from any immediate contingency, support, nevertheless, was ultimately based on the value of applications as yet unknown which research alone could reveal. Although not usually broached in extreme form in the nineteenth century, the doctrine of 'pure science' can be seen as entailing a commitment to a system of values which had 'objective knowledge' as the sovereign good. In other words, scientific knowledge was not a means to the attainment of ends sanctioned by some political or religious system, but was a supreme end in itself. The ethic of 'objective knowledge' imposed on a scientist the obligation to pursue his inquiries irrespective of their implications for his fellow men.[53] In science, as perhaps in no other school subject, there were the seeds of discord with accepted norms of behaviour and belief.

As long as education was conceived as a process of initiation into a stable and enduring value system, the contribution of science to social and moral development of learners was a restricted one. Today we are more ready to accept that values are derived, in part at least, from the patterns of choice which characterize the behaviour of individuals and their societies; and equally, that this choice is influenced by the options available at any given time.[54] It follows that science and technology have a direct impact on human values by virtue of their ability to extend the range of possible courses of action. As has been pointed out by Edward Shils, 'the scope of individual choice and action today is greater than in previous times, in the choice of consumer products, marital partner, occupation, place to live, objects of loyalty and allegiance to religious, political and other social groups.'[55] In similar vein, the Nobel prize-winner, Dennis Gabor, has indicated the alternatives which confront the people of an industrialized state. The technologist, according to Gabor, is in a position to say: 'I can give you your exponential growth for a while, with fly-overs, on top of fly-overs on which hundreds of millions of motor-cars will race to and from your city centres, and I can provide power for these cars even when the last barrel of natural oil will be exhausted. But I cannot guarantee the exponential growth for ever. On the other hand, I can also give you a world in which nobody need live at more than walking distance from his work, and where people use fast transport only for pleasure. A world in which people will have to work only as much or as little as is good for them.'[56]

It is in this ability to act as an influence conducive to freedom – and by freedom one means enlightened choice taken in the full awareness of all possibilities – that science makes its claim to be one of the humanities.[57] To the extent that the teaching of science is concerned exclusively with technique and encourages the performance of operations with no sense of their human significance, it is a dehumanizing activity. Brewster's instinct for the centrality of relevance was doubly sound;[58] without it, the contribution of science to the personal development of learners was impoverished and, in the longer run, the scientific enterprise itself was placed in jeopardy.

Three points arise from this brief discussion of the relation of science to human values. First, it is largely through the intervention of technology that science influences values.[59] The need, again, is for a careful appraisal of the implications and potentialities of their work by scientists so that they may make their contribution as 'cartographers of the future',[60] expounding the options which are open to individuals and society as a result of scientific inquiry and technological application. In Baconian terms, the scientist as dowry-man is as essential as the scientist as interpreter of nature.[61] The degree of scientific literacy on the part of the general population which is necessary to make this a meaningful exercise is by no means clear; decision-making in such fields as national fuel policy, development of supersonic transport and siting of new reservoirs involves considerations of both a scientific and non-scientific kind. Perhaps after a basic acquaintance with the central concepts, laws and theories of the major sciences, the most important requirement is a sense of what the public can reasonably expect from science and scientists, an awareness of the limits beyond which a question passes from the realm of science into that of trans-science.[62]

The second point is that it is unrealistic for science itself to expect to remain untouched by those very shifts in the societal and ideational balance to which it has itself contributed. The dependence of science upon public confidence, expressed in material terms, is now so total that, as Alvin Weinberg has remarked, 'The republic of science can be destroyed more surely by withdrawal of public support than by intrusion of the public into its workings.'[63] It seems inevitable that in the years ahead science will increasingly be seen in a neo-Baconian light; it may even be that future historians will come to regard the emphasis on 'pure science', which has characterized the last century, as a limited interlude in the evolution of mankind's most remarkable intellectual achievement. Nevertheless, the extent to which science should accept a servicing role in its relations to the community is an issue on which opinions are at present divided sharply. At one extreme, science is the radical transformer of society, its ethic of objective knowledge the begetter of a new enlightened humanism;[64] at the other, science is the resourceful handmaid, subservient to imperatives derived from larger ends. Arguments are advanced both for and against the disestablishment of science.[65] From an educational standpoint, however, the significance of recent concerns, of which the movement for social responsibility in science is a manifestation, lies in the recognition that the neutrality of science is a myth; science is indissolubly linked to a world of values, a fact which adds a new dimension to its educational capabilities.

Maturity, no less than adolescence, has its trials and the third point is that the view of science just expounded brings in its train a series of formidable pedagogical problems. Yet, if science is to serve as an instrument for the social and moral development of children it must accept an association with specific controversial issues which call into play children's discriminational and judgemental powers. This is a new undertaking for which science teachers have had little training; indeed, many may feel themselves ill-qualified for the task; the room for discussion of alternative viewpoints is much less in the traditional science courses, with which they are familiar, than in the arts. At least when dealing with Avogadro's hypothesis or electromagnetic induction a science teacher is not vulnerable to a charge of bias; he may be incompetent, idle, careless or even ill-informed; but he can scarcely be corrupting or prejudicial. The situation is different when controversial value issues are involved. The choice of issue on which to focus attention and the selection of teaching materials to illustrate particular points of view are both matters which prevent a teacher adopting a position of procedural neutrality. Quite simply, it is impossible to be value-free, and, as has been pointed out in connection with the teaching of politics in schools, 'attempts to achieve this blissful state of moral suspension involve high degrees of either boredom or hypocrisy.'[66] The alternatives, the stance of 'honest bias' and that of genuine striving after empathy for conflicting points of view, impose, in their different ways, new professional demands on already hard-pressed science teachers. Perhaps just as the isolation of science in society is a thing of the past, so should be the isolation of the science teacher; courses should be planned by teams of teachers covering different disciplines and value positions.[67]

COMMON OR COMMUNITY CURRICULUM

Whilst not uniquely an issue of science education, the question of the most appropriate curriculum for the schools of a culturally diverse society was raised in sharp form by the work of Dawes and Moseley. As has been seen, their principle of curriculum design was criticized on a number of grounds.[68] By some it was regarded as an instrument of social dissolution, whose application would result in a widening gap between the various classes in society. Far from liberating children from a state of cultural deprivation, the argument ran, the community-related curriculum would be likely to imprison them within the confines of their immediate environment: introversion and disjunction, rather than assimilation and cohesion, were the probable social outcomes. From an economic standpoint also there were deficiencies; if able children were to ascend Huxley's ladder from the gutter to the university, educational institutions needed to be linked by a common set of studies. The distinctive curriculum proposed for the elementary schools for the masses might inhibit upward social mobility and the fostering of talents important for the economy because continuity of studies would be difficult to achieve.

The alternative to the community-related curriculum appeared to be the common curriculum, reflecting in its educational objectives a view of what Matthew Arnold later termed 'a high best self'.[69] Arnold, who entered the school inspectorate in the year of the Great Exhibition, was to make explicit in *Culture and Anarchy* (1869) a concept of culture as the study of 'the best which has been thought and said in the world'.[70] To this end all members of society, irrespective of class, might hope to aspire. 'Plenty of people', wrote Arnold, 'will try to give the masses . . . an intellectual food prepared and adapted in the way they think proper for the actual condition of the masses.' In contrast, culture 'seeks to do away with classes; to make the best that has been thought and known in the world current everywhere; to make all men live in an atmosphere of sweetness and light'. 'This is the social idea', he continued, 'and the men of culture are the true apostles of equality.'[71]

Culture and Anarchy was written at a time of extension of the franchise to the working class; in Arnold's view the educational objectives which he outlined were ones urgently needed by the new democracy.[72] The expansion of man's humanity, in accordance with his doctrine of culture, had to be a general expansion, a national movement, supported by state intervention.[73] Arnold's unwearying opposition to the form of the elementary school curriculum as shaped by the Revised Code was on the grounds of an inadequate concept of a common culture. That all children, irrespective of social background, should have an identical curriculum, was seen as a virtue rather than a defect of the system.

Even in his own day, Arnold's view was criticized as being too academic and refined a distillate. Henry Sidgwick's response to the early chapters of *Culture and Anarchy* as these appeared in the *Cornhill Magazine* was to require that Arnold's culture should learn 'to call nothing common or unclean'. 'It can only propagate itself', argued Sidgwick, 'by shedding the light of its sympathy liberally; by learning to love common people and common things, to feel common interests.'[74] Such an enlargement did not run counter to Arnold's ideas; at the same time it led to a position remarkably close to that of Dawes and Moseley with their emphasis on a respect for 'the springs of opinion amongst the poor'.[75] Indeed, it raises the question of whether the community-related curriculum and the common curriculum were as antithetic as had been supposed.

It is noteworthy that this issue is as alive today, rather more than a century after Arnold was writing, as it was in the 1850s and 1860s. The Educational Priority Area community school, 'rooted in the values of the particular community which it serves and capable of eliciting and sustaining a sense of fraternity from those who are involved in its life' is fundamental to recent attempts to achieve equality of educational outcomes as between different social groups.[76] Its existence is justified in terms of the prime importance which must be assigned to the social determinants of learning, a truth intuitively recognized by Dawes and Moseley, and now formally established on a basis of empirical research.[77] Yet, as one of its leading advocates points out, the community school emphasizes the differences rather than the similarities of schools,[78] and it is difficult to escape the conclusion that the more accurately schools reflect the different ways of life in a pluralistic society, the less capable they will be of achieving a greater equality of educational attainment. From a community standpoint, the educational arguments for the inclusion of 'black studies' or 'community science' in the curriculum might seem compelling; but so long as life chances are distributed by an educational system which reflects a different definition of what constitutes important knowledge, the students of 'black studies' and 'community science', however successful in their chosen fields, will be handicapped. The point has been well expressed in another way by Martin Shipman. 'Educating the culturally different must not involve an attack on their culture. To organize such an education and yet not simultaneously further disadvantage the children we are trying to help is the major issue for education today.'[79]

Perhaps the work of Dawes and Moseley in the nineteenth century provides at least a hint towards a solution. Neither man saw the community-related curriculum as an end in itself. Instead, the science of common things was a specific resource, a well-adapted means for the acquisition by elementary school children of those general powers of intellect and conduct which Arnold associated with the humanization of man in society. Its basic purpose, in Dawes' phrase, was 'to raise them in the scale of thinking beings'. The underlying and unifying idea was indeed that of a common culture, albeit a dynamic one of rich complexity, in continuous process of social reconstruction, which embraced scientific as well as other modes of understanding. The curriculum they devised was a first sketch towards an instrument of initiation and regeneration for the people; initiation in the sense of comprehending the images and traditions which had shaped their present; regeneration, in the sense of deriving confidence and power to create their future.

References

Chapter 1

1 R. Lowe, *Middle Class Education. Endowment or Free Trade* (London 1868), p. 13.
2 Census of Great Britain, 1851, *Education. England and Wales. Report and Tables* (London 1854), p. xv.
3 Harry Chester, *Address on National Education*, quoted in James Hole, *Light, More Light* (London 1860), pp. 14–15.
4 David Layton, 'The Educational Exhibition of 1854', *Journal of the Royal Society of Arts*, Vol. 120, Nos 5187 and 5188 (1972), pp. 183–7 and 253–6.
5 See, for example, Andreas M. Kazamias, ' "What Knowledge is of Most Worth?" A Historical Conception and a Modern Sequel', *Harvard Educational Review*, Vol. 30, No. 4 (Fall 1960), pp. 307–30.
6 Liebig's letter was cited by C. Lyell, *Travels in North America*, Vol. 1 (London 1845), p. 309 and passages from it were quoted in the House of Commons by William Tite, *Hansard's Parliamentary Debates*, third series, CXLII, columns 1263–1273 (1856). The full text can also be found in W. A. Shenstone, *Justus von Liebig, His Life and Work* (London 1895), pp. 201–3.
7 Lord Lytton, *England and the English* (London 1874), pp. 290–300. First published in 1833.
8 See, for example, R. M. MacLeod, 'The Royal Society and the Government Grant: Notes on the Administration of Scientific Research, 1849–1914', *The Historical Journal*, Vol. 14 (1971), pp. 323–58.
9 The first four of the institutions listed owed their existence in large measure to the efforts of Sir Henry de la Beche. The Geological Survey was established under Treasury grant in 1835, the Mining Records Office in 1839, the Museum of Practical Geology and the Government School of Mines and of Science applied to the Arts in 1851. The Royal School of Chemistry began as a private venture in 1845, but was rescued from financial difficulties by being affiliated to the School of Mines in 1853.
  See M. Reeks, *History of the Royal School of Mines* (London 1920) and A. Geikie, *Life of Sir Roderick I. Murchison*, Vol. 2 (London 1875), pp. 177–87.
10 Basil Willey, 'Darwin and Clerical Orthodoxy' in P. Appleman, W. A. Madden, M. Wolf, *1859: Entering an Age of Crisis* (Bloomington 1959), p. 60.

11 *Report of the 25th Meeting of the British Association for the Advancement of Science* (London 1856), p. lxxxii.

12 T. G. Bonney, *Annals of the Philosophical Club of the Royal Society* (London 1919), pp. 5–26.

13 J. E. Bicheno, *An Address Delivered at the Anniversary Meeting of the Zoological Club of the Linnean Society* (London 1826), pp. 23–5.

14 See, for example, David Layton, 'Lord Wrottesley, F.R.S., Pioneer Statesman of Science', *Notes and Records of the Royal Society of London*, Vol. 23, No. 2 (December 1968), pp. 230–46.

15 For Hamilton's views on the Cambridge mathematics course see G. E. Davie, *The Democratic Intellect, Scotland and her Universities in the Nineteenth Century* (Edinburgh 1961), particularly Chapter 4, 'The Humanistic Bias of Scottish Science'.
The Scottish pedagogical emphasis on geometry as opposed to algebraic analysis is examined by Richard Olson, 'Scottish Philosophy and Mathematics 1750–1830', *Journal of the History of Ideas*, Vol. 32, No. 1 (January–March 1971). pp. 29–44.

16 Davie, pp. 170–2. Brewster's views on the importance of applied science and on the need for state support for scientific activity are well exemplified in his critical review of Whewell's *History of the Inductive Sciences* in *Edinburgh Review*, Vol. 66 (Edinburgh 1838), pp. 110–51.

17 Census of Great Britain, 1851, *Education England and Wales. Report and Tables* (London 1854), p. cxxxvi.

18 Further information on Mayo's contribution to education is to be found in Hugh M. Pollard, *Pioneers of Popular Education 1760–1850* (London 1956) and W. A. C. Stewart and W. P. McCann, *The Educational Innovators* (London 1967).

19 The 1845 edition of *Lessons on Objects* included details of suppliers of cabinets. By 1859 a 16th edition had been published; the work was also translated into Spanish.

20 *The Quarterly Educational Magazine and Record of the Home and Colonial School Society*, Vol. 1 (1848), p. 51.

21 Ibid.

22 Ibid., pp. 62–6.

23 In a statistical study of scientific activity in Scotland during the nineteenth century, the period 1830–70 is described as the golden age of Scottish science with a peak in science output (measured as discoveries per million inhabitants) in the first half of the century. A. G. Clement and R. H. S. Robertson, *Scotland's Scientific Heritage* (Edinburgh 1961), p. 127.

24 Stow claimed to be the first to introduce lessons on natural science into the training of teachers. An advertisement bound into the 10th edition of his book, *The Training System*, claimed that 2,600 male and female teachers had been trained under his

system by 1854. The first edition appeared in the mid-twenties. David Stow, *The Training System Adopted in the Model Schools of the Glasgow Education Society* (Glasgow 1826). The arrangement and contents were modified as the book went through its numerous editions, achieving an 11th in 1859.

25 Frank Smith, *The Life and Works of Sir James Kay-Shuttle-worth* (London 1923), p. 49.

26 Central Society of Education, *First Publication* (London 1837), pp. 172–213.

27 M. Faraday, 'On Wheatstone's Electric Telegraph in Relation to Science (being an argument in favour of the full recognition of Science as a branch of Education)', *Proceedings of the Royal Institution*, Vol. 2 (1854–8), p. 555.

28 Francis Galton, *English Men of Science: Their nature and nurture* (London 1874), pp. 215–6.

29 *Sketches from the Life of Edward Frankland* (London 1902), pp. 3–8.

30 Stair Douglas (Mrs), *The Life and Selections from the Correspondence of William Whewell* (London 1881), p. 6.

31 John Dalton, *Meteorological Observations and Essays* (Manchester 1834), 3rd edition, preface to the 2nd edition, p. xvii.

32 W. Airy (Ed.), *Autobiography of Sir George Biddell Airy* (Cambridge 1896), p. 14.

33 A. R. Wallace, *My Life* (London 1905), Vol. 1, pp. 20 and 192.

34 F. Darwin (Ed.), *The Life and Letters of Charles Darwin* (London 1888), Vol. 1, p. 35.

35 William Johns, *Practical Botany* (London 1826), p. vi.

36 E. G. R. Taylor, *The Mathematical Practitioners of Hanoverian England, 1714–1840* (Cambridge 1966), p. 479.

37 G. Tate, 'On the Progress and Diffusion of Science during the Present Century', *The Educational Expositor*, Vol. 3 (London 1855), pp. 165–72.

38 R. K. Webb, *The British Working Class Reader* (London 1955), p. 77.

39 Richard D. Altick, *The English Common Reader* (Chicago 1957), pp. 390–4. The circulation of the more narrowly scientific periodicals would clearly be much less than that of general publications like the *Penny Magazine*. In 1824, the circulation of the *Mechanics' Magazine* is given as 16,000.

40 *D.N.B.* Jane Marcet. See also L. Pearce Williams, *Michael Faraday* (London 1965), p. 19, and H. Bence-Jones, *The Life and Letters of Faraday* (London 1870), Vol. 2, pp. 401–2.

41 A graduate of Glasgow University, Rennie was for four years the holder of a chair of natural history and zoology at King's College, London. In 1834 his chair was allowed to lapse and Rennie migrated to Australia where he was able to indulge his passion for studying the habits of rare birds. F. J. C. Hearn-

shaw, *The Centenary History of King's College London* (London 1929), pp. 89 and 109.

42 Joyce, whose book, *Scientific Dialogues*, was much influenced by the educational views of the Edgeworths, was the author of several elementary works of science intended for children. The earliest edition of *Scientific Dialogues* listed in the British Museum Catalogue is one of seven volumes, dated 1809–8–9. After Joyce's death in 1816, a succession of enlarged and revised single volume editions continued to appear until well into the second half of the century.

43 Altick, op. cit., p. 164.

44 E. G. R. Taylor, *The Mathematical Practitioners of Hanoverian England, 1714–1840* (Cambridge 1966).

45 Frank Smith, *The Life and Works of Sir James Kay-Shuttleworth* (London 1923), p. 4.

46 D. B. Reid, 'Notice of a System Proposed for Introducing Chemistry as a Branch of Elementary Education' in Central Society of Education, *First Publication* (London 1837), pp. 65–72.

Chapter 2

1 *Royal Commission on Scientific Instruction and the Advancement of Science*, Second Report (London 1872), p. xi.

2 See, for example, *Hansard's Parliamentary Debates*, third Series, Vol. 241 (London 1878), column 778 and Vol. 248 (London 1879), column 1639.

3 Walter F. Cannon, 'The Role of the Cambridge Movement in Early Nineteenth-Century Science', *Ithaca: Proceedings of the 10th International Congress of the History of Science, 1962* (Paris 1964), pp. 317–20 and 'Scientists and Broad Churchmen: An Early Victorian Intellectual Network', *J. British Studies*, Vol. 4 (1964), pp. 65–88.

4 A study of the work and influence of Dawes is given in David Layton, 'Science in the Schools: The First Wave', *British Journal of Educational Studies*, Vol. 20, No. 1 (February 1972), pp. 38–57.
Biographical material is to be found in: W. C. Henry, *A Biographical Notice of the Late Very Rev. Richard Dawes, M.A., Dean of Hereford* (London 1867). J. P. T. Bury, *Romilly's Cambridge Diary, 1832–42* (Cambridge 1967). H. W. Petit Stevens, *Downing College* (London 1899).

5 Petit Stevens, op. cit., p. 169.

6 Ibid., p. 69.

7 *Sketches from the Life of Edward Frankland* (London 1902), p. 51.

8 *Correspondence of John Tyndall*, Vol. 1, Mary Helen Dawes to John Tyndall, 6 December 1863.
9 Moseley's account is given in: Committee of Council on Education, *Minutes 1847–8* (London 1848), Vol. 1, pp. 7–27.
Later studies of Dawes' School include: C. K. Francis Brown, *The Church's Part in Education 1833–1941* (London 1942), pp. 55–9. N. Ball, 'Richard Dawes and the Teaching of Common Things', *Educational Review*, Vol. 17 (1964), pp. 59–68. W. A. C. Stewart and W. P. McCann, *The Educational Innovations, 1750–1880* (London 1967), pp. 124–35. J. W. Adamson, *The Illiterate Anglo-Saxon* (Cambridge 1946), pp. 142–54.
10 Committee of Council on Education, *Minutes 1845* (London 1846), Vol. 1, p. 103.
11 Committee of Council on Education, *Minutes 1847–8* (London 1848), Vol. 1, p. 24.
12 R. Dawes, *Suggestive Hints towards Improved Secular Instruction* (6th edition, London 1853), p. viii.
13 *J. of the Society of Arts*, Vol. 1 (1852–3), p. 266 and Committee of Council on Education, *Minutes 1847–48* (London 1848), Vol. 1, pp. ccxxxviii–cclxxxix.
14 Donald H. Akenson, *The Irish Education Experiment* (London 1970), p. 229. J. M. Goldstrom, *The Social Content of Education, 1808–1870* (Shannon 1972), pp. 52–90.
15 R. Dawes, *Hints on an Improved and Self-Paying System of National Education . . . with Observations, from Personal Inspection, on the Irish National Schools* (3rd edition, London 1848), pp. 35–52.
16 Committee of Council on Education, *Minutes 1844* (London 1845), Vol. 2, p. 102.
17 R. Dawes, *Hints*, p. 16.
18 R. Dawes, *Effective Primary Instruction: the only sure road to success in the Reading Room, Library, and Institutes for Secondary Instruction* (London 1857), pp. 6–7.
19 R. Dawes, *Suggestive Hints*, p. ix.
20 Ibid.
21 A list of scientific apparatus used in his school and copies of the tables of scientific data enscribed on the walls are appended to the text of *Suggestive Hints*, pp. 212–20.
22 *Suggestive Hints*, p. 111.
23 J. F. W. Herschel, *Preliminary Discourse on the Study of National Philosophy* (London 1830), p. 50. Herschel's insight into the condition and needs of the working classes is well illustrated in 'Address to the subscribers to the Windsor and Eton Public Library and Reading Room, 29 January 1833' included in *Essays from the Edinburgh and Quarterly Reviews* (London 1857), pp. 1–20.
24 *Quarterly Review*, Vol. 45 (April–July, London 1831), p. 405.

25 *D.N.B.*, Dionysius Lardner.

26 Title page of Lardner's *Treatise on Heat* (new edition, London 1837).

27 Cited by H. Hale Bellot, *University College London* (London 1929), p. 133.

28 *Hints*, p. 28.

29 *Suggestive Hints*, p. xviii–xix.

30 Commissioners of National Education in Ireland, *Report* for 1847, Appendix 30, p. 139.

31 Committee of Council on Education. *Minutes 1846* (London 1847), Vol. 2, pp. 477–8.

32 *D.N.B.*, James Finlay Weir Johnston. See also J. R. Partington, *A History of Chemistry*, Vol. 4 (London 1964), p. 254.

33 A. W. von Hofmann: letter to J. Liebig, October–November 1845. Liebig Papers, Bayerische Staatsbibliothek, Munich. Translation by Mrs M. Whitrow. I am grateful to Dr W. H. Brock (University of Leicester) and Mrs J. Pingree (Imperial College) for help in connection with this Letter.

34 David Alec Wilson, *Carlyle at his Zenith (1848–53)*, (London 1927), p. 300. In Wilson's view, 'There can hardly be room for a doubt that if only Peel had been spared a few years longer, Ashburton would have re-organized an elementary education far better than was done about twenty years afterwards'. Without detracting from Ashburton's perception and ability, it must be said that this judgement underestimates the complexity of the problems involved in establishing a system of elementary education.

35 *Suggestive Hints*, pp. x–xi.

36 Mrs Tyndall, *Life of John Tyndall (Preliminary Drafts), 1830–51*, p. 169. For an account of science teaching at Queenwood College, see D. Thompson, 'Queenwood College, Hampshire. A mid-nineteenth-century experiment in science teaching', *Annals of Science*, Vol. 11 (1955), pp. 246–54.

37 *J. of Chemical Society*, Transactions 1905, Vol. 87, Part 1, pp. 575–6.

38 *Sketches from the Life of Edward Frankland* (London 1902), p. 51. Frankland's Journal, deposited in the Library of the Royal Institution, London, also contains references to his early relations with Dawes and his assistance to pupils at King's Somborne.

39 John Tyndall, *Sound* (London 1867).
Dawes died in March 1867. The preface to the first edition of Tyndall's book, which appeared in June 1867, contained a tribute to Dawes.

40 D. B. Reid, *Illustrations of the Theory and Practice of Ventilation* (London 1844), pp. x–xi.

41 Wemyss Reid, *Memoirs and Correspondence of Lyon Playfair* (London 1899), p. 107.

N

42 *Suggestive Hints*, p. 148.
43 Ibid., p. xxviii.
44 Ibid., p. xix.

Chapter 3

1 Charles Darwin, *The Autobiography of Charles Darwin, 1809–1882*, Edited with Appendix and Notes by his grand-daughter, Nora Barlow (London 1958), p. 58.
2 Information about Darwin's Cambridge acquaintances is to be found in his *Autobiography*, pp. 58–70; his *Journal* entry for 1831 describes the spring meeting with Dawes. See also *Darwin and Henslow: the growth of an idea, Letters 1831–1860* edited by Nora Barlow (London 1967), p. 9.
3 *Biographical Sketch of the Rev. John Stevens Henslow* (Reprinted from the *Gardeners' Chronicle*), (London 1861), p. 8. When Henslow's Friday evening parties were terminated at the end of 1836, the Cambridge Ray Club was established to take their place. Babington's *Journal* gives an account of the inauguration of the new Club. *Memorials, Journal and Botanical Correspondence of Charles Cardale Babington* (Cambridge 1897), p. 60.
4 *Autobiography*, p. 64.
5 'A kind of machine for grinding general laws out of large collections of facts' was, of course, Darwin's description of his own mind, given in his *Autobiography* at the point where he laments the loss of aesthetic tastes (p. 139). For Darwin's relationship with Hooker, see *Darwin and Henslow*, p. 18. Also Mea Allan, *The Hookers of Kew* (London 1967) and W. B. Turrill, *Joseph Dalton Hooker* (London 1963).
   Henslow's defence of Darwin, following an attack by Sedgwick at a meeting of the Cambridge Philosophical Society is described in a letter to Hooker: L. Huxley, *Life and Letters of Sir Joseph Dalton Hooker* (London 1918), Vol. 1, pp. 512–14.
6 *Darwin and Henslow*, p. 124.
7 *Life, Letters and Journals of Sir Charles Lyell* (edited by his sister-in-law, Mrs Lyell), (London 1881), Vol. 1, p. 366.
8 A. R. Hall, *The Cambridge Philosophical Society: a history, 1819–1969* (Cambridge 1969).
9 *Autobiography*, p. 67.
10 *Quarterly Review*, Vol. 45, April–July 1831 (London 1831), p. 381.
11 *Report of Her Majesty's Commissioners appointed to Inquire into the Revenues and Management of Certain Colleges and Schools, and the Studies pursued and instruction given therein*. Vol. IV, Evidence Part 2, p. 385. In his evidence to the Public

School Commissioners Hooker describes how he accompanied Henslow on these visits to the Palace.

See also *Biographical Sketch of the Rev. John Stevens Henslow* (London 1861), p. 16.

12 Committee of Council on Education, *Report 1858–9* (London 1859), p. 70 and *Gardeners' Chronicle*, 7 July 1856), p. 453.

13 *Report of Her Majesty's Commissioners appointed to Inquire into the Revenues and Management of Certain Colleges and Schools, and the Studies pursued and instruction given therein*, Vol. 3, Evidence Part 1, p. 345.

14 J. S. Henslow, *Illustrations to be employed in Practical Lessons on Botany: adapted to beginners of all classes* (London 1858), p. 1, and 'Example of Botany in Village Education', *Gardeners' Chronicle* (7 July 1856), p. 453.

15 Joan Thirsk and Jean Imray (Eds), *Suffolk Farming in the Nineteenth Century*, Suffolk Records Society, Vol. 1 (Ipswich 1958), p. 24.

16 *Quarterly Review*, Vol. 45, April–July 1831 (London 1831), pp. 402–4.

17 *Darwin and Henslow*, p. 159.

18 George Henslow's description of his father's course is given in *The Leisure Hour* (1862), p. 676. Details of the contents of J. S. Henslow's lesson notes are given in Professor D. Oliver's *Lessons in Elementary Botany* (London 1864), p. vii, which was based on Henslow's uncompleted manuscript.

19 L. Huxley, *Life and Letters of Sir Joseph Dalton Hooker* (London 1918), Vol. 1, p. 399.

20 *Gardeners' Chronicle*, (2 August 1856), p. 517.

21 George Wilson and A. Geikie, *Memoir of Edward Forbes, F.R.S.* (London 1861), p. 355.

22 *Quarterly Review*, Vol. 45, April–July 1831 (London 1831), pp. 391–7.

23 *Gardeners' Chronicle*, (2 August 1856), p. 516.

24 L. Huxley, *Life and Letters of Sir Joseph Dalton Hooker* (London 1918), Vol. 1, p. 403, and *Memorials, Journal and Botanical Correspondence of Charles Cardale Babington* (Cambridge 1897), p. xxxii.

25 *Gardeners' Chronicle*, (2 August 1856), p. 517, and *Life and Letters of Sir Joseph Dalton Hooker*, Vol. 1, p. 399.

26 *Gardeners' Chronicle*, (2 August 1856), p. 517.

27 J. S. Henslow, *Illustrations to be employed in Practical Lessons on Botany* (London 1858), p. 28.

28 Henslow's biographer, his brother-in-law the Rev. Leonard Jenyns, a naturalist of some reputation, provides a detailed account of the state of the parish of Hitcham in the late 1830s. L. Jenyns, *Memoir of the Rev. John Stevens Henslow* (London 1862), p. 68 et. seq.

Although Henslow's school was not at the time in union with
the National Society, a general indication of the educational
difficulties characterizing a rural situation in Suffolk is provided
by the report of the Society's inquiry into National Schools
undertaken in 1846–7.
National Society, *Church School Inquiry 1846–7* (London
1849), p. 11.

29 When Henslow commenced negotiations with a view to receiving grant for his school from the Committee of Council on
Education he made clear how limited were the resources that
had sustained his educational efforts at Hitcham.
'If it be made a *sine qua non* that we are to lay out much
money before a grant can be obtained, there is an end of the
matter. Our school cost 50 1. in building and furnishing, and
it has answered our purpose for fifteen years,' he wrote to the
regional inspector. Committee of Council on Education,
Minutes 1855–6 (London 1856), p. 305.

30 *Darwin and Henslow*, p. 171.

31 An account of Henslow's pastoral activities is given in L. Jenyns,
Memoir of the Rev. John Stevens Henslow (London 1862). The
description of Babington as 'that mighty man of minute dif-
ferences' is from a letter from Darwin to Henslow: *Darwin
and Henslow*, p. 153. Babington's account of the visit of the
Hitcham parishioners to Cambridge is recorded in his journal,
*Memorials, Journal and Botanical Correspondence of Charles
Cardale Babington* (Cambridge 1897), p. 174.

32 *Darwin and Henslow*, pp. 167 and 190–1.

33 Henslow described his matured course in a letter to the Rev. M.
Mitchell, H.M.I., the government inspector responsible for
Norfolk, Suffolk and Essex, dated 7 January 1859.
Committee of Council on Education, *Report 1858–9* (London
1859), pp. 70–1. The evolution of his teaching of botany is
referred to in the advertisement for the nine botanical diagrams
which he produced for the Department of Science and Art. See
J. S. Henslow, *Illustrations to be employed in Practical Lessons
on Botany: adapted to beginners of all classes* (London 1861).
A more detailed account of his *Practical Lessons in Botany for
Beginners of all Classes* was given in a series of fourteen contributions to the *Gardeners' Chronicle* between 12 July and
27 December 1856.

34 *Gardeners' Chronicle*, (27 December 1856), p. 853.

35 *Darwin and Henslow*, p. 184.

36 Committee of Council on Education, *Report 1858–9* (London
1859), pp. 70–1.

37 *Life and Letters of Sir Joseph Dalton Hooker*, Vol. 1, p. 370.

38 Ibid., pp. 347–8.

39 Ibid., p. 386.

40 Ibid., p. 388.
41 L. Jenyns, *Memoir of the Rev. John Stevens Henslow* (London 1862), p. 150.
42 G. Wilson and A. Geikie, *Memoir of Edward Forbes, F.R.S.* (London 1861), pp. 281–2.
In October 1853 when Forbes was appointed to deliver the introductory lecture on the opening of the autumn session of the Government School of Mines, he chose as his subject *The Educational uses of Museums*. His address was published as a pamphlet; (London 1853).
43 *Life and Letters of Sir Joseph Dalton Hooker*, Vol. 1, p. 434; Jenyns, p. 159.
44 *Third Report of the Department of Science and Art* (London 1856), p. xxx.
45 *Life and Letters of Sir Joseph Dalton Hooker*, Vol. 1, p. 392.
46 Ibid., p. 161.
47 See, for example, Roy M. MacLeod, 'The X-Club. A Social Network of Science in Late-Victorian England,' *Notes and Records of the Royal Society of London*, Vol. 24 (1970), p. 305. Also J. Vernon Jenson, 'The X-Club: Fraternity of Victorian Scientists,' *British Journal for the History of Science*, Vol. 5 (1970), pp. 63–72.
48 *Life and Letters of Sir Joseph Dalton Hooker*, Vol. 1, pp. 368–9.
49 Ibid.. pp. 393 and 399–401.
50 Henslow fully recognized the need for trained teachers; his view was that 'sufficient knowledge of British Botany' could be acquired in a twelve month to enable a start to be made in the teaching of systematic botany but he doubted whether enough teachers would be willing to prepare themselves for this work. The solution seemed to be to make Natural History a compulsory part of the course of education in training colleges. *Illustrations to be employed in Practical Lessons in Botany* (London 1858), pp. 30–1.
51 J. M. Wilson, *An Autobiography 1836–1931* (London 1932), pp. 61–4. Wilson's letter to Temple describing the state of science teaching at Rugby in 1861 is given in *Report on the Past, Present and Future of the Royal Institution* (London 1862), p. 14. Temple's letters to Playfair (5.vi.1860 and 12.xii.1860) are in the archives of Imperial College London.
52 The changes at Rugby following the report of the Public Schools Commission are described by Wilson in Board of Education, *Educational Pamphlets, No. 17* (London 1909), pp. 3–4; and by Kitchener in E. G. Sandford (Ed.), *Memoir of Archbishop Temple* (London 1906), pp. 196–8.
For information on George Henslow see *Journal of Botany*, Vol. 64 (1926), pp. 55–6.
53 *Report of the British Association for the Advancement of*

Science (London 1868), pp. xxxix–liv. Besides Huxley, Tyndall and Wilson, the committee included the Rev. F. W. Farrar, assistant master at Harrow, the Rev. T. N. Hutchinson, Wilson's colleague at Rugby, George Griffith, Assistant General Secretary to the British Association (who taught science at Winchester) and Joseph Payne. An appendix to the report gave an account of the teaching of science at Rugby where Henslow's diagrams and Oliver's text (based on Henslow's notes) were employed in the teaching of botany (p. 1). See also Schools Inquiry Commission, Vol. 2, *Miscellaneous Papers* (London 1868), pp. 218–30. F. W. Farrar, *Essays on a Liberal Education* (London 1867), pp. 272–8.

54 E. G. Sandford (Ed.), *Memoir of Archbishop Temple* (London 1906), pp. 133–41. Schools Inquiry Commission, Vol. 1, *Report of the Commissioners* (London 1868), p. 35.

55 Jenyns, p. 108.

56 *Darwin and Henslow*, pp. 171, 182 and 192.
Life and Letters of Sir Joseph Dalton Hooker, pp. 393–8.

57 Information about Oliver's amendments to Henslow's manuscript is given in the preface to *Lessons in Elementary Botany*, p. vii. The reviewer was Asa Gray writing in *The American Journal of Science and Arts*, second series, Vol. 38 (November 1864). p. 125. Along with Lockyer's *Elementary Lessons in Astronomy*, Huxley's *Lessons in Elementary Physiology*, Roscoe's *Lessons in Elementary Chemistry* and Balfour Stewart's *Lessons in Elementary Physics*, Oliver's text become one of MacMillan's celebrated 'Elementary Class-Book' series. Jean Bremner, *The teaching of the biological sciences in English schools during the second half of the nineteenth century* (unpublished M.A. thesis, University of London, 1955) gives the number of copies of Oliver published before 1900 as 67,000 (p. 140).

58 *Royal Commission on Scientific Instruction and the Advancement of Science*. Sixth Report (London 1875), pp. 25–7. On the limited development of the teaching of botany in elementary schools, see Vol. 1, Minutes of Evidence (London 1872): evidence of the Rev. Canon Norris, Inspector of elementary schools from 1849 to 1864 (p. 584) and of the Rev. Frederick Watkins, an inspector for twenty-seven years (p. 591).

Chapter 4

1 B. C. Bloomfield (Ed.), *The Autobiography of Sir James Kay-Shuttleworth* (London 1964), p. 50.

2 See, for example, Frank Smith, *The Life and Work of Sir James Kay-Shuttleworth* (London 1923).

3 Supra, p. 33.
4 Smith, op. cit., p. 11.
   See also F. Darwin (Ed.), *The Life and Letters of Charles Darwin* (London 1888), Vol. 1, p. 40.
5 Smith, op. cit., pp. 48–50.
6 Smith, op. cit., p. 94.
7 Thomas Adkins, *The History of St John's College, Battersea* (London 1906), pp. 49–50. A brief account of Tate's background and career is to be found in Temple's letter to Lingen, Kay-Shuttleworth's successor as Secretary to the Committee of Council, requesting that consideration be given to Tate's claims for a pension. Committee of Council on Education, *Minutes 1856–7* (London 1857), p. 32.
8 Smith, op. cit., pp. 305–10.
9 The chemistry lessons are described in a letter to Kay-Shuttleworth from his son, dated 26 January 1859. A month later a letter from Harrow, where Ughtred was at school with Moseley's son, raised the problem of the clash of physiology with other studies. *Papers and Correspondence of Sir James Kay-Shuttleworth.*
10 Committee of Council on Education, *Minutes 1842–3* (London 1844), p. iii.
11 Smith, op. cit., p. 139.
12 Moseley, somewhat surprisingly, has never been the subject of a biographical study. General information about his life is available in a number of sources including: *D.N.B.* Henry Moseley; *The Times*, 23 January 1872, p. 5; *Transactions of the Institution of Naval Architects*, Vol. 13 (1872), pp. 328–30.
13 F. J. C. Hearnshaw, *The Centenary History of King's College London 1828–1928* (London 1929), p. 110.
14 Forbes' letter to Moseley, dated August 1833, is part of the collection of correspondence and papers of Forbes held by the University Library, St Andrews. Part is quoted, although without reference to Moseley, in J. Campbell Shairp, P. G. Tait and A. Adams-Reilly, *Life and Letters of James David Forbes, F.R.S.* (London 1873), p. 98.
15 The quotation is from Robison's article on the Scottish geometer Robert Simpson in the *Encyclopaedia Britannica*, 8th edition (Edinburgh 1860). See Richard Olson, 'Scottish Philosophy and Mathematics 1750–1830', *Journal of the History of Ideas*, Vol. 32, No. 1 (January–March 1971), pp. 29–44.
16 Hearnshaw, op. cit., p. 147.
17 'Civil Engineering and Mining' in 1838 became 'Civil Engineering and Science as applied to Arts and Manufactures' in 1839. The following year 'Architecture' was added to the title, with a further broadening of scope to 'Engineering, Architecture, Arts and Manufacturers' in 1841.

The subsequent development of mining education in Cornwall is discussed in *Report from the Select Committee on Provision for giving Instruction in Theoretical and Applied Science to the Industrial Classes*, Parl. Paper 1867–8, xv, p. 95.

18 Committee of Council on Education, *Minutes 1851–2* (London 1852), pp. 356–60 and 363–6.

19 Committee of Council on Education, *Minutes 1842–3* (London 1844), p. 68.

20 Hearnshaw, op. cit., p. 124.

21 Moseley was one of five new inspectors. Kay-Shuttleworth's part in training them is described in Smith, op. cit., pp. 154–6. Moseley's acknowledgement of his debt to Kay-Shuttleworth is given in a letter dated 24 July 1856. *Papers and Correspondence of Sir James Kay-Shuttleworth.*

22 Committee of Council on Education, *Minutes 1845* (London 1846), Vol. 1, pp. 247–8.

23 Ibid., pp. 250–5.

24 Committee of Council on Education, *Minutes 1844* (London 1845), Vol. 2, p. 519.

25 Committee of Council on Education, *Minutes 1845* (London 1846), Vol. 1, p. 229.

26 Ibid., p. 230.

27 Committee of Council on Education, *Minutes 1844* (London 1845), Vol. 2, pp. 507–8.

28 Ibid., p. 508.

29 Committee of Council on Education, *Minutes 1845* (London 1846), Vol. 1, p. 271.

30 Ibid., pp. 266–7.

31 Ibid., p. 268.

32 Ibid., p. 262.

33 Ibid., pp. 233–40.

34 Ibid., p. 269.

35 Ibid., p. 264.

36 Committee of Council on Education, *Minutes 1847–8* (London 1848), Vol. 1, p. xvi.

37 Ibid.. p. 26.

38 Committee of Council on Education, *Minutes 1853–4* (London 1854), p. 203.

39 With other correspondence Moseley's letters to Henslow were bound into a volume originally deposited at Kew, but later presented to the library of the Botany School, Cambridge.

40 For excellent discussions of the proposals for civil service reform see E. Hughes, 'Sir Charles Trevelyan and Civil Service Reform, 1853–5', *The English Historical Review*, Vol. 64 (1949), pp. 53–88 and 206–34; and E. Hughes, 'Civil Service Reform 1853–5', *Public Administration*, Vol. 32 (1954), pp. 17–51.

The former source reprints the letters between Dawes, Jowett and Trevelyan. The Trevelyan–Northcote Report is reprinted in the latter, pp. 1–16. Moseley's reply to Trevelyan is given in *Papers relating to the Reorganization of the Civil Service*, Parl. Paper 1854–5, xx, pp. 36–42.

41 Ibid., p. 39.

42 An interesting account of Rigg's work is given in F. E. Foden, 'The Rev. Arthur Rigg: Pioneer of Workshop Practice', *The Vocational Aspect of Secondary and Further Education*, Vol. 11, No. 23 (Autumn 1959), pp. 105–18.

43 Committee of Council on Education, *Minutes 1844* (London 1845), Vol. 2, pp. 626–55.

44 Committee of Council on Education, *Minutes 1845* (London 1846), Vol. 1, pp. 368–9.

45 Ibid., pp. 369–70.

46 The curriculum and organization of the Trade School at Bristol was a subject on which Moseley gave evidence to a number of committees and commissions in the second half of the century. For example, *Report from the Select Committee on Provisions for giving Instruction in Theoretical and Applied Science to the Industrial Classes*, Parl. Paper 1867–8, xv, pp. 192–9; *Royal Commission: Schools Inquiry, Minutes of Evidence: Part 1*, Parl. Paper 1867–8, xxviii, Part 3, pp. 187–214.

47 For Moseley's work on the Council of Military Education, see the *General Reports of the Council of Military Education*, Parl. Papers 1860, xxiv; 1865, xxxiv; and 1868–9, xxii. Moseley was one of the original Vice-Presidents of the Institution of Naval Architects in 1860.

48 Moseley's unpublished scientific papers, together with the reports of referees, are deposited in the archives of the Royal Society.

49 The account of H. G. J. Moseley in the *Dictionary of National Biography: 1912–21* was from the pen of Rutherford.

Chapter 5

1 Committee of Council on Education, *Minutes 1844* (London 1845), Vol. 1, pp. 6, 113–18.

2 Committee of Council on Education, *Minutes 1847–8* (London 1848), Vol. 1, p. ccxxxvi.

3 Committee of Council on Education, *Minutes 1848–9–50* (London 1850), Vol. 1, p. lxxix.

4 Committee of Council on Education, *Minutes 1851–2* (London 1852), pp. 213–14.

5 J. S. Furnivall, *Colonial Policy and Practice* (New York 1948), p. 375.

6 M. C. Morgan, *Cheltenham College* (Chalfont St Giles 1968), pp. 34 and 38.

7 C. H. Bromby, *A Lecture on Education; its principles, instruments, and present prospects, delivered at the Literary and Philosophical Institution at Cheltenham on Tuesday evening, 6 December 1853* (London n.d.), pp. 11–13.
See also *Journal of the Society of Arts*, Vol. 2 (1854), p. 313.

8 Committee of Council on Education, *Minutes 1852–3* (London 1853), p. 154.

9 Ibid., pp. 154–214.

10 Supra, p. 53.

11 Committee of Council on Education, *Minutes 1854–5* (London 1855), pp. 311–12.

12 Each of the three firms appointed to provide apparatus had displayed wares in the 1851 Exhibition and each had been awarded a prize medal, Griffin and Knight for their chemical apparatus and Horne for photographic equipment.

13 Fownes' text, first published in 1844, was repeatedly revised and corrected, first by H. Bence Jones and A. W. Hofmann, later by H. Watts, achieving a 12th edition in 1877. Fownes himself died in 1849 at the early age of 34, being professor of practical chemistry in the Birkbeck laboratory, University College, London.
Wilson's *Chemistry*, first published in Chambers' Educational Course, was another text which enjoyed an extended life. Wilson, on whom Dr D. B. Reid's mantle as a chemistry teacher in Edinburgh fell when Reid moved to London in 1840, became the first occupant of the new chair of Technology in the University of Edinburgh, created by the crown in 1855.

14 See, for example, Board of Trade. Department of Science and Art. *Correspondence between the Lords of the Committee of Privy Council for Trade and the Lords Commissioners of Her Majesty's Treasury, on the constitution of the Department of Science and Art* (London 1853), p. 2.

15 Supra, pp. 20, 70.

16 *Second Report of the Commissioners for the Exhibition of 1851* (London 1852), p. 41. The Commissioners included the Prince Consort; Lord Derby, the Prime Minister, (who was responsible for the reference to science and art in the Queen's speech); the Earl of Rosse, President of the Royal Society; Lord John Russell; Sir Charles Lyell, President of the Geological Society; and Henry Labouchere, President of the Board of Trade.

17 *First Report of the Department of Science and Art* (London 1854), p. xxx.

18 Ibid., Appendix C, p. 33. Correspondence between Playfair and Lingen.

19 Committee of Council on Education, *Minutes 1852–3* (London 1853), p. 155.
20 Moseley to Playfair: 12 November 1853. Collection of letters to Lyon Playfair: Royal Society of Arts. In December 1854 the first batch of eleven schoolmasters presented themselves for examination and all were successful.
21 See, for example, the letter from Colonel Grey, one of the Prince Consort's officials, to Playfair: Wemyss Reid, *Memoirs and Correspondence of Lyon Playfair* (London 1899), pp. 137–8.
22 *Journal of the Society of Arts*, Vol. 1 (London 1853), pp. 344–5.
23 Dawes was elected an Honorary Member of the Society of Arts early in 1853 (Society of Arts, *Council Minutes*, 18 May 1853) and immediately played an active part as a member of Council. He received the Society's medal for his paper describing the principles on which the King's Somborne schools had been organized and at the dinner following the conference between Institutes and the Council in June 1853 he proposed the toast 'Success to Instruction in Science and Art', to which Playfair responded. *Journal of the Society of Arts*, Vol. 1 (London 1853), pp. 352–5.
24 Chester, a neglected figure, is the subject of a biographical study by J. S. Hurt in *Journal of the Royal Society of Arts*, Vol. 116 (London 1968), pp. 156–60, 262–4, and 321–3.
25 David Layton, 'The Educational Exhibition of 1854', *Journal of the Royal Society of Arts*, Vol. 120, Nos 5187 and 5188 (1972), pp. 183–7 and 253–6.
26 The criticisms were expressed with particular trenchancy by Thomas Tate, who had taught science for ten years at the Battersea Training School, and who had designed much apparatus for teaching and had written science texts for teachers. See *The Educational Expositor, specially designed for Schoolmasters and Schoolmistresses* edited by T. Tate and J. Tilleard (London 1854), Vol. 2, pp. 337–44.
27 *Journal of the Society of Arts*, Vol. 2 (London 1854), pp. 411–13.
28 *Journal of the Society of Arts*, Vol. 3 (London 1854–5), p. 3.
29 Committee of Council on Education, *Minutes 1854–5* (London 1855), p. 312.
30 Figures taken from financial statements in *Minutes* of the Committee of Council on Education for the years in question.
31 Committee of Council on Education, *Minutes 1847–8* (London 1848), Vol. 1, pp. xvi–xxxix.
32 Education (Ireland), Parl. Paper 1852–3, xciv, p. 489.
33 *Fifteenth Report of the Commissioners of National Education In Ireland for the year 1848*, Parl. Paper 1848, xxiii, p. 6.
34 Donald H. Akenson, *The Irish Education Experiment* (London and Toronto 1970), pp. 228–74.

See also Akenson's article, 'The Irish Textbook Controversy and the Gospel of Free Trade' in *Journal of Educational Administration and History*, Vol. 3 (Leeds 1970), pp. 19–23. Akenson's conclusion that the prohibition on direct sale of the Irish books to the public led to price increases is not supported by an examination of book lists over the period 1848 to 1860. In 1848 the price per copy from the Committee of Council of the first five Irish readers was 1d, 4d, 8d, 9d and 11d respectively. In the late 1850s, the same readers, now published by A. Thom and Sons, were priced in the Committee of Council's list at $\frac{1}{2}$d, $2\frac{3}{4}$d, $5\frac{1}{4}$d, $6\frac{1}{4}$d and $6\frac{3}{4}$d. Over the same period the price of similar readers, e.g. those of the British and Foreign School Society, showed no comparable reduction.

35 James Tilleard, 'On Elementary School Books', *Transactions of the National Society for the Promotion of Social Science 1859* (London 1860), p. 391.

36 Ibid., p. 389.

37 Ibid., p. 392.

38 The events which followed Kay-Shuttleworth's proposal can be traced from letters included in the papers of Sir James Kay-Shuttleworth (University of Manchester Library) and in the collection of Playfair's letters in the library of the Royal Society of Arts.

39 Playfair to Kay-Shuttleworth: 6 April 1853.

40 C. J. Blomfield to Kay-Shuttleworth: 1 August 1853.

41 Harriet Mantineau to Kay-Shuttleworth: 7 April 1853.

42 The Journals of John Tyndall, 17 October 1853.

43 *The London, Edinburgh and Dublin Philosophical Magazine and Journal of Science*, Vol. 10, 4th series, July–December 1855, p. 441.

44 Chambers to Playfair: 27 December 1853.

45 Kay-Shuttleworth to Playfair: 6 February 1854.

46 Tilleard, op. cit., p. 388.

47 Indispensable aids in any attempt to acquire an accurate picture of the texts available to schools in the 1850s are the *Catalogues of the Educational Division of the South Kensington Museum*, 1st edition (London 1857); 2nd edition corrected to November 1857; 3rd edition corrected to April, 1858.

48 Dr E. C. Brewer, *A Guide to the Scientific Knowledge of Things Familiar* (London 1873), Preface to the 31st edition, p. vi.

49 *Royal Commission on Scientific Instruction and the Advancement of Science*, Vol. 1 (London 1872), Minutes of Evidence, p. 576.

50 Dawes to Playfair: 1 February 1854. Collection of letters to Lyon Playfair: Royal Society of Arts.

51 E. K. Blyth, *Life of William Ellis* (London 1889), p. 125.

52 Dawes to Playfair: 7 February 1854. Collection of letters to Lyon Playfair: Royal Society of Arts.
53 *Ashburton Prizes for the Teaching of 'Common Things'*. An account of the proceedings at a meeting between Lord Ashburton and the elementary schoolmasters assembled at Winchester on Friday, 16 December 1853 (London 1854).
See also Ashburton to Kay-Shuttleworth: 1 August 1853, Kay-Shuttleworth Papers. Wemyss Reid, *Memoirs and Correspondence of Lyon Playfair* (London 1899), p. 157.
54 *A Summary Account of Prizes for Common Things offered and awarded by Miss Burdett Coutts at the Whitelands Training Institution*, 2nd edition (London n.d.).
55 *Ashburton Prizes*, op. cit., p. 12.
56 Ibid., p. 31.
57 Select Committee on Scientific Instruction, *Report* (London 1868), p. 108.
58 R. Dawes, *Remarks occasioned by the Present Crusade against the Educational Plans of the Committee of Council on Education* (London 1850), p. 40.
59 Committee of Council on Education, *Minutes 1854–5* (London 1855), p. 311.
60 Ibid., p. 10.
61 Ibid.. p. 288 and pp. 14–17.
62 Ibid., p. 16.
63 Ibid., p. 17.
64 Committee of Council on Education, *Minutes 1850–1* (London 1851), p. 47.
65 Committee of Council on Education, *Minutes 1856–7* (London 1857), pp. 713–17.
66 *Report of the 25th Meeting of the British Association for the Advancement of Science* (London 1856), p. lxxxi.
Argyll. who retained a life-long interest in science, was a member of the Committee of Council on Education in both Aberdeen's coalition and Palmerston's first government.

Chapter 6

1 See, for example, *Royal Commission on Scientific Instruction and the Advancement of Science*, second report (London 1872), pp. xiii–xiv, and D. M. Turner, *History of Science Teaching in England* (London 1927), p. 109.
2 Moseley to Kay-Shuttleworth, 24 July 1856. *Papers and Correspondence of Sir James Kay-Shuttleworth*.
3 *J. of the Society of Arts*, Vol. 2 (1853–4), p. 565.
4 *The Educational Expositor*, Vol. 3 (1855), pp. 41–2.
5 James Hole, *Light, More Light* (London 1860), p. 72.

6 *First Report of the Department of Science and Art* (London 1854), p. xlv. *Second Report of the Department of Science and Art* (London 1855), p. xxxii.
7 F. Engels, *The Condition of the Working Class in England in 1844* (London 1892), pp. 238–9.
8 William Lovett, *The Life and Struggles of William Lovett, in the pursuit of bread, knowledge and freedom* (London 1876). The 'Address on Education', printed on pp. 135–46, included detailed curriculum recommendations. Lovett's text-books on science are referred to in Chapter 21, pp. 399–410.
9 *Report from the Select Committee on Scientific Instruction* (London 1868), Appendix, p. 474.
10 Supra, pp. 92–4.
11 Quoted by Somervell, D. C., *English Thought in the Nineteenth Century* (London 1929), p. 84.
12 Ashburton to Kay-Shuttleworth, 1 August 1853 and a further (undated) letter, probably later in August. *Papers and Correspondence of Sir James Kay-Shuttleworth.*
13 *Ashburton Prizes for the Teaching of 'Common Things'* (London 1854).
14 Kay-Shuttleworth to Playfair, 6 February 1854. Collection of letters to Lyon Playfair: Royal Society of Arts.
15 Committee of Council on Education, *Minutes 1854–5* (London 1855), pp. 14–17.
16 T. Tate, *The Philosophy of Education*, 2nd American edition (Syracuse, N.Y. 1885), pp. 262–3.
17 *The Educational Expositor*, Vol. 3 (1855), p. 42.
18 *Ashburton Prizes*, op. cit., pp. 10–11.
19 Supra, pp. 47–8.
20 T. Tate, *The Philosophy of Education*, op. cit., p. 24.
21 The different perceptions of objectives by teachers and by those outside the classroom who are involved in the promotion of change, remains a major source of resistance to curriculum reform: see, for example, Marshall Heron, 'On Teacher Perception and Curriculum Innovation', *Curriculum Theory Network, Monograph Supplement, Elements of Curriculum Development*, Ontario Institute for Studies in Education (Ontario 1971), pp. 47–52.
22 Committee of Council on Education, *Minutes 1853–4* (London 1854), pp. 199–201.
23 Ibid., p. 203.
24 R. W. Lingen, MS. Confidential Memorandum by Lingen on the Committee of Council on Education in the House of Commons, 6 June 1855, para. 8.
25 Supra, p. 20. A typical reaction was that of a schoolmaster witness before the Public School Commissioners in 1862. Although by no means antipathetic to science, his opinion was

that 'the theory of geology cannot be received by mere boys without a violent disturbance of their religious beliefs'. *Report of Her Majesty's Commissioners appointed to Inquire into the Revenues and Management of Certain Colleges and Schools, and the Studies pursued and Instruction given therein*. Vol. 3, Evidence, Part 1, p. 159 (London 1864).

26 David Layton, 'Lord Wrottesley, F.R.S., Pioneer Statesman of Science', *Notes and Records of the Royal Society of London*, Vol. 23, No. 2 (December 1968), pp. 230–46. The twelve resolutions are printed as an appendix to the above paper.

27 A deputation, led by Huxley as President of the Association, and including Lyon Playfair as one of its members, presented an address to the Vice-President of the Committee of Council in 1870. See *Nature*, Vol. 3 (1871), p. 149. By the end of the decade a committee of the B.A. had been established to study and report on aspects of science teaching in elementary schools. *Report of the British Association for the Advancement of Science* (London 1880), p. lxv. This committee reported annually over the next two decades.

28 The title page of Rumford's proposal for the formation of the Royal Institution is reproduced in E. Ironmonger, 'The Royal Institution and the Teaching of Science in the Nineteenth Century', *Proc. of the Royal Institution of Great Britain, 37*, Part 2, p. 141 (1958).

29 Ibid., p. 143.

30 *The Journals of John Tyndall*, 4 February 1954.

31 Supra, pp. 101–2, 107–12.

32 Wemyss Reid, *Memoirs and Correspondence of Lyon Playfair* (London 1899), *passim*. Playfair served as a member of commissions of inquiry into a variety of matters including the health of towns, the sanitary condition of Buckingham Palace, town water supplies, graveyards, accidents in coal mines and the Irish potato blight. Whilst he appeared to enjoy cordial relations with some of the most eminent figures in the land, the nature of some of the requests for his help is indicative that he was seen by many government officials as very much a scientist 'on tap, but not on top'. Trevelyan could write brusquely 'Pray analyse the coal from Moldavia, Mount Lebanon and Tripoli and let us know the result.' (Trevelyan to Playfair, 10 April 1854) and Cardwell, President of the Board of Trade at the time of the establishment of the Department of Science and Art, expected detailed advice on the means of ensuring a supply of pure water to a house he was proposing to buy in Eaton Square (Cardwell to Playfair, 26 October 1853).

33 *Fourth Report of the Department of Science and Art* (London 1857), p. xxxi.

34 The lectures were published as *Records of the School of Mines*

and of Science applied to the Arts, Vol. 1, Part 1 (London 1852).

35 Ibid., pp. 51–2.

36 Ibid., p. 64.

37 R. Hunt, 'On classes for scientific observation in mechanics' institutes', in *Lectures in Connection with the Educational Exhibition of the Society of Arts* (London 1854), pp. 172–4.

38 *Records of the School of Mines and of Science Applied to the Arts*, Vol. 1, Part 1 (London 1852), p. 27.

39 Ibid., p. 48.

40 *Cole Diaries*, 28 January 1853 and 8 March 1853.

41 *Cole Correspondence*, Library of the Victoria and Albert Museum, Box 15, Playfair to Colonel Phipps, 18 July 1853.

42 Ibid.

43 Playfair to Cole, 19 July 1853. The relationship between the Director of the School of Mines, the professors, and the Government was, nevertheless, a continuous source of friction throughout the period under study. See Cardwell to Playfair, 26 October 1853, Playfair to Cole, 7 June 1855.

44 The Royal Institution lectures were published as a book in 1855. Six of the seven were included in a collection of addresses on *Modern Culture; its true aims and requirements* (London 1867) edited by the American E. L. Youmans, and all were reprinted, with an introduction by Sir E. Ray Lankester, in a volume entitled *Science and Education* (London 1917).

45 E. L. Youmans, *Modern Culture; its true aims and requirements* (London 1867), p. 270.

46 M. Faraday, 'On Wheatstone's Electric Telegraph in relation to Science (being an argument in favour of the full recognition of Science as a branch of education)', *Procedings of the Royal Institution*, Vol. 2 (1854–8), p. 555. Also reprinted in *Proceedings of the Royal Institution*, Vol. 37 (1958), p. 215.

47 Youmans, op. cit., p. 28.

48 D. Thompson, unpublished M.A. thesis, *The Development of scientific education during the second half of the nineteenth century, with special reference to the influence of John Tyndall* (Sheffield 1955), p. 36.

49 G. Combe, *Discussions on Education* (London 1893), pp. 211–12.

50 *Minutes of the Department of Science and Art*, P.R.O. Ed. 28/2, 11 February 1854. The physiology diagrams were but one set of several produced by the Department for science teachers. Their circulation was considerable: Miss Florence Nightingale applied for a set for use with the army in the Crimea; another set was presented to the King of Siam on the ratification of a treaty between Siam and Britain. P.R.O. Ed. 28/5, 29 November 1955 and 3 December 1855.

51 Youmans. op. cit., p. 54.

52 David Layton, 'The Educational Exhibition of 1854', *J. of the Royal Society of Arts*, Vol. 120 (February and March 1972), pp. 183–7 and 253–6. See also *J. of the Society of Arts*, Vol. 2 (1853–4), p. 531.

53 G. E. L. Cotton, 'The necessity of an extended education for the educator' in *Lectures in Connection with the Educational Exhibition of the Society of Arts* (London 1854), p. 147.

54 R. Hunt, 'On familiar methods of instruction in Science', Ibid., pp. 176–7. See also R. Hunt, *The Poetry of Science* (London 1848), p. 397.

55 Ibid., p. 178.

56 G. Wilson and A. Geikie, *Memoir of Edward Forbes, F.R.S.* (Edinburgh 1861), p. 494.

57 *Cole Correspondence*, Playfair to Cole, 21 March 1853. Despite Playfair's support, Hunt was not appointed. The following year, in accordance with arrangements suggested by the Treasury, he became full-time Keeper of the Mining Records. He was succeeded as lecturer in physical science in the School of Mines by G. G. Stokes. P.R.O. Ed. 28/2, 5 August 1854.

58 Supra, pp. 46 and 59.

59 David Layton, 'Lord Wrottesley', op. cit., p. 242.

60 See, for example, John Dillenberger, *Protestant Thought and Natural Science* (London 1961), pp. 89, 98, 113.

61 Youmans, op. cit., p. 162.

62 R. Hunt, *The Poetry of Science* (London 1848), p. 397.

63 Committee of Council on Education, *Minutes 1847–8* (London 1848), p. 35, and *Minutes 1845*, Vol. 1 (London 1846), p. 263.

64 R. Hunt, 'On classes for scientific observation in mechanics' institutes', *Lectures in Connection with the Educational Exhibition* (London 1854), pp. 159–74, and *J. of the Society of Arts*, Vol. 2 (1853–4), pp. 684–5.

65 *J. of the Society of Arts*, Vol. 2 (1853–4), p. 625. See also Committee of Council on Education, *Minutes 1854–5* (London 1855), p. 316.

66 Supra, pp. 67–72.

67 T. H. Huxley, *On the Educational Value of the Natural History Sciences* (London 1854).

68 Ibid., p. 12.

69 On the differences between the views of Mill and Whewell on 'scientific method' see, for example, L. Laudan, 'Theories of Scientific Method from Plato to Mach', *History of Science*, Vol. 7 (Cambridge 1968), pp. 30–2; E. W. Strong, 'William Whewell and John Stuart Mill: their controversy about scientific knowledge', *J. of the History of Ideas*, Vol. 16 (1955), pp. 209–31. Walter F. Cannon. 'William Whewell: contributions to science and learning', *Notes and Records of the Royal Society*, Vol. 19 (1964), pp. 176–91.

Huxley acknowledged his debt to Mill in a footnote to his lecture; the view of science as an extension of common sense was elaborated in his introduction to the famous series of Science Primers published by MacMillan later in the century. T. H. Huxley, *Science Primers: Introductory* (London 1880), pp. 5–19.

70 The essay 'On the educational value of the natural history sciences' was included by Huxley in his *Lay Sermons, Addresses, and Reviews* (London 1870), and later in his *Science and Education* (London 1893).

71 William Whewell, *'On the Principles of English University Education'*, second edition (London 1838), p. 15.

72 William Whewell, 'On the influence of the history of science upon intellectual education' in Youmans, *Modern Culture*, op. cit., pp. 185–6.

73 Ibid., pp. 187–9.

74 The evidence is reviewed in: Board of Education, *Report of the Consultative Committee on Secondary Education* (London 1938). Appendix 4 (by Cyril Burt) and Appendix 5 (by H. R. Hamley), pp. 429–52. See also 'Final report of the Committee appointed to consider the bearing on school work of recent views of formal training' in *Report of the British Association for the Advancement of Science* (London 1931), pp. 279–86.

75 *Report of Her Majesty's Commissioners appointed to Inquire into the Revenues and Management of Certain Colleges and Schools and the Studies pursued and instruction given therein*, Vol. 4, Evidence, Part 2, p. 377 (London 1864).

76 T. H. Huxley, op. cit., pp. 28–9. Huxley also advanced the extraordinary argument that knowledge of the pain and evil associated with the life of worms would enable a person to 'bear his own share with more courage and submission'.

77 Basil Willey, *Nineteenth-Century Studies: Coleridge to Matthew Arnold* (London 1964), p. 78.

78 The Department of Science and Art was formally transferred from the Board of Trade to the Committee of Council on Eduction in February 1856.

Chapter 7

1 R. Lowe, *Primary and Classical Education* (Edinburgh 1867), p. 13.

2 Census of Great Britain, 1851. *Education England and Wales. Report and Tables* (London 1854), pp. xxxvi–xxxvii.

3 Ibid., p. xli.

4 See, for example, C. H. Bromby, 'On Voluntary Half-Time

Schemes' in Alfred Hill (Ed.) *Essays Upon Educational Subjects* (London 1857), p. 264.

5 Census of Great Britain, 1851, op. cit., p. xc.

6 Supra, p. 93.

7 See, for example, Richard Johnson, 'Educational Policy and Social Control in Early Victorian England', *Past and Present*, Vol. 49 (November 1970), p. 119.

8 Ibid.

9 C. G. B. Daubeny, 'On the Importance of the Study of Chemistry as a Branch of Education for all Classes' in E. L. Youmans, *Modern Culture: its true aims and requirements* (London 1867), pp. 57–8.

10 *Report of Her Majesty's Commissioners appointed to Inquire into the Revenues and Management of Certain Colleges and Schools, and the Studies pursued and instruction given therein*, Vol. 4, Evidence, Part 2, p. 374 (London 1864).

11 It is not, of course, suggested here that the various functions – political, cultural, economic – are necessarily independent.

12 *Second Report of the Commissioners for the Exhibition of 1851* (London 1852), pp. 11, 15.

13 Joshua G. Fitch, *The Relative Importance of Subjects Taught in Elementary Schools* (London 1854), p. 5.

14 A. L. Lilley, *Sir Joshua Fitch* (London 1906). In his years of early manhood Fitch appears to have been a High Churchman. He was appointed Principal of the Borough Road Training College in 1856 and to the inspectorate in 1863, on the recommendation of Matthew Arnold. His election to the Athenaeum Club in 1888 was proposed by Archbishop Temple and seconded by Arnold.

15 Fitch, pp. 3–5.

16 Ibid., pp. 6–17.

17 Ibid., p. 19.

18 Ibid., p. 21.

19 Supra, p. 124.

20 Committee of Council on Education, *Minutes 1855–6* (London 1856), p. 4.

21 G. S. R. Kitson Clark, *An Expanding Society: Britain 1830–1900* (Cambridge 1967), pp. 174–5. Lingen, apparently, relied much on the recommendations of Jowett in appointing examiners and inspectors from Oxford. Four successive permanent heads of the Education Office – Lingen, Sandford, Cumin and Kekewich – were Balliol men.

22 Committee of Council on Education, *Minutes 1856–7* (London 1857), p. 32.

23 E. G. Sandford (Ed.), *Memoir of Archbishop Temple* (London 1906), Vol. 1, p. 197.

24 *Report of Her Majesty's Commissioners appointed to Inquire*

o*

into the Revenues and Management of Certain Colleges and Schools, and the Studies pursued and Instruction given therein, Vol. 4, Evidence, Part 2, pp. 270–1 (London 1864).

25 Ibid.

26 Joseph Payne, *Lectures on the Science and Art of Education* (London 1880), p. 263.

27 Matteo Palmieri, *Libro della Vita Civile* (Firenze 1529), p. 20. Cited by William Harrison Woodward, *Studies in Education during the Age of the Renaissance, 1400–1600* (New York 1967), p. 76. For a more recent statement of the same point see, for example, A. L. Rowse, *The Use of History* (London 1946), p. 191. ('History is an essential part of the mind of a cultivated man. One may be a cultivated man without knowing mathematics or chemistry or engineering, for these are specialisms. We expect the technicians in question to know them and do our sums and sanitation for us. But some knowledge of history . . . is . . . part of the self-awareness of our environment.')

28 Committee of Council on Education, *Minutes 1856–7* (London 1857), p. 684.

29 Ibid., pp. 6–8.

30 Ibid., p. 686.

31 Committee of Council on Education, *Report 1859–60* (London 1860), pp. 302–7.

32 *First Report of the Department of Science and Art* (London 1854), p. xxiii.

33 Ten years previously de la Beche had been at great pains to secure Playfair's services: see, for example, M. Reeks, *History of the Royal School of Mines* (London 1920), p. 25.
After Playfair's appointment to the Department of Science and Art he appears to have seen his former protégé as a malevolent influence bent on remodelling the School of Mines. *Cole Diaries*, 2 July 1853.

34 *Cole Diaries*, 16 August 1853.

35 Ibid., 2 November 1853.

36 *Cole Correspondence*: Playfair to Cole, 17 April 1855.

37 Ibid., 25 April 1855.

38 Murchison to Playfair, 2 April 1855. Collection of letters to Lyon Playfair: Royal Society of Arts.

39 Ibid., Murchison's views were made abundantly clear in a letter to Phillips, dated 18 April 1855. 'Notwithstanding your *mot* on the triple directorate', he wrote, 'I view it simply as the School of British Geology and Mines. The affiliated sciences are all subordinate to that fundamental point.' M. Reeks, *History of the Royal School of Mines* (London 1920), p. 88.

40 The Prince Consort's memorandum written at the time of Murchison's appointment made the point bluntly. 'Sir H. de la Beche cannot be said to have extended the usefulness of his

department, but has rather counteracted the plans of the Commissioners by confining his attention to simple geology.' A. Geikie, *Life of Sir Roderick Murchison* (London 1875), Vol. 2, p. 186.

The title of the school changed from the Metropolitan School of Science in 1853 to the Royal School of Mines in 1861. *Tenth Report of the Science and Art Department* (London 1863), p. xiii.

41 *Second Report of the Department of Science and Art* (London 1855), p. xxxi. The arrangement whereby college students in the London area were offered free admission to lectures in Jermyn Street was not successful. See Moseley's comments on the scheme: Committee of Council on Education, *Minutes 1853-4* (London 1854), p. 202.

42 *Second Report of the Department of Science and Art* (London 1855), p. xxxii. *Third Report* (London 1856), Appendix p. 21. These lectures to 'the middle classes and schoolmasters' were distinct from the celebrated and highly successful series of lectures to working men.

43 *Fifth Report* (London 1858), p. 21. P.R.O. Ed. 28/8, p. 60 (11 November 1857).

44 *Cole Diaries*, 7 January 1854. The Jermyn Street professors lectured to both science and art students. Forbes, for example, delivered a series on the forms and colours of the animal and vegetable kingdom to art students (P.R.O. Ed. 28/2, p. 45); Huxley, also, lectured on animal forms to the training masters and students in the normal school (P.R.O. Ed. 28/2, p. 167).

45 M. Reeks, *History of the Royal School of Mines* (London 1920), p. 96. Murchison's letter was apparently lost in one or other of the Departments into whose hands it came: when it was required to be printed, in obedience to an order of the House of Commons, a copy had to be obtained from the letter book of the Survey Office. A. Geikie, *Life of Sir Roderick Murchison* (London 1875), Vol. 2, p. 248.

46 N. MacLeod to Playfair, 1 July 1854 and P.R.O. Ed. 28/2, p. 204.

47 As a result of de la Beche's insistence that all scientific diagrams be examined by a competent authority, the extraordinary situation arose in which Playfair's own diagram, showing the nutritional value of foods, was submitted for approval to Hofmann, his successor as teacher of chemistry in the Metropolitan School of Science. P.R.O. Ed. 28/2, p. 209.

48 Wemyss Reid, *Memoir and Correspondence of Lyon Playfair* (London 1899), pp. 140-1. *Cole Diaries*, 31 December 1856.

49 Playfair to Cole, 12 July 1855. *Cole Correspondence*. There is some evidence that uncertainty about the disposal of

the 1851 surplus prevented students coming forward from the provinces to the School of Mines: see M. Reeks. *History of the Royal School of Mines* (London 1920), p. 63.

50 A. Geikie, *Life of Sir Roderick Murchison* (London 1875), Vol. 2, p. 185.

51 Dr. Copleston, Provost of Oriel College, Oxford: cited by J. H. Newman, *On the Scope and Nature of University Education* (London 1915), Everyman edition, p. 162.

52 C. G. B. Daubeny, 'On the importance of the study of chemistry as a means of education' in E. L. Youmans, *Modern Culture: its true aims and requirements* (London 1867), pp. 57–8.

53 J. H. Newman, op. cit., p. 164. Newman was in fact quoting a critical review of Edgeworth's work on Professional Education.

54 *Cole Diaries*, 9 January 1853 and 12 July 1853.
Hansard's Parliamentary Debates, Third Series, Vol. 125 (London 1853), Col. 549–50.

55 *Cole Diaries*, 12 January 1853.

56 P.R.O. Ed. 28/1, p. 301 and Ed. 28/2, p. 38.

57 Board of Trade. *Department of Science and Art. Correspondence between the Lords of the Committee of Privy Council for Trade and the Lords Commissioners of Her Majesty's Treasury, on the constitution of the Department of Science and Art* (London 1853), pp. 9–11.

58 P.R.O. Ed. 28/3, p. 123.
Third Report of the Department of Science and Art (London 1856), Appendix pp. 7–8.
Hansard's Parliamentary Debates, Third Series, Vol. 134 (London 1854), Col. 1004–6.
Cole's absence due to his involvement in the Paris Exhibition of 1855 might have been a further reason for the change. Although one secretary's post was abolished, there was in fact no financial saving.

59 P.R.O. Ed. 28/7, 10 February 1857.

60 A. S. and H. Cole, *Fifty Years of Public Work of Sir Henry Cole* (London 1884), Vol. 1, pp. 309–10.

61 Playfair to Tyndall, 7 January 1857. *Tyndall Correspondence*, Vol. 3, letter 982.

62 P.R.O. Ed. 28/11, p. 122.

63 Royal Commission on Scientific Instruction, Vol. 1, *Minutes of Evidence* (London 1872), A. 183, p. 14.
See also H. Butterworth, 'South Kensington and Whitehall: a conflict of educational purpose', *Journal of Educational Administration and History*, Vol. 4 (December 1971), pp. 9–19.

64 Supra, p. 153.

65 *Cole Diaries*, 13 March 1857.

66 Figures taken from financial statements in *Minutes* and *Reports* of the Committee of Council on Education for the years in

question. The large expenditure in 1857 conceals a transfer to the Department of Science and Art of £1,500 towards the expense of establishing the Educational Division of the new museum at South Kensington. Committee of Council on Education, *Report 1863–4* (London 1864), p. lxxi.

67 *Cole Diaries,* 7 July 1857.

68 Committee of Council on Education, *Minutes 1857–8* (London 1858), p. 22.

69 *Seventh Report of the Science and Art Department* (London 1860), p. 35.

70 Ibid., p. 8.

71 Lowe to Lingen, March 17 1882. Quoted in A Patchett Martin, *Life and Letters of the Right. Hon. Robert Lowe, Viscount Sherbrooke* (London 1893).

72 Almost thirty years later the Cross Commissioners could state with accuracy that, in 1888, the teaching of science in elementary schools was as yet in its infancy.
Royal Commission appointed to inquire into the Elementary Education Acts, England and Wales, *Final Report* (London 1888), p. 141.

Chapter 8

1 D. J. de Solla Price, *Little Science, Big Science* (New York 1963).

2 David Layton, 'Lord Wrottesley, F.R.S., Pioneer Statesman of Science', *Notes and Records of the Royal Society of London*, Vol. 23, No. 2 (December 1968), pp. 230–46.
J. B. Morrell, 'Individualism and the Structure of British Science in 1830', *Historical Studies in the Physical Sciences*, Vol. 3 (1971), pp. 183–204.

3 J. Perrin, *Atoms* (London 1916), translated by D. Ll. Hammick, p. vii.

4 Galileo puts the words into the mouth of Salviati during the third day of discussions on *Two Principal Systems. Due Massimi Sistemi*, iii (Opere, vii) 355: English translation by T. Salusbury, *Mathematical Collections and Transactions* (London 1661), p. 301.

5 A. N. Whitehead went so far as to describe the achievement of the seventeenth century as 'a scheme of scientific thought framed by mathematicians, for the use of mathematicians'. *Science and the Modern World* (Cambridge 1929), p. 70.

6 Sir Cyril Hinshelwood, *The Vision of Nature* (Cambridge 1961), pp. 17, 19 and 21.
For a more detailed account of the crucial change in the con-

ception of a scientific explanation which took place in the seventeenth century see E. A. Burtt, *The Metaphysical Foundations of Modern Physical Science*, 2nd edition (London 1932).

7 A. N. Whitehead, *Science and the Modern World* (Cambridge 1929), p. 41.

8 This point was elaborated in the inaugural lecture of A. B. Pippard, F.R.S., Cavendish Professor of Physics in the University of Cambridge. A. B. Pippard, *Reconciling Physics with Reality* (Cambridge 1972). At the secondary school level it manifests itself in a naïve belief that the physical world is much simpler than it really is.

9 Supra, p. 80.

10 The process was described by a distinguished theoretical physicist of the present century, J. L. Synge, as

'i. A dive from the world of reality into the world of mathematics.

ii. A swim in the world of mathematics.

iii. A climb from the world of mathematics back into the world of reality, carrying the prediction in our teeth.'

Quoted by C. A. Coulson, *The Spirit of Applied Mathematics* (Oxford 1953), pp. 12–13.

Coulson points out that not everything encountered in 'the world of mathematics' has direct physical significance, e.g. the wave function. The same image of land and sea is used by Hinshelwood in his Eddington Memorial Lecture (1961), although investigators now sail, rather than swim, across the mathematical deep. As he remarks, some never quite recover from their seasickness and others, when conceptions like negative energy are inferred from the formulae themselves, 'are destined like the Flying Dutchman to sail the seas forever with no prospect of reaching port' (p. 22).

11 This particular reservation was even expressed by mathematicians, for example, I. Todhunter, *The Conflict of Studies* (London 1873), p. 27. However, a distinction between pedagogical and research requirements must again be drawn. 'Thoughtless technique' is an important aspect of the work of a mathematician, according to C. W. Kilmister, *The Times Higher Educational Supplement*, 29 October 1971: it enables 'operations to be carried out without burdening the mind with the intolerable labour of understanding what is happening'.

12 This was the main criticism of those who, like Sir David Brewster, (supra, p. 22) regarded an emphasis on the applications of science as essential if science was to succeed as an instrument of general education.

13 J. Piaget and B. Inhelder, *The growth of logical thinking* (London 1958). See also J. Piaget, 'Development and Learning',

Journal of Research in Science Teaching, Vol. 2 (1964), pp. 176–86.

The stage of formal operational thought is achieved by ordinary pupils around the ages of fourteen and fifteen years, and by outstandingly able pupils around the ages of eleven and twelve years.

14 Supra, p. 129.

Criticisms of Nuffield science curriculum developments have been made in terms of the heavy conceptual demands being made on learners, for example, R. B. Ingle and M. Shayer 'Conceptual demands in Nuffield O-level Chemistry', *Education in Chemistry*, Vol. 8 (September 1971), pp. 182–3.

15 A helpful review of Piagetian research on intellectual growth as it pertains to the learning and understanding of mathematics is to be found in the paper by my colleague Professor Kenneth Lovell, *Intellectual Growth and Understanding Mathematics*, Science and Mathematics Education Information Report (February 1971), ERIC Information Analysis Center for Science and Mathematics Education, 1460 West Lane Avenue, Columbus, Ohio 43210.

On the introduction of highly abstract concepts into the teaching of science and mathematics in schools, the view of one eminent applied mathematician, Professor H. Bondi, is that such concepts should be introduced to large numbers of children 'so that later in life, if necessary, these concepts won't be total strangers to them.' H. Bondi, 'Mathematics, the universities and social change', *Universities Quarterly*, Vol. 20 (September 1966), p. 414.

16 K. Lovell, op. cit., pp. 12–13.

For a good modern statement of the requirements for effective teaching of science, see: The Association for Science Education, *Science for the Under-Thirteens* (1971).

17 An interesting discussion which draws on recent work in the philosophy of science, particularly the views of T. S. Kuhn, is to be found in: Robert G. Bridgham 'Conceptions of Science and Learning Science', *University of Chicago School Review*, Vol. 78 (November 1969), pp. 25–40.

18 Supra, p. 88.

19 Francis Bacon, Preface (to the people) to *The Great Instauration*, in *The Philosophical Works of Francis Bacon*. Reprinted from the Texts and Translations . . . of Ellis and Spedding. Edited . . . by John M. Robertson (London 1905), p. 247.

20 Supra, p. 141.

21 *Gardeners' Chronicle* (London 1856), p. 517. and *Life and Letters of Sir Joseph Dalton Hooker* (London 1918), Vol. 1, p. 399.

22 For the relationship between the conceptions of science of Mill

and Whewell, and those of more recent philosophers of science, such as Karl Popper, see P. B. Medawar, 'Anglo-Saxon Attitudes', *Encounter*, Vol. 25 (August 1965), pp. 52–8.

The existence of great research schools in which budding scientists learn 'how to select worthwhile problems and how to create the tools required to achieve a solution' is, of course, evidence that the art of investigation can be taught: see H. A. Krebs, 'The Making of a Scientist', *Nature*, Vol. 215 (1967), p. 1441. The master-apprenticeship relation which characterises such schools is, however, a very different matter from the general and systematic teaching of the process of scientific inquiry.

23 There is, of course, a danger in equating science with common-sense empiricism and inflating the claims in the ways indicated. Other studies than science can foster 'critical thinking' and 'problem solving'; consequently there is no special justificaton for the inclusion of science in the school curriculum.

24 For a recent discussion of this issue see: Bentley Glass, *The Timely and the Timeless: the interrelations of science education and society* (London 1970), pp. 11–21.

25 J. Myron Atkin, 'A Critical Look at "Process" in Science Education', *EPIE Forum*, Vol. 1, No. 8 (April 1968), p. 9. Quoted by Bentley Glass, op. cit., p. 20.

26 For critical views on conceptions of scientific activity in recent curriculum developments see M. D. Herron, 'Nature of Science: panacea or Pandora's Box', *Journal of Research in Science Teaching*, Vol. 6 (1969), pp. 105–7; F. M. Connelly, 'Philosophy of Science and the Science Curriculum', *Journal of Research in Science Teaching*, Vol. 6 (1969), pp. 108–13; Mary E. Deiderich, 'Physical Sciences and Processes of Inquiry: a critique of CHEM, CBA and PSSC', *Journal of Resarch in Science Teaching*, Vol. 6 (1969), pp. 309–15.

27 The Nuffield Foundation Science Teaching Project, *Progress Report October 1964* (London 1964), p. 5.

Writing of the American Biological Sciences Curriculum Study, Bentley Glass makes a similar point: a pupil was 'to learn about science by doing, by gradually broadening his understanding of the methods of investigation through personal use of them'. B. Glass, *The Timely and the Timeless* (London 1970), p. 30.

28 A detailed critique of 'discovery learning' will be found in L. S. Shulman and E. R. Keislar (Eds), *Learning by Discovery: a critical appraisal* (Chicago 1966).

29 To claim, for example, that when a child looks down a spinthariscope he is seeing what Rutherford saw and stands in the same relation to the experimental evidence as Rutherford did, is to assume that perception is unaffected by previous experience, knowledge, and expectations. This is clearly not so.

30 N. Koertge, 'Towards an Integration of Content and Method in the Science Curriculum', *Curriculum Theory Network 4* (Ontario, Winter 1969–70), pp. 38–9.
Karl R. Popper, *Conjectures and Refutations*, 3rd edition (London 1969), pp. 220–87.

31 A nineteenth-century critic of the introduction of science into education, Isaac Todhunter, F.R.S., in a discussion of the complexity of genuine experimentation, recalled the case of the student who, watching a demonstration of Focault's experiment for proving the rotation of the earth and seeing the pendulum moving in the wrong direction, withdrew in order that he might retain his faith in astronomy. I. Todhunter, *The Conflict of Studies* (London 1873), p. 18.
Anyone who has stood before a class of students and performed demonstration experiments will recognize the truth in the statement attributed to Theobald Smith, an eminent American bacteriologist: 'it is the care we bestow on apparently trifling, unattractive and very troublesome minutiae which determines the result.' Cited by W. Bullock in his obituary notice to T. Smith, *Journal of Pathology and Bacteriology*, Vol. 40 (1935), p. 621.

32 I. Lakatos, 'Falsification and the Methodology of Scientific Research Programmes' in I. Lakatos and A. Musgrave, *Criticism and the Growth of Knowledge* (Cambridge 1970), pp. 91–195.

33 An example of a study of competing systems is to be found in year five of the Nuffield Ordinary Level Physics course where the Aristotelian and Copernican are treated in some detail.
It should be added that the record of the history of science in science teaching is not encouraging: whilst I share the conviction of Professor F. R. Jevons that 'the history of science holds immense educational possibilities which are crying out to be exploited and which we have barely begun to tap', equally I endorse his reservation that poor teaching of the history of science is worse than none at all. F. R. Jevons, *The Teaching of Science* (London 1969), p. 42.

34 Thomas Kuhn's description of science education as 'a relatively dogmatic initiation into a pre-established problem-solving tradition that the student is neither invited nor equipped to evaluate', expresses the position succinctly, if somewhat brutally. Thomas S. Kuhn, 'The Function of Dogma in Scientific Research' in A. C. Crombie (Ed.), *Scientific Change* (London 1963). Also in: Barry Barnes (Ed.), *Sociology of Science* (London 1972), pp. 84–5.

35 See, for example, The Science Masters' Association and The Association of Women Science Teachers, *Chemistry for Grammar Schools* (1961), p. 3; J. Schwab, *Biology Teacher's Handbook, B.S.C.S.* (New York 1964), p. 39.

36 Alvin M. Weinberg, 'The Two Faces of Science', *Journal of Chemical Education*, Vol. 45 (February 1968), p. 74.

37 Ministry of Education, *Half our Future* (London 1963), p. 32.

38 Organization for Economic Co-operation and Development, *Science, Growth and Society – a new perspective* (1971).

39 Lord Zuckerman, 'Public Knowledge, Hopes and Fears', *The Times Literary Supplement*, 12 November 1971, p. 1422.
    Alvin Weinberg makes a similar point about the encouragement of participation by the public in debate on what he terms trans-science issues: 'Science and Trans-Science', *Minerva*, Vol. 10 (April 1972), p. 222.
    See also Joseph Ben-David, 'The Profession of Science and its Powers', *Minerva*, Vol. 10 (July 1972), pp. 362–83.

40 Agreement on this need comes from widely differing scientific sources. See, for example, Sir Frederick Dainton, *Science: salvation or damnation* (University of Southampton 1971), pp. 18–22.
    Barry Commoner, 'Science and Social Action', *The Science Teacher*, Vol. 39 (May 1972), p. 24.

41 Alvin M. Weinberg, 'The Two Faces of Science', op. cit., p. 77.

42 Richard Dawes, *Suggestive Hints towards Improved Secular Instruction making it bear upon Practical Life* (London 1847).

43 *Report of Her Majesty's Commissioners appointed to Inquire into the Revenues and Management of Certain Colleges and Schools, and the Studies pursued and Instruction given therein*, Vol. 4, Evidence, Part 2, pp. 270–1 (London 1864).

44 The problem of social and moral development is perhaps most acute in the case of children of average or less than average ability (the Newsom children in England, the Brunton children in Scotland) and in the case of socially disadvantaged children. It is interesting to note how close the correspondence is between Dawes' statement of aims (*Suggestive Hints*, 6th edition, London 1853, p. viii) and that in a modern document, for example Scottish Education Department, Curriculum Papers – 3, *Modern Studies for School Leavers* (Edinburgh 1968), p. 10, Schools Council Working Paper No. 27, *Cross'd with Adversity* (London 1970), pp. 65–7.

45 R. H. Syfret, 'Some early critics of the Royal Society', *Notes and Records of the Royal Society of London*, Vol. 8 (October 1950), pp. 20–64.

46 A. N. Whitehead, *Science and the Modern World* (Cambridge 1929), p. 245.

47 Ibid., p. 177.

48 Sir Frederick Dainton, *Science: salvation or damnation* (University of Southampton 1971), p. 18.

49 Even when, within the study of a 'pure' science such as botany, such issues arose, the opportunity was not seized. Consideration

of the origin of species and of evolution had to await the publication of Hooker's science primer on *Botany* in 1876 for its
first muted treatment in a school text.

50 The case for broadening the objectives of school science education is examined in David Layton, 'Science as General Education', *Trends in Education*, No. 25 (London 1972), pp. 11–15.
51 Supra, p. 146.
52 Supra, pp. 131–2.
53 For a modern statement of this position see the lecture by the
Nobel Laureate, Jacques Monod, *From Biology to Ethics* (The
Salk Institute: Occasional Papers 1: California 1969).
54 Emmanuel G. Mesthene, *Technological Change: its impact on
man and society* (Harvard 1970), pp. 48–53.
55 Ibid., p. 85.
56 D. Gabor, 'Technology, Life and Leisure', *Nature*, Vol. 200,
No. 4906 (9 November 1963), pp. 513–18.
57 A profound and illuminating discussion of science as a humanity
is to be found in Ralph Barton Perry, 'A definition of the
humanities', in T. M. Greene (Ed.), *The Meaning of the
Humanities* (Princeton 1940).
58 Supra, p. 22.
59 Emmanuel G. Mesthene, *Technological Change*, op. cit., p. 50.
60 Sir Frederick Dainton, *Science: salvation or damnation* (University of Southampton 1971), p. 21.
61 Bacon used the terms in his description of Salomon's House
(*The New Atlantis*): 'interpreters of nature' were the theoreti-
cians who transformed experimental results into 'axioms and
aphorisms'; 'dowry-men or benefactors' were those who, 'looking
into the experiments of their fellows . . . cast about how to
draw out of them things of use and practice for man's life'.
62 Alvin M. Weinberg, 'Science and Trans-Science', *Minerva*,
Vol. 10, No. 2 (April 1972), pp. 209–22. See also the remarks
of Edward E. David, Jr., science adviser to the President of the
U.S.A., on the inflated public expectations of science and technology.
'Reflections on the Objectives of Science Teaching', *The Science
Teacher*, Vol. 38 No. 5 (May 1971), pp. 27–8.
63 Alvin M. Weinberg, op. cit., p. 222.
64 See, for example, Jacques Monod, op. cit. p. 22, and 'On the
logical relationship between knowledge and values' in Watson
Fuller (ed.) *The Social Impact of Modern Biology* (London
1971), pp. 11–21.
65 J. Bronowski, 'The disestablishment of science' in Watson
Fuller (ed.) *The Social Impact of Modern Biology* (London
1971), pp. 233–46.
For commentary on the above by Sir Peter Medawar, Gerard

Piel, Anthony Wedgwood Benn and Eugene Rabinowitch see *Encounter*, Vol. 37, No. 3 (September 1971), pp. 91–5.
Recent disavowals of the need for a national science policy are clearly related to the view that scientific research and development should 'flow from the imperatives of other policies'. The point was made by Sir William Pile, permanent secretary at the Department of Education and Science, in evidence to the Select Committee on Science and Technology at the time of the Rothschild debate. *New Scientist*, 23 March 1972, p. 627.

66 Bernard Crick, 'How politics should be taught', *The Times Higher Education Supplement*, 16 June 1972, p. 14.

67 For a further discussion of some of the problems arising from the association of science teaching with controversial issues see David Layton, 'The Secondary School Curriculum and Science Education' in *Physics Education*, Vol. 8, No. 1 (January 1973), pp. 19–23.

68 Supra, pp. 146–7.

69 Matthew Arnold, *Culture and Anarchy* (edited by J. Dover Wilson), (Cambridge 1961), p. 113.

70 Ibid., p. 6.

71 Ibid., pp. 69–70.

72 Ibid., p. 65.

73 Ibid., p. 48.

74 Ibid., p. xxxv.

75 Supra, pp. 40 and 86.

76 The quotation is taken from Robert Jackson, 'Community versus equality', *The Times Higher Education Supplement*, 3 November 1972, p. 2. For other descriptions of E.P.A. Community Schools see A. H. Halsey (ed.), *Educational Priority Vol. 1 E.P.A. Problems and Policies*, HMSO (London 1972), esp. Chapters 9–12. Eric Midwinter, *Priority Education* (Harmondsworth 1972). Equality of educational outcome is achieved if the proportion of people from different social, economic or ethnic categories at all levels and in all types of education are more or less the same as the proportion of these people in the population at large.

77 See, for example, A. H. Halsey, op. cit., p. 9.

78 E. Midwinter, op. cit., p. 22.

79 M. D. Shipman, 'The Unbridgable Gap', *The Times Educational Supplement*, 30 June 1972.

Index

abstraction 18, 27, 129, 167–71, 178
agricultural chemistry 48–53, 95, 98, 130
Airy, G. B. 22, 29, 80
Akenson, D. H. 106
Allen, J. 39, 82
Altick, R. 32
Apothecaries' Company 68
applied science 18–19, 22, 28, 43, 46, 52–3, 59, 81, 92, 107, 130–2, 138, 143, 178–9, 183
Argyll, Duke of 20, 117
Arnold, M. 17, 185–6
Ashburton, Lord 49, 107, 113, 119, 122, 123, 149
Atkin, M. 174
authoritarian teaching 33, 177
autodidactic tradition 29–32, 46, 77

Babbage, C. 18, 22, 135
Babington, C. C. 57, 64
Bacon, F. 59, 172, 183
Battersea Training College 77, 82, 111, 120, 162
Bence Jones, H. 128, 134
Blomfield, C. J. 107, 108
Board of Health 52, 121
Board of Ordnance 19
Board of Science 21
Board of Trade 20, 100, 133, 156–8, 160
Borough Road School 33
botany 21, 56, 58, 61–3, 67–9, 72, 140
Brewer, E. C. 111–12
Brewster, D. 22, 26, 47, 80, 182
Bristol Trade School 94
British and Foreign School Society 15, 40–1, 111, 148
British Association for the Advancement of Science 20, 28, 69, 73, 126–7, 155
Bromby, C. H. 96–7, 119, 120

Buckland, W. 20
Burdett Coutts, A. 113

Cambridge Philosophical Society 36, 57, 79
Carpenter, W. B. 114, 139
Census: 1851 Report on Education 15, 20, 144–5
Central Society of Education 28
Chambers, R. 110
Cheltenham Training College 96–7
chemistry 33, 48–50, 51–3, 61, 73, 98–100, 107, 131, 134–5
Chester Diocesan Training College 92–4, 146, 157
Chester, H. 15, 16
civil service 53, 90–1
Cole, H. 70, 132, 137, 155, 160–5
colonial office 96
Combe, G. 135
Committee of National Education in Ireland 41, 43, 48, 105–6
Committee of Council on Education 14, 15, 17, 67, 75–6, 78, 87, 95–102, 105, 113, 114–17, 119, 121, 125, 133, 155, 156
common curriculum 147, 149–50, 185–7
community-related curriculum 86–7, 92–3, 146–8, 160, 185–7
controversial issues 184
conversational lectures 44, 89, 104
Coutts Trotter 175
cultural deprivation 14, 85, 150, 185, 187
curriculum change 13–14, 17, 34, 75, 89, 95, 118, 163–4

Dainton, F. S. 180
Dalton, J. 29, 30
Darwin, C. 30, 33, 55–7, 59, 64, 67, 74, 76, 138, 156
Daubeny, C. B. 134, 135, 146–7, 160
Davy, H. 30, 128